FOOD&**WINE**

Wine Guide
2011

WINE GUIDE 2011

editor in chief **Dana Cowin**
executive wine editor **Ray Isle**
deputy editor **Christine Quinlan**
volume editor **Kristen Wolfe Bieler**
associate wine editor **Megan Krigbaum**
copy editor **Amy K. Hughes**
tastings coordinator **Colleen McKinney**
tastings assistant **Scott Rosenbaum**
chief researcher **Janice Huang**
researchers **Jenny Choi, Erin Laverty, Lawrence Marcus**
indexer **Andrea Chesman**

contributors **Robert Bohr (Burgundy), Sue Courtney (New Zealand), Victor de la Serna (Spain), Jamie Goode (Portugal), Peter Liem (Champagne), Fiona Morrison (Bordeaux), Jeremy Parzen (Italy)**

produced for FOOD & WINE magazine by gonzalez defino, ny
gonzalezdefino.com
principals **Joseph Gonzalez, Perri DeFino**

map illustrations **Ethan Cornell**

cover photography **Con Poulos**
food stylist **Susan Spungen**
prop stylist **Jessica Romm**

AMERICAN EXPRESS PUBLISHING CORPORATION
president/ceo **Ed Kelly**
chief marketing officer & president, digital media **Mark V. Stanich**
senior vice president/chief financial officer **Paul B. Francis**
vice presidents/general managers **Frank Bland, Keith Strohmeier**

vice president, books & products/publisher **Marshall Corey**
director, book programs **Bruce Spanier**
senior marketing manager, branded books **Eric Lucie**
assistant marketing manager **Lizabeth Clark**
director of fulfillment & premium value **Phil Black**
manager of customer experience & product development **Charles Graver**
director of finance **Thomas Noonan**
associate business manager **Uma Mahabir**
operations director (prepress) **Rosalie Abatemarco Samat**
operations director (manufacturing) **Anthony White**

ISSN 1522-001X

FOOD & WINE

Wine Guide 2011

by Anthony Giglio

FOOD & WINE
BOOKS
American Express Publishing Corporation
New York

contents

old world

new world

old & new worlds

foreword

If you've ever had any doubts about whether we're a wine-drinking country, consider this: There are more than 5,500 wineries in the U.S., in all 50 states, and American wineries produced more than 650 million gallons of wine last year. And that doesn't count the remarkable variety of great wines imported into the country. That might sound daunting—or, if you love wine, exciting—but either way it's one of the reasons the information in our 2011 FOOD & WINE Wine Guide is so invaluable.

There's an extraordinary amount of advice packed into our 13th annual edition—more than 1,000 recommended wines, plus not-to-be-missed travel tips for some of the world's top wine regions, insights into the latest wine trends and a 31-page comprehensive guide to pairing wine with food. And for the first time we have recipes in the book, including Pappardelle with Veal Ragù and Thai

Green Salad with Duck Cracklings. This year the wine recommendations, selected from more than 4,000 wines that New York–based wine writer Anthony Giglio tasted over the year, particularly emphasize affordable bottles—the wines that offer the best possible value for the dollar.

Whether you're a beginner or a connoisseur, our 2011 Wine Guide offers the information you need to make sense of the ever-expanding world of wine.

Dana Cowin
Editor in Chief
FOOD & WINE

Ray Isle
Executive Wine Editor
FOOD & WINE

acknowledgments

The author would like to thank the following people not named in the masthead, without whose help this seemingly small book would have been a far bigger task.

Deepest thanks to wine authority and friend Jeffery Lindenmuth for going above and beyond—again—to see this book to fruition.

A Champagne salute to the Wine Guide Tasting Room's neighbors at The Hired Guns for allowing wave after wave of wine deliveries to clutter their beautiful office loft. Here's to you, Allison Hemming, Bart Codd, Jeffrey Wernecke, Jennifer Pugh and Jude Sanjek. A special shout-out to concierge Eric Perkins for signing for all of those wine boxes and directing deliveries over the course of five months.

A giant pat on the back to our intern, Ben Shapiro, for opening endless boxes and sorting thousands of bottles.

My sincere appreciation goes to colleague and office-mate Larry Smith of smithmag.net for keeping me focused—if not always calm—with his fresh-brewed Gorilla brand Zambica Estates coffee day after day.

A toast to Waterford Crystal for generously donating their Mondavi Fume/Sauvignon Blanc and Mondavi Cabernet Sauvignon glasses to the Wine Guide Tasting Room.

Thank you to my friends at Wine Enthusiast Catalog for donating their fabulous wooden wine racks for individually storing more than 100 bottles in the Wine Guide Tasting Room closet.

To Tom Geniesse of Bottlerocket Wine & Spirit in New York City for the ample supply of sturdy wine-case boxes used to keep bottles stacked and organized. Special thanks to Nicole Serle for putting up with our ceaseless requests, no matter how busy she was.

And finally, to my wife, Antonia LoPresti Giglio, and our two greatest vintages, Sofia and Marco, for their patience during my long absences while writing this book.

how to use this book

All of the wines in this guide—a total of more than 1,000 bottles—are for sale this year. For ease of reference, the wines are listed alphabetically by producer name, followed by the vintage year and region. There is an emphasis throughout the book on affordable bottles that offer the best value for the dollar. The quality and price symbols used to rate each wine are described below.

You may note that certain wines have significantly older vintage dates than others. This is because some wines are released within months after harvest, while others are aged for years before release.

Wineries that make excellent wines every year without fail are featured in the "Star Producers" sections in various chapters throughout the guide. Other features include wine trend reports by wine writers around the world ("From the Wine Frontier") and, new this year, recurring travel boxes ("Where to Go Next") and short travel sidebars ("Eat Here Now," "Taste Here Now," "Stay Here Now," etc.) highlighting noteworthy restaurants, hotels, wineries and tasting rooms in wine regions around the world.

For more expert advice from FOOD & WINE magazine on wine and food pairings, go to foodandwine.com/wine.

Key to Symbols

QUALITY

★★★★ **OUTSTANDING** Worth a search

★★★ **EXCELLENT** Top-notch of its type

★★ **VERY GOOD** Distinctive

★ **GOOD** Delicious everyday wine

PRICE

$$$$ **OVER $60**

$$$ **$31 TO $60**

$$ **$16 TO $30**

$ **$15 AND UNDER**

food & wine's american wine awards 2010

To find the winners of FOOD & WINE magazine's annual American Wine Awards, F&W editors polled a select group of wine professionals, including writers, restaurateurs, sommeliers, retailers and past award winners. Here are our picks for the year's top winemaker, best importer, most promising new winery and best American wines under and over $20.

winemaker of the year

Thomas Rivers Brown A South Carolina native, Brown began making wine at Napa Valley's Schrader Cellars in 2000, following a four-year stint as assistant winemaker at Turley Wine Cellars. Eight years later he became the youngest winemaker ever to earn not just one but two perfect, 100-point scores from Robert M. Parker's *The Wine Advocate,* for two of Schrader Cellars' Cabernet Sauvignons. It has been a rapid ascent from wine lover to consultant to lauded winemaker, but as Brown will tell you from behind the wheel of his Aston Martin Vantage, he likes to move fast.

wine importer of the year

Domaine Select Wine Estates Paolo Domeneghetti had more than 20 years' experience in the restaurant and wine business when he and his wife, Allison, a wine enthusiast and fine arts professional, started their wine importing and wholesale company, Domaine Select, in 1999. Today, the Domeneghettis' portfolio features 75 world-class wine and spirits partners, among them top producers from France, Italy and Austria, many of whom are committed to natural winemaking practices. "Our relationships with our producer-partners are based on friendship," says Paolo Domeneghetti, "and we see ourselves as an extension of their philosophies."

most promising new winery

Gramercy Cellars Master Sommelier Greg Harrington tasted countless bottles of great wine while working as partner and director of beverage for BR Guest Restaurants. But it was a handful of wines from Walla Walla, Washington, that inspired him and his wife, Pam, to open a winery there. Beginning with the 2005 vintage, Harrington has been making wines with a sommelier's eye toward balance and an affinity for food. A combination of "great vineyards, minimalist winemaking, time and patience" is the formula for Gramercy Cellars' sellout Cabernet Sauvignons, Syrahs, Tempranillo and Grenache.

best wines $20 and under

Honig | 2008 | SAUVIGNON BLANC

Mount Eden Vineyards Wolff Vineyard | 2008 | CHARDONNAY

Elk Cove Vineyards | 2008 | PINOT GRIS/PINOT GRIGIO

Wallace Brook | 2008 | PINOT NOIR

Columbia Crest H3 | 2007 | MERLOT

Four Vines Old Vine Cuvee | 2007 | ZINFANDEL

Red Car Boxcar | 2008 | SYRAH

Louis M. Martini Sonoma County | 2007 | CABERNET SAUVIGNON

best wines over $20

Merry Edwards | 2009 | SAUVIGNON BLANC

Hanzell Vineyards Estate | 2007 | CHARDONNAY

Brewer-Clifton Mount Carmel | 2008 | PINOT NOIR

Pepper Bridge | 2007 | MERLOT

A. Rafanelli | 2007 | ZINFANDEL

Qupé Bien Nacido Hillside Estate | 2006 | SYRAH

Buccella | 2007 | CABERNET SAUVIGNON

Continuum Estate | 2007 | BORDEAUX BLEND

Schramsberg Blanc de Blancs Brut | 2006 | SPARKLING WINE

sommeliers of the year

The seven master sommeliers honored here by FOOD & WINE magazine have created incredible, forward-thinking wine lists at new restaurants. This eclectic group of men and women includes industry veterans and new talents, ex-chefs (Rajat Parr, John Wabeck and Ercolino Crugnale), a former cheesemonger (Emilie Garvey) and even one beer fanatic (Greg Engert).

Stephanie Caraway | Chef's Table
Iowa City, IA

223 E. Washington St.; chefstableiowacity.com

WHY SHE WON For finding truly amazing wine values from southern France.

FAVORITE PAIRING 2006 Château du Donjon Minervois with chef Eric McDowell's hearty bison rib eye with mushrooms and root vegetables confit.

Ercolino Crugnale | JORY at the Allison Inn
Newberg, OR

2525 Allison Ln.; theallison.com

WHY HE WON For a list that perfectly balances local Oregon wines with terrific selections from the rest of the world.

FAVORITE PAIRING 2005 Soter Brut Rosé and gnocchi with lamb and beef ragù.

Greg Engert | Birch & Barley
Washington, DC

1337 14th St. NW; birchandbarley.com

WHY HE WON For bringing the same passionate ambition to beer that other sommeliers bring to wine, sourcing 555 artisanal brews.

FAVORITE PAIRING WinterCoat Vildmoseol, a funky Danish peat-smoked ale, with chef Kyle Bailey's smoky charred octopus with capers.

Emilie Garvey | SHO Shaun Hergatt
New York, NY

40 Broad St.; shoshaunhergatt.com

WHY SHE WON For creating a beautifully edited list of small-production wines.

FAVORITE PAIRING 2006 Mas d'En Compte Priorat white with chef Shaun Hergatt's cinnamon-dusted rabbit loin.

David Mokha | Hakkasan at the Fontainebleau
Miami Beach, FL

4441 Collins Ave.; fontainebleau.com

WHY HE WON For tasting thousands of bottles to find wines that work with every dish on the family-style Chinese menu at this branch of Alan Yau's acclaimed London restaurant.

FAVORITE PAIRING 2007 Huet Clos du Bourg Vouvray with chef Wen Sian Tan's jasmine tea–smoked ribs.

Rajat Parr | RN74
San Francisco, CA

301 Mission St.; michaelmina.net

WHY HE WON For his 2,500-bottle list, including 47 pages of vintages from Burgundy's top producers and 100 excellent, diverse choices for $100 or less.

FAVORITE PAIRING 2006 Reynard Cornas from Thierry Allemand with chef Jason Berthold's flavorful roast chicken with runner beans and Swiss chard.

John Wabeck | Inox
McLean, VA

1800 Tysons Blvd.; inoxrestaurant.com

WHY HE WON For his incredibly thoughtful, food-friendly list that's heavy on great Burgundy.

FAVORITE PAIRING 2005 Bodegas Carrau Amat Tannat and chef Jon Mathieson's decadent, spice-crusted venison with foie gras and Madeira sauce.

great wine from unexpected places

It's tempting—and much easier—to purchase wine solely from the world's many well-known, established wine regions. But wineries in less familiar wine-producing territories around the globe are making terrific wines worth hunting for. Try these off-the-beaten-path producers.

molio family vineyards, brazil

Brazil produces a substantial amount of wine from its main growing regions, most of it from hilly vineyards in the southern Rio Grande do Sul state. Not much of it reaches the U.S., but one of the country's top producers, Miolo (for whom superstar winemaker Michel Rolland consults), does have a presence here.

A light, fragrant red from the Vale dos Vinhedos region, the 2008 Miolo Family Vineyards Pinot Noir has bright berry flavors and an appealing briskness.

sula vineyards, india

Most of this vast country is unsuitable for producing fine wine, but a few regions—Nashik, in India's western Maharashtra state, chief among them—are making great strides. The winery with the largest U.S. presence is undoubtedly Sula Vineyards, founded in 1997.

Lodged somewhere between New Zealand and California Sauvignons in style, Sula Vineyards' zesty 2008 Sauvignon Blanc from the Nashik region displays green grass and gooseberry aromas and flavors. It's a light, vivid and surprisingly intense wine.

domaine du castel, israel

The number of Israeli wineries is growing steadily, as is the quality of their wines. Regions crafting modern-style wines—Golan Heights, Upper Galilee and Judean Hills—have had success with Syrah and Chardonnay, though many wineries make wines from Bordeaux varieties as well.

Domaine du Castel is a family producer that makes a pricey but high-quality range of wines from the Judean Hills. Crafted from Chardonnay grown on a hilltop vineyard, Domaine du Castel's 2008 C Blanc du Castel has impressive length and luscious crème brûlée notes.

château musar, lebanon

Lebanon has been producing wine since biblical times, and dozens of wineries operate here. Most vineyards are located in the Bekaa Valley, and are planted with French varieties such as Cabernet Sauvignon, Merlot, Cinsault, Carignane and Grenache. Some obscure native varieties—Obaideh, Merweh—are planted as well.

The country's most respected winery is Château Musar, and its flagship wine is a graceful, distinctive and long-aging red blend of Cinsault, Carignane and Cabernet Sauvignon from the Bekaa Valley. The 1999 vintage offers flavors of black currants and exotic spice and a velvety texture.

movia winery, slovenia

Slovenia's long winemaking tradition was set back during the postwar Communist era (when the country was part of Yugoslavia) but has been revived with impressive results. The country's three main wine regions are Podravje, Posavje and Primorska. While a number of good reds are made from international grape varieties, Slovenia's greatest viticultural strength is its minerally, complex whites. Many are made with grapes common in northwestern Italy's Friuli region—Pinot Grigio, Sauvignon Blanc, Friulano and Ribolla Gialla (known here as Rebula). Among the top producers are Movia, Edi Simcic, Cotar and Sutor.

Ales Kristancic, the offbeat and visionary owner-vintner at Movia Winery, keeps his whites in oak barrels for long periods of time. The result is wines that are rich and substantial, like Movia's spicy, peachy 2006 Brda Pinot Grigio.

wine tasting guide

Tasting wine is like any other acquired skill: the more you practice, the better you become. Most of us possess the necessary tools to taste wine. Our tastebuds can detect sweet, salty, bitter and sour sensations, plus "umami," the savory flavor found in mushrooms and meat. And our noses can differentiate among hundreds of aromas. The most important thing to learn is how to pay attention to the wine in your glass. Here are a few tips to help get your palate into tasting shape.

set the mood For each wine you want to taste, find a clear, stemmed glass that is comfortable to hold. Choose a well-lit place that's relatively odor-neutral. It is best not to wear perfume or scented lotion.

set the scene Pour just enough wine in the glass so it barely reaches the widest part of the bowl. This way you'll have room to swirl the wine without spilling it.

check the color A light color generally indicates a light-bodied wine; a darker color, a fuller-bodied wine. Also, white wines deepen in color with age; reds get lighter and take on an orangish or even brown hue. If you've poured more than one wine, compare the colors and guess which wine will taste more concentrated. Young wines that appear brown may be the result of poor winemaking or storage.

swirl & sniff Hold the glass by its stem and swirl it gently to release the wine's aromas. Sniff. What do you smell? Sniff again. Do you smell fruit? What sort? The wine might evoke herbs, flowers, spices, vanilla or wood. Some wines smell like bell pepper, leather, roasted meat or even manure. Don't worry about cataloguing every aroma. Just articulate what you smell. Doing so will help you tell the difference between one wine and another. Sharing your impressions will help you learn and remember. Noxious smells like sulfur or must might dissipate with air. If the wine smells bad, give it a few minutes and swirl the glass to bring more contact with oxygen. If the wine still has an unappealing odor, move on to another one. If a wine smells like wet, moldy cork or cardboard, it may be "corked," meaning it has been infected by an unpleasant-smelling compound called TCA that can be found in corks. TCA is harmless, but it makes wine taste bad.

sip & swish Sip the wine and swish it around in your mouth. Try to suck air into your mouth while wine is still in it (this takes practice). This allows the wine to release more aromas. How does it feel? Does it coat your mouth? Is it light, prickly and refreshing? Does it taste bitter or sweet? Does it recall specific fruits or spices? Smell again. Does it smell like it tastes? Do you like it? There are no wrong answers; it's all about what you perceive.

to spit or swallow? If you're tasting more than a couple of wines at one sitting and want to be able to detect as much as possible from every glass (and remember your impressions tomorrow), it's important to spit.

taste in context In a horizontal tasting, you sample a range of wines that are alike in all but one way. This could be a group of wines from the same region and vintage, but made by different producers, or a group of wines from the same producer, same grape and same vintage, but from different vineyards. Comparing the differences among such similar wines will expand your knowledge. In a vertical tasting, you sample the same wine from the same producer made in different years. It's a great demonstration of how vintage can make a difference, as well as how age can change a wine's look and taste.

wine terms

You won't find much fussy wine jargon in this guide, but some of the terms commonly used to describe the taste of wine might be unfamiliar or used in an unfamiliar way. Many tasting notes mention specific flavors or describe a wine's texture. These references to flavors and textures other than "grape" are meant to serve as analogies: All the wines in this guide are made from grapes, but grapes have the ability to suggest the flavors of other fruits, herbs or minerals. A wine said to taste like raspberries, for example, isn't infused with raspberries. Rather, it evokes flavors similar to those of raspberries. Here's a mini glossary to help you become comfortable with the language of wine.

acidity The tart, tangy or zesty sensations in wine. Ideally, acidity brightens a wine's flavors as a squeeze of lemon brightens fish. Wines lacking acidity taste "flabby."

balance The harmony between acidity, tannin, alcohol and sweetness in a wine.

body How heavy or thick a wine feels in the mouth. Full-bodied or heavy wines are often described as "big."

corked Wines that taste like wet cork or newspaper are said to be "corked." The cause is trichloroanisole (TCA), a contaminant sometimes transmitted by cork.

crisp A term used to describe well-balanced, light-bodied wines that are high in acidity.

dry A wine without perceptible sweetness. A dry wine, however, can have powerful fruit flavors. "Off-dry" describes a wine that has a touch of sweetness.

earthy An earthy wine evokes flavors like mushrooms, leather, damp straw or even manure.

finish The length of time a wine's flavors linger on the palate. A long finish is the hallmark of a more complex wine.

fruity Wine with an abundance of fruit flavors. Sometimes fruity wines can give the impression of sweetness, though they are not actually sweet.

herbaceous Calling a wine "herbaceous" or "herbal" can be positive or negative. Wines that evoke herb flavors can be delicious. However, wines with green pepper flavors are less than ideal, and are also referred to as "vegetal."

mineral Flavors that reflect the minerals found in the soil in which the grapes were grown. The terms "steely," "flinty" and "chalky" are also used to describe these flavors.

nose How a wine smells; its bouquet, or aroma.

oaky Wines that transmit the flavors of the oak barrels in which they were aged. Some oak can impart "toast" flavors.

oxidized Wines that have a tarnished quality due to exposure to air are said to be oxidized. When intended, as in the case of Sherry (see p. 259), oxidation can add fascinating dimensions to a wine. When unintentional, oxidation can make a wine taste tired and unappealing.

palate The various sensations a wine gives in the mouth, including sweetness, flavors, texture and alcohol. The term "mid-palate" refers to the way these characteristics evolve with time in the mouth.

powerful Wine that is full of flavor, tannin and/or alcohol.

rustic Wine that is a bit rough, though often charming.

tannin A component of grape skins, seeds and stems, tannin is most commonly found in red wines. It imparts a puckery sensation similar to over-steeped tea. Tannin also gives a wine its structure and enables some wines to age well.

terroir A French term that refers to the particular attributes a wine acquires from the specific environment of a vineyard, i.e., the climate, soil type, elevation and aspect.

wine buying guide

Buying wine should be fun and easy, yet too often it isn't. Thankfully, there are several ways to gain confidence and make wine buying enjoyable no matter where you shop.

in shops

scope out the shops Visit local wineshops and determine which has the most helpful salespeople, the best selection and the lowest prices. Ask about case discounts, and whether mixing and matching your own assorted case is allowed. Expect at least a 10 percent discount; some stores will offer 20 percent. As wine shoppers have become more value-conscious, many retailers have increased their discounts and are offering one-liter bottles and three-liter wine boxes that deliver more wine for the money. Finally, pay attention to store temperature: The warmer the store, the more likely the wines are to have problems.

ask questions Most wine-savvy salespeople are eager to share their knowledge and recommend some of their favorite wines. Let them know your likes, your budget and anything else that might help them select a wine you'll love.

become a regular The better the store's salespeople know you, the better they can suggest wines that will please you. They may also alert you to sales in advance.

online

know your options The two most common ways to buy wine online are via online retailers or directly from wineries. Retailers may offer bulk discounts if you buy a case and shipping discounts if you spend a certain amount. Wineries don't often discount, but their wines can be impossible to find elsewhere. A great advantage of online shopping is price comparison: Websites like wine-searcher.com allow you to compare prices at retailers around the world.

know the rules The difference between browsing for wine online and actually purchasing it has everything to do with where you live and how "liberal" your state is about interstate wine shipments. The laws governing direct-to-consumer interstate shipments differ from state to state. If you're considering buying wine from an out-of-state vendor, find out first whether it can ship to your state.

in restaurants

check out the list Most good lists feature wines in all price ranges. A poor list might be limited in selection, have too many wines from one producer or fail to list vintages. When faced with a bad wine list, order the least expensive bottle that you recognize as being reasonably good.

ask questions Treat the wine list as you would a food menu. You should ask how the Bordeaux tastes in comparison to the California Cabernet as readily as you'd ask the difference between two fish dishes. The first question should always be "May I speak to the wine director?" Then, tell that person the type of wine you're looking for—the price range, the flavor profile—as well as the dishes you will be having. With this information, the wine director should be able to recommend several options.

taste the wine When the bottle arrives, make sure it's exactly what you ordered—check the vintage, the producer, the blend or variety. If it's not, speak up. If the listed wine is out of stock, you might prefer to choose something else. You may be presented with the cork. Ignore it. Instead, sniff the wine in your glass. If it smells like sulfur, cabbage or skunk, tell your server that you think the wine might be flawed and request a second opinion from the wine director or the manager. If there's something truly wrong, they should offer you a new bottle or a new choice.

france

Other countries may make (or drink) more wine, but France is still the first country that comes to mind when people think of wine. The best-known grape varieties—Cabernet, Pinot Noir, Chardonnay—are French; many of the greatest wines come from France. And thanks to a constant push-pull between tradition and innovation here, France remains one of the world's most dynamic wine-producing nations.

Paris ☆

• Reims

Champagne

Strasbourg •

Alsace

Orléans •

Loire Valley

• Nantes

• Dijon

Burgundy

Atlantic Ocean

• Limoges

• Lyon

Bordeaux •

Rhône Valley

Bordeaux

• Avignon

Nîmes •

• Nice

Southwest

Provence

Languedoc-Roussillon

Marseille

Mediterranean Sea

■ **Principal Wine Region**

France: An Overview

France makes slightly less wine than Italy, the world's top producer, but most experts (and connoisseurs) agree that French vintners produce more *fine* wine than any other nation on earth. Thanks to its varied topography and climate, and centuries of experimentation in winemaking, France produces excellent wines in nearly every category. Red wines dominate in Bordeaux and the Rhône Valley. Alsace and the Loire Valley specialize in white wines. Burgundy is acclaimed for both reds and whites.

France has maintained its long-standing position as the center of the wine universe partly because it is home to the world's most esteemed wine grape varieties—Chardonnay, Cabernet Sauvignon, Merlot, Pinot Noir, Syrah and Sauvignon Blanc. But while the French care about grape varieties—and strictly regulate where and how different grapes are planted and grown—what really matters to them is a wine's *terroir*. The idea of terroir, a term that refers to all the distinguishing elements of a place, such as climate, sun exposure, soil makeup and surrounding flora, is fundamental to French winemaking philosophy. It is the belief that nature and geography make the wine, not man. Perhaps that is why, quite surprisingly, there is no French word for winemaker; someone who makes wine is called a *vigneron*—literally, a vine grower.

French Wine Labels

Most French wine labels list appellation (i.e., region or subregion) but not the grape variety used to make the wine. (Alsace labels are an important exception; see p. 25.) A wine bearing its appellation name is required to satisfy certain regulations designed to guarantee high quality and authenticity. The complex system governing these regulations is known as the *Appellation d'Origine Contrôlée* (AOC), or "controlled region of origin." The AOC hierarchy from top to bottom is:

• **AOC** This category encompasses the majority of French wines exported to the U.S. and ensures that the wines meet regional requirements. While standards vary by region, they typically spell out permitted grapes, winemaking practices, minimum alcohol levels (higher alcohol levels mean that the grapes were riper when they were picked, which in theory translates to more flavorful wines) and harvest size (overly large grape harvests tend to yield dilute wines). There are AOC regions *within* larger AOC regions as well; generally, the more specific the subregion, the higher the standards. In Burgundy, for example, a wine bearing a district name such as Côte de Nuits–Villages must meet more stringent requirements than those labeled with the region-wide appellation Bourgogne. Wines from the Vosne-Romanée, a *village* within the Côte de Nuits, must conform to stricter standards. The standards are even higher for wines from Vosne-Romanée Les Suchots, for example, a Premier Cru denomination of Vosne-Romanée.

• **VIN DÉLIMITÉ DE QUALITÉ SUPÉRIEURE (VDQS)** The VDQS category is an intermediary step to AOC status, so wines with this designation have always been few in number because of their transitional nature. In an effort to simplify the system, the VDQS designation is being phased out.

• **VIN DE PAYS** Translated as "country wines," Vins de Pays are subject to lower standards than AOC or VDQS wines, but they are allowed to list the wine's region and grape. Most Vins de Pays are forgettable, but there are a growing number of innovative winemakers who wish to work beyond the constraints of AOC requirements, and many are producing exemplary wines with this designation.

• **VIN DE TABLE** The lowest rung on the quality ladder of wines that fail to meet AOC requirements, Vins de Table (literally, "table wines") are not permitted to mention vintages or grape varieties on their labels, or give a place of origin more specific than "France." Most are dull, but certain iconoclasts who have chosen to ignore some of the AOC demands (which they believe inhibit quality production) are currently making some great Vins de Table.

alsace

It is easy to mistake wines from Alsace for their German counterparts: They share the same slim, tapered bottles, German surnames and even a history, as Alsace changed hands between France and Germany at various times between the 17th and 20th centuries.

Alsace Grapes & Styles

Alsace produces almost exclusively white wine, and two of the area's most notable grapes are German: Riesling and Gewurztraminer. However, while some German Rieslings are sweet, Alsace examples are almost always dry. French Pinot Blanc, Pinot Gris, Muscat and Auxerrois make up the bulk of Alsace's other white varieties and are all widely planted. Pinot Noir is the region's only red variety and makes both lighter red and rosé wines. Alsace is also known for its wonderful dessert wines (see p. 264) and for Crémant d'Alsace, a sparkling wine (see p. 252).

Alsace Wine Labels

Alsace labels are wonderfully simple compared to those of most other French regions. Taking a cue from Germany, Alsace labels its wines by grape variety. While European Union standards require that the listed grape make up at least 85 percent of a bottle's contents, Alsatian standards are higher, calling for 100 percent of the listed grape (wines labeled Pinot Blanc are an exception; see p. 26). Blended white wines are labeled with the official designation *Edel-zwicker* or *Gentil,* or the label may name the vineyard that grew the grapes. Most of the wine produced in Alsace meets AOC standards. Unlike the complex hierarchy in Burgundy or Bordeaux, Alsace has three AOC designations: Alsace, Alsace Grand Cru (which indicates the grapes were sourced from select vineyards) and Crémant d'Alsace (for sparkling wines). Wines labeled *Réserve,* a term used fairly liberally in Alsace to indicate wines of higher quality, may also list a place name.

alsace whites

Among Alsace grapes, four are regarded as noble, yielding the highest quality wines—Riesling, Gewurztraminer, Pinot Gris and Muscat. Riesling is the region's most widely planted grape, usually creating wines in a medium-bodied, dry style that tends to reflect the mineral and flinty quality of the terroir. Wines made from Gewurztraminer, another aromatic white grape, offer distinctive lychee and floral aromas and dry, spicy flavors, though a good number are made in an off-dry style. Pinot Gris, a white mutation of Pinot Noir, is the same grape as Italy's Pinot Grigio. Alsace Pinot Gris tends to be creamier and fuller-bodied than its Italian counterparts, with apricot and orange peel aromas. The least planted of the noble grapes, Muscat includes several sub-varieties, two of which are cultivated in Alsace.

Alsace white wine blends often include the noble grapes in combination with Sylvaner, Auxerrois and Chasselas—good if unexceptional varieties that don't generally make great wines on their own. Any of these grapes may be combined in an Edelzwicker blend, but a Gentil blend must be made up of at least 50 percent noble varieties. Pinot Blanc, the lighter-bodied sibling of Pinot Gris, is also permitted in these blends. However, Alsace wines labeled *Pinot Blanc* are likely to be a blend of Pinot Blanc and Auxerrois, with possible inclusions of Pinot Gris or Pinot Noir that has been vinified as white wine. Chardonnay is approved for AOC Crémant d'Alsace wines but not for still wines.

alsace white recommendations

Albert Seltz Réserve Riesling | 2008 |
★★ **$** This Riesling is all about peaches, limes and flowers. Complete with crisp acidity, pronounced minerality and great length, it is an immensely satisfying wine.

Audrey et Christian Binner les Saveurs | 2007 |
★★ **$ $** This organic blend of Riesling, Muscat and Pinot Gris comes from a small, 15-acre vineyard and offers a lovely mix of lychee, flower, citrus and tropical fruit flavors.

Domaine Ostertag Fronholz Pinot Gris | 2007 |

★★★ $ $ $ Domaine Ostertag's spectacular, full-bodied Pinot Gris possesses a depth and complexity that are rare for this grape variety. Honey-coated apricot and baked ripe peach flavors linger long after the final sip.

Domaines Schlumberger Les Princes Abbés Pinot Blanc | 2007 |

★★ $ As is the case with many Alsace Pinot Blancs, this wine is actually made with primarily the Auxerrois grape. It has a medium-full body and a clean, zippy palate comprised of tasty green apple and soft pear flavors.

star producers
alsace

Domaine Marcel Deiss

Jean-Michel Deiss is a committed terroirist, cultivating single-vineyard field blends that emphasize the soil rather than the specific variety.

Domaine Marc Kreydenweiss

At this winery—established in 1650—Marc Kreydenweiss made the switch to biodynamic viticulture in 1989 and has been a terroir evangelist ever since.

Domaine Weinbach

The widow and daughters of legendary Alsace advocate Théo Faller honor his dedication to excellence by crafting some of the region's most spectacular wines.

Domaine Zind-Humbrecht

Olivier Humbrecht was the first Frenchman ever to qualify as a Master of Wine. He's especially gifted at showing how low-yielding vines can translate to fantastic wines.

Hugel & Fils

This family winery's strict adherence to its central winemaking philosophy that "the wine is already in the grape" has kept it in business since the 17th century.

Trimbach

This esteemed family property is the top-selling Alsace brand in America—about a third of its entire wine production is exported to the U.S.

Domaine Weinbach Clos des Capucins Réserve Muscat
| 2008 |

★★★ $ $ $ Made partially with grapes grown in the historic 12-acre Clos des Capucins vineyard, this dry, fruity Muscat charms with its grape and elderflower perfume. Citrus zest dominates the palate through the long, crisp finish.

Helfrich Gewurztraminer | 2008 |
★★ $ Pleasantly off-dry and round-textured, this Gewurztraminer is a terrific value, offering perfume, rose and tropical fruit aromas and flavors and a somewhat oily texture.

Hugel et Fils Cuvée Les Amours Pinot Blanc | 2007 |
★★ $ $ Thanks to aromas of green apple and pear, and a fairly weighty palate, this nicely built Pinot Blanc is a great alternative for those who like unoaked Chardonnay.

Josmeyer L'Exceptíon Grand Cru Hengst Riesling | 2006 |
★★★★ $ $ $ $ Josmeyer's exceptional Hengst vineyard (the name means "stallion" in German) has yielded a truly stunning Riesling. Seductive aromas of petrol, peach and honey come on strong, and the rich, off-dry palate shows incredible length.

Léon Beyer Riesling | 2007 |
★ $ $ Tangy and tart, this medium-bodied Riesling is completely dry and presents a lovely mix of white peach and lime aromas and a citrus-driven palate.

Lucien Albrecht Cuvée Marie Gewurztraminer | 2007 |
★★★★ $ $ $ The grapes for this ethereal, concentrated Gewurztraminer hailing from the incredible 2007 vintage were harvested by hand and put through a pneumatic press. It is luscious, off-dry and brimming with wonderful flavors of honeysuckle, perfume and spice.

bordeaux

Bordeaux's legendary reputation throughout the world is based predominantly on its long-lived, earthy reds, and even more specifically on a handful of elite and expensive "first-growth" châteaux with notable names such as Lafite, Latour and Haut-Brion. Beyond this select sampling of renowned wines, Bordeaux yields many affordable reds, whites and even sweet wines.

Bordeaux Grapes & Styles

Nearly 90 percent of Bordeaux wines are red, made from some combination of Cabernet Sauvignon, Merlot, Cabernet Franc, Malbec, Petit Verdot and, in the past, Carmenère. Cabernet Sauvignon excels on the Left Bank of the Gironde; Merlot is at its best on the Right Bank, though blending is vital in all Bordeaux. In addition, the region makes many excellent whites, from Sauvignon Blanc, Sémillon and Muscadelle, or some combination thereof, that exhibit stone-fruit flavors. The greatest Bordeaux blancs are the sweet wines from Sauternes and its satellite regions (see p. 264).

■ Principal Wine Region

Bordeaux Wine Labels

Bordeaux wines are labeled by region, and generally, the more specific the regional designation, the better the wine. Wines labeled simply *Bordeaux* can be made anywhere in Bordeaux. The next level up is *Bordeaux Supérieur;* these wines are required to be higher in alcohol, which implies they were made from riper grapes—often a measure of higher quality. Wines from Bordeaux's districts—such as Médoc, Graves and St-Émilion—are required to meet even higher standards. And within the districts are communes—Pauillac and Margaux in Médoc, for example—which must meet more stringent requirements still. Bordeaux's system for ranking wines was established with the famous 1855 classification, which created a hierarchy of wineries (or châteaux) considered superior based on the prices their wines were able to command over time. Known as the *Cru Classé* system, this ranking grouped 61 superior wineries by *cru* (growth), from first (*Premier Cru*) on top to fifth. Châteaux that didn't make the cut, but were still considered quite good, received the rank *Cru Bourgeois*. The 1855 system is limited to châteaux in Médoc and Sauternes, and a single château in Graves. In 1955 a similar system was set up to rank wines from the St-Émilion district, but it is subject to revision every ten years or so. The famed wines of Pomerol are not ranked. An attempt to revise the Cru Bourgeois ranking in 2003 was overturned by a French court in 2007, and the designation was reestablished as of the 2008 vintage. It is now viewed as a stamp of approval rather than a true classification.

bordeaux whites

The finest white Bordeaux—made in Pessac-Léognan, Graves and Blaye—are worth seeking out for their dry flavors of citrus, peach, grass and stone. The district of Entre-Deux-Mers, literally "between two seas," produces the bulk of Bordeaux white wine. These whites display similar light, citrusy flavors; many of them are quite good and affordable, if not terribly complex.

bordeaux white recommendations

Château Bonnet | 2009 | ENTRE-DEUX-MERS

★ **$** A blend of 50 percent Sauvignon Blanc, 40 percent Sémillon and 10 percent Muscadelle, this unoaked white offers crisp, dry grapefruit flavors and a tangy finish.

Château Carbonnieux Grand Cru | 2006 | PESSAC-LÉOGNAN

★★★★ **$ $ $** Dating back to the 14th century, Château Carbonnieux was owned by the Benedictine monastic order for many years. This golden-hued, elegant wine delivers a complex mix of sweet vanilla, wildflower and vibrant citrus flavors that linger impressively on the palate.

Château Graville-Lacoste | 2008 | GRAVES

★★★★ **$ $** Owner-vintner Hervé Dubourdieu crafts this magnificent white Graves, which is the château's Grand Vin. Unfiltered, unoaked and wonderfully bright and refreshing, it is characterized by aromas and flavors of lime zest and fresh-cut grass and a rather weighty mouthfeel that nicely coats the palate.

stay here now

THE REGENT GRAND HOTEL BORDEAUX Facing the Opéra National de Bordeaux in the city's premier shopping district, this beautifully renovated hotel features the excellent restaurant Le Pressoir d'Argent and in-room wine bars in the Prestige Suites (with private sommelier service upon request). An ultra-deluxe spa is set to open in early 2011. *Bordeaux; theregentbordeaux.com*

Château Lamothe de Haux | 2009 | BORDEAUX

★★ **$** This likable wine is an ideal aperitif. Aged *sur lie* (on lees) for about three weeks, the 2009 vintage is a combination of 40 percent Sauvignon Blanc, 40 percent Sémillon and 20 percent Muscadelle. The result is a white wine full of flowers, ripe gooseberry flavors and an invigorating acidity.

Château Les Maines Cuvée Soleil d'Or | 2009 | BORDEAUX

★ **$** Unoaked and very dry, this crisp white is ripe and citrusy, the perfect companion for oysters. It's also available in a party-friendly three-liter box.

Château Rahoul | 2007 | GRAVES

★★ **$ $** Château Rahoul crafted this in a modern style compared with most other whites from the region. Aromas of toasted oak and citrus are at the forefront, and a moderate acidity nicely offsets the full body and round texture.

bordeaux reds

Made from mostly Cabernet Sauvignon and Merlot, plus small amounts of Cabernet Franc, Petit Verdot and Malbec, the red wines of Bordeaux differ from subregion to subregion. Those from Pauillac are tannic and full-bodied; those from St-Julien are more taut. The wines of Margaux are delicate, while those from St-Émilion are plush. Most Bordeaux reds share earthiness and finesse.

bordeaux red recommendations

Blason de l'Evangile | 2007 | POMEROL
★★★ $ $ $ This Right Bank estate is owned by the Rothschilds. The 2007 boasts aromas of blackberry, spice and charred oak, while the full-bodied palate shows the classic ripe plum flavors of Merlot.

Blason d'Issan | 2006 | MARGAUX
★★★★ $ $ The historic third-growth Château d'Issan was referenced in a 1787 letter from Thomas Jefferson (it was then called Château de Candale). This stunning second wine, a blend of more Cabernet than Merlot, is marked by layers of oak, spice, cigar box and currant.

Château Bibian Cru Bourgeois | 2005 | LISTRAC-MÉDOC
★★★ $ $ Château Bibian holds the distinction of being situated at the highest point in the Médoc. The vineyards' elevation contributes a lovely firmness to flavors of cassis and baking spice in this medium-bodied and affordable gem.

Château Brane-Cantenac | 2007 | MARGAUX
★★★★ $ $ $ Cabernet-dominated Brane-Cantenac is a powerful, full-bodied and velvety wine made in a thoroughly modern style. Low yields and 18 months in oak impart vanilla and spice nuances to ripe, dark cherry flavors that linger on the palate.

Château La Garde | 2005 | PESSAC-LÉOGNAN
★★★ $ $ $ This clean and polished red offers flavors of cassis, smoke and vanilla. Chewy tannins, a medium-full body and a good depth make it balanced and immensely enjoyable.

Château Palmer | 2007 | MARGAUX
★★★★ $ $ $ $ Since Thomas Duroux took the helm as winemaker at this third-growth neighbor of Château Margaux in 2004, the wines just keep getting better. Plum and licorice flavors meld nicely with bright acidity in this silky, medium-bodied wine.

Château Palmer Alter Ego | 2007 | MARGAUX
★ ★ ★ $ $ $ Château Palmer's second label is polished yet brawny, displaying ripe black fruit and notes of mocha and spice. Its long finish and firm but approachable tannins indicate that it will benefit from a decade in the cellar.

Château Pimpine | 2005 | BORDEAUX CÔTES DE FRANC
★ ★ $ $ Located near Pomerol and St-Émilion, Château Pimpine crafts this biodynamic wine from 80 percent Merlot and 20 percent Cabernet Sauvignon. Medium in body but full in flavor, it's intensely earthy, with notes of cigar box and blackberry.

Château Recougne | 2006 | BORDEAUX SUPÉRIEUR
★ $ This charming red is not about power or concentration; lithe and delicate in body, it features pure, delicious flavors of baking spice, black fruit and smoke.

news from bordeaux

Vintage Notes

The 2009 harvest is being hyped as Bordeaux's best since 2005. The 2008 vintage will be released in early 2011; it was small, but the wines are fresh and elegant. These wines will likely be bargains compared to those from the 2009 vintage, which will undoubtedly fetch very high prices.

Bordeaux value-seekers should also note that the 2008 vintage marks the return of Cru Bourgeois–labeled wines from the Left Bank. These are high-quality wines from cru-classified vineyards that are significantly less expensive than Cru Classé bottlings.

Regions to Watch

Right Bank satellite appellations like Côtes de Castillon and Fronsac are turning out more and more stellar wines. Young superstar producers such as Guillaume Halley, Thibault Despagne and Thierry Valette are all making wine in these more affordable regions.

Winemaker to Watch

All eyes are on Olivier Berrouet, who took over winemaking at Château Pétrus in 2008 after his father, Jean-Claude Berrouet, retired from the position after 44 years. The younger Berrouet's first vintage will be the 2009.

Château Reysson Réserve du Château Cru Bourgeois
Supérieur | 2005 | **HAUT-MÉDOC**
★★ **$ $** This 50-50 blend of Cabernet Sauvignon and Merlot is typical Bordeaux—structured and elegant. It displays more red fruit than black in flavor, a subtle oakiness and ripe tannins.

Château Teyssier | 2005 | **MONTAGNE ST-ÉMILION**
★★ **$ $** Made primarily from Merlot, this well-crafted wine shows off blackberry, cherry and earth on the palate and juicy tannins on the medium-long finish.

Dourthe La Grande Cuvée | 2007 | **BORDEAUX**
★ **$** Both oaky and smoky, this medium-bodied value red offers black fruit flavors along with a plush texture and fleshy tannins.

star producers
bordeaux reds

Château Angélus
Over the last 20 years, Angélus has made a dizzying number of standout wines, maintaining its position in the upper echelon of Bordeaux estates.

Château Haut-Brion
Throughout its rich, storied history this first-growth vintner has consistently produced world-class wines.

Château Lafleur
For 40 years, until the mid-1980s, this château was run by sisters Marie and Thérèse Robin. Today, their niece and nephew run Lafleur, which produces exceptional Merlot-based wines.

Château Léoville Barton
Founded by an Irishman, this nearly 200-year-old second-growth producer makes relatively affordable wines that are loved by critics and oenophiles alike.

Château Margaux
Under the direction of longtime owner Corinne Mentzelopoulos and manager Paul Pontallier, this first-growth producer continues to shine.

Château Pétrus
Christian and Jean-François Moueix carry the torch for their late father, Jean-Pierre, who is credited with putting Pomerol and St-Émilion on the map.

Haut Beyzac I Second | 2005 | HAUT-MÉDOC
★ ★ $ $ This blend of 60 percent Merlot and 40 percent Cabernet Sauvignon spends 12 months in barrel, and although it's only six years old, it's already showing some lovely signs of maturity. Flavors of cassis and spice are underscored by dried leaves and leather notes.

Les Fiefs de Lagrange | 2006 | ST-JULIEN
★ ★ ★ $ $ $ Since purchasing Château Lagrange in 1983, Japanese conglomerate Suntory has spent over $40 million refurbishing it. This, the Grand Cru estate's second label, is packed with dark fruit and forest floor aromas that meld beautifully with soft tannins on the impressive, long finish.

Michel Lynch Merlot | 2008 | BORDEAUX
★ $ Blackberry and plum notes define the palate of this bright, juicy red. While simple, it's highly enjoyable, proving that it's still possible to find great value in Bordeaux.

burgundy

Burgundy has a reputation that far exceeds its small size. Its wines are among the most highly prized in the world. Yet because it is one of France's northernmost and coolest grape-growing regions, it can produce some highly variable (and often disappointing) vintages. Winemakers here value terroir above all else, and the most esteemed names are vineyards, such as Montrachet, rather than producers. The rigid and elaborate hierarchy in Burgundy is every bit as complex as the region's ethereal, smoky wines.

Burgundy Grapes & Styles

Burgundy's fame is tied to two grape varieties: Chardonnay and Pinot Noir. Basically, all whites here are made from Chardonnay, except for a bit of Sauvignon Blanc (grown in and around St-Bris) and Aligoté (mostly from the Côte Chalonnaise)—both of which are indicated on labels—and tiny amounts of Pinots Blanc and Gris. Pinot Noir is responsible for the lion's share of Burgundy reds, with the major exception of Beaujolais reds, which are made with Gamay. Though considered part of the Burgundy region, Beaujolais has a distinctly different climate, terroir and style of wine.

Burgundy Wine Labels

All wine labels in Burgundy list region; some also list subregion, and the most prestigious include a vineyard name. Generally, the more specific the place information on a label, the finer the wine, but vintage is also extremely important when it comes to assessing quality in this unpredictable region. Many of the familiar producers of Burgundy are *négociants*, merchants who purchase wine or grapes from the region's many small grower-producers.

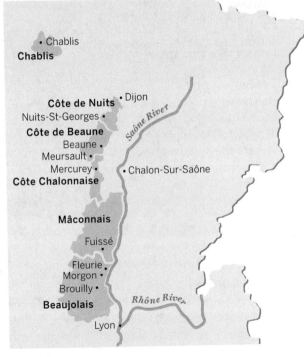

■ Principal Wine Region

• **REGION** The most basic wines of Burgundy are labeled with just the name of the region, *Bourgogne,* and occasionally with the grape variety. Though these wines are essentially unassuming, some of them nonetheless offer good quality at an excellent price.

• **DISTRICT** A district appellation (such as Chablis or Mâconnais) is the next step up in terms of quality in Burgundy. The grapes must be grown exclusively in the named district. Wines labeled with *Villages* after the district name are theoretically superior.

• **VILLAGE** A wine is permitted to take the name of a specific village if all of its grapes have been grown within that village's boundaries. This is often a good sign, as grapes from the same terroir typically display similar characteristics and flavors.

• **PREMIER CRU** Certain vineyards with a lengthy history of producing truly superior wines have earned the Premier Cru distinction. These special wines account for only about 10 percent of Burgundy's entire production, and they must be made only with grapes grown in these designated vineyards, which are sometimes included in the wine's name (Meursault Premier Cru Genevrières, for example). Premier Cru is the second-highest distinction in Burgundy, after Grand Cru. (Confusingly, in Bordeaux, *Grands Crus Classés* refers to the entire classification system, and Premier Cru is the highest rank.)

• **GRAND CRU** The exceptional Grand Cru vineyards of Burgundy are so elite (fewer than 2 percent hold the honor), and the wines so famous throughout the world, that some, like Montrachet, don't even include the *Grand Cru* title on their labels, as it is considered unnecessary. These are the region's finest wines, requiring many years of age to reach their fullest potential. So great is the prestige of these wines that some villages added the name of the local Grand Cru vineyard to their own names decades ago. Thus the wines from Chassagne, for example, became Chassagne-Montrachet; while many of them are indeed superb, they are not true Montrachet.

burgundy whites

Basic white Burgundy takes two forms, Bourgogne Blanc, made from Chardonnay, and the much scarcer Bourgogne Aligoté, made from the grape of the same name. For affordable Chardonnay wines, look to Côte Chalonnaise, as well as Mâconnais, which benefits from limestone soils well suited to the grape. The simplest Mâconnais wines are labeled Mâcon; more complex wines typically have a village name as well—Mâcon Verzé and Mâcon Lugny, for instance. Pouilly-Fuissé, distinguished by its ripe, rich and oaky style, is regarded as the apex of the Mâconnais region's wines.

The Côte d'Or is Burgundy's premier region. It is split into two halves: Côte de Nuits in the north and Côte de Beaune in the south. While the Côte d'Or produces both reds and whites, the Côte de Beaune is responsible for some of the world's most prestigious Chardonnays, from villages such as Puligny-Montrachet and Meursault.

Far to the north is Chablis. With its cool climate and limestone-rich soils, Chablis is known for high-acid, mineral-laden Chardonnays. They are considered distinct among all other white Burgundies in that they spend very little if any time in oak barrels, which leaves them particularly fresh and pure. The region's best wines are labeled with their Grand or Premier Cru vineyard names, followed by the Chablis appellation; lesser wines are labeled *Petit Chablis.*

burgundy white recommendations

Bouchard Père & Fils Clos Saint-Landry | 2007 |
BEAUNE PREMIER CRU

★★★ $ $ $ Richly layered aromas of hazelnut and spice are echoed on the palate alongside honeyed fruit, nut and subtle toast flavors in this exceptional white. The driving acidity and mineral nuances on the finish provide great balance.

Cave de Lugny Les Charmes Chardonnay | 2008 |
MÂCON-LUGNY

★★ $ $ With vines averaging 40 years of age, the Les Charmes vineyard yields fresh, lively whites. This unoaked example delivers inviting bread aromas followed by apple, peach and citrus flavors.

Collin-Bourisset | 2007 | POUILLY-FUISSÉ
★★ $ $ Wonderfully fresh, this light-bodied Pouilly-Fuissé offers grapefruit and lime zest flavors, hints of toast and warm spice and a zippy, acidic finish.

Didier Montchovet | 2007 | HAUTES–CÔTES DE BEAUNE
★★ $ $ Established in 1984, the pioneering Didier Montchovet was one of the early adopters of biodynamic viticulture. Its rustic Chardonnay is quite distinctive, with a fleshy palate, rich cider and pear flavors and a spicy, lime-infused acidity.

news from burgundy

Vineyard News

Corton, one of Burgundy's most famous Grand Cru districts, has seen a lot of recent changes. Etienne de Montille of Domaine Hubert de Montille and winemaker David Croix of Domaine des Croix and Maison Camille Giroud have both purchased land here. More recently, Burgundy's most fabled property, Domaine de la Romanée-Conti, acquired the Corton holdings of Domaine Prince Florent de Mérode. This marks DRC's first venture into the Côte de Beaune; the 2009 will be its first vintage.

Vintage Notes

The best 2007 reds show the ethereal side of Burgundy and resemble the 2000 reds in their elegance. Across the board, 2007 was a good vintage for whites, and prices will be lower than the 2006 vintage. For upcoming vintages, 2008 will be a long-lived year, reminiscent of 2003; unfortunately, it was a tiny harvest. Most agree 2009 is a top vintage, though many wines won't be on the market until late 2011 or early 2012.

Finding Value

Chablis remains undervalued. Basic village bottles are good deals, priced in the mid-$20s; even Premier Cru wines are in the low $40s. Among large producers, Maison Joseph Drouhin and William Fèvre are both making excellent wines. Among boutique producers, Vincent Dauvissat continues to craft some of the best white wine values in France.

Domaine J.A. Ferret | 2008 | POUILLY-FUISSÉ

★ ★ $ $ Enticing notes of oak, toast and flowers mingle with zippy citrus and mineral on the nose of this lively Pouilly-Fuissé, while flavors of sweet butter, green apple and grapefruit take over in the mouth.

Domaine Montanet-Thoden Le Galerne | 2006 | BOURGOGNE VÉZELAY

★ ★ $ $ Bracing acidity expertly balances the supple creamy character of this buttery wine. Hints of herbal verbena and nutmeg add complexity to flavors of honey and almonds.

Guillot-Broux Sélection | 2008 | MÂCON VILLAGES

★ ★ $ $ Here's a refreshing, organic wine that's a great value. Six months in oak barrels contribute some weight, while leaving the stone-fruit and citrus flavors fresh and inviting.

JJ Vincent Chardonnay | 2008 | BOURGOGNE

★ ★ $ $ This starts off somewhat subdued, but opens up to reveal zesty citrus and vanilla flavors with hints of hazelnut and spice on a medium-bodied palate.

Joseph Faiveley Chardonnay | 2007 | BOURGOGNE

★ ★ $ $ Caramel candy and toffee aromas join abundant apple and spice in Faiveley's stellar Chardonnay. It has a medium weight, sharp acidity and flavors of golden apple and Asian pear that linger nicely.

Labouré-Roi Les Chevaliers | 2006 | MEURSAULT

★ ★ ★ $ $ $ A particularly robust Meursault, this is loaded with hazelnut, straw, earth and dried flower aromas. There's a creaminess to the apple flavors, underscored by golden raisin, dates and honey on the long, dry finish.

Louis Jadot | 2007 | PULIGNY-MONTRACHET

★ ★ ★ $ $ $ From one of the biggest names in Burgundy comes this toast- and hazelnut-accented wine. Peach and citrus are balanced with dry minerals and herbs on the well-built palate.

Louis Latour | 2007 | CHASSAGNE-MONTRACHET

★ ★ $ $ $ This is quite ripe, with tropical fruit and juicy peach flavors joined by hints of macadamia and piecrust. The plump texture is wonderfully rich, offset by grapefruit-like acidity.

Nicolas Maillet | 2007 | MÂCON VERZÉ

★ ★ ★ $ $ Honey, acacia flower, caramelized nut and spice aromas lead to a palate that opens with ripe white peach and pineapple flavors. Nervy acidity balances the subtle sweetness, and bold minerals take over on the finish.

Olivier Leflaive Rabource | 2008 | **RULLY PREMIER CRU**
★★★ **$ $ $** Equal parts lively and rich, this plush white reverberates with loads of acidity, which provides nice lift. Luscious flavors of grapefruit, lemon and apple share the stage with nuts, cinnamon, butterscotch and toast.

Paul Jacqueson | 2007 | **RULLY PREMIER CRU GRÉSIGNY**
★★★ **$ $ $** Paul is the son of Rully pioneer Henri Jacqueson. His elegant white starts off with enchanting aromas of toasted almonds, flowers, pears and orange blossoms, followed by flavors of peach and apricot that are broad and round.

chablis recommendations

A. & F. Boudin Domaine de Chantemerle | 2008 | CHABLIS
★★ **$ $** Made without oak, this Chardonnay is clean and lightly fragrant, with delicate apple, mineral and pear aromas. On the palate, tart citrus joins the mix, along with a stroke of refreshing acidity.

Christian Moreau Père & Fils | 2008 | CHABLIS
★★★ **$ $** This tasty, zippy white, made with grapes from 45-year-old vines in the village of Chablis, features a generous body, with spice and abundant limestone permeating a core of ripe stone fruit. It finishes taut, with minerals and acidity adding a nice lift.

Domaine Oudin | 2007 | CHABLIS PREMIER CRU VAUGIRAUT
★★ **$ $ $** Yeast character meets stone fruits and mandarin orange in this delightful white. Its texture is broad and its body relatively full for a Chablis.

Drouhin Vaudon Réserve de Vaudon | 2008 | CHABLIS
★★★ **$ $** Showing a touch of creaminess, this stunning Chablis is defined by ripe pear, quince and citrus. Notes of lemon oil, orange zest and oyster shell appear toward the long, bright finish.

Régnard Saint Pierre | 2004 | CHABLIS
★★★ **$ $** A gorgeous chalky nose introduces this flavorful Chablis, with fresh hay, herbs, seashell and peach pit coming in on the palate. The body is robust—even a touch oily—and elegantly framed by herbs and minerals.

William Fèvre | 2007 | CHABLIS PREMIER CRU MONTMAINS
★★★ **$ $ $** There's nothing shy about this stunning wine, which shows off Chardonnay's bold, plump side. Toast and citrus flavors with nuances of flint, herbs and vanilla course through the round body; lively acidity holds it all together beautifully.

burgundy reds

Whether it's made into basic Bourgogne Rouge or world-famous benchmark reds, Pinot Noir is Burgundy's pride. The finest Burgundy reds hail from the Côte d'Or region and are characterized by seductive cherry flavors under-scored by a pronounced minerality. The more renowned of Burgundy's villages and Grands Crus are in the Côte de Nuits, including Chambolle-Musigny, Gevrey-Chambertin and Nuits-St-Georges. Corton is the only red Grand Cru in the Côte de Beaune, where most reds tend to be lighter in body and flavor. Wines labeled simply *Côte de Nuits–Villages* may be red or white, while *Côte de Beaune–Villages* are always red. Such wines either don't qualify for a village designation or are blends made up of wines from several villages. The Côte Chalonnaise is less important for red wine than for white, although the villages of Mercurey and Givry do produce some good-value reds.

burgundy red recommendations

Bouchard Père & Fils Caillerets Ancienne Cuvée Carnot
| 2007 | VOLNAY PREMIER CRU

★★★★ $ $ $ $ Tart berries meet barnyard and hints of rose petal on the nose of this exceptional Volnay, while dark plum flavors take over on the beautifully textured palate. The initial sweet fruit is lay-ered with baking spice and refined tannins, which see the wine through the firm, tasty finish.

Catherine & Dominique Derain La Plante Chassey | 2007 | MERCUREY

★★★ $ $ $ With prices much lower than those of the great Côte d'Or villages, Mercurey is a good source for value wines. Silky and smooth, with a good acidic backbone, this stellar example starts off with aromas of spiced berries, pine and rose petal, followed by bright cherry, wild strawberry and raspberry on the fruit-driven palate.

Domaine Eric Boussey | 2007 | MONTHÉLIE

★★ $ $ A nice entry-level Burgundy, this features an abundance of black fruit alongside loads of earthy, damp forest flavors, with toasted oak, smoke and cedar sweeping in on the finish. Its supple texture and firm tannins are very inviting.

Domaine Montanet-Thoden | 2007 | BOURGOGNE

★★ $ $ Bright and ripe, with a sweet cherry nose, this wine shows a distinct herbaceous edge—its leafy sassafras and eucalyptus flavors are fresh and enjoyable.

Domaine Patrick Miolane Pinot Noir | 2005 | BOURGOGNE

★★★★ $ $ An exceptional bargain from Burgundy, this Pinot Noir offers a complex, concentrated mix of ripe black fruit flavors layered with spice cake, earth, smoke and star anise. It's creamy and plush, with a crescendo of plums, licorice, tobacco and cedar that builds toward the long finish.

Domaine Poulleau Père & Fils Les Mondes Rondes | 2008 | CÔTE DE BEAUNE

★★ $ $ Vivid aromas of cherry and strawberry are joined by classic barnyard and berry flavors in this medium-bodied Côte de Beaune. The dense palate is wonderfully balanced by a refreshing acidity.

Julien Guillot | 2007 | BOURGOGNE

★ $ $ Light-bodied, with crackling acidity and some candied red cherry flavors, this basic Burgundy red features hints of spice and citrus.

Louis Jadot | 2007 | GEVREY-CHAMBERTIN

★★ $ $ $ There's nice weight and length to the fruit and earth flavors in this somewhat firm, structured red, and enough tannins to ensure that it will age well for a few more years.

Maurice Chapuis Les Taillepieds | 2006 | VOLNAY PREMIER CRU

★★★ $ $ $ Flavors of blackberry, currant and plum display good intensity in this ripe and dark Premier Cru. Some cedary oak notes are woven in, and the palate is tightly laced with firm tannins.

Michel Picard | 2006 | ST-AUBIN PREMIER CRU LE CHARMOIS

★★ $ $ $ The alluring floral aromas of this cherry-saturated red wine are punctuated by notes of cinnamon, clove and sandalwood. Fine, drying tannins provide just the right amount of structure, while the finish is wonderfully spicy.

eat here now

AUBERGE DE LA CHARME At Auberge de la Charme's new incarnation in a 1780s stone house, chef Nicolas Isnard prepares dishes like roasted pigeon with fresh porcini mushrooms and black Burgundy truffles. His wife, pastry chef Cécile Isnard, tweaks French classics, using a confit of figs to fill flaky tarts. The restaurant quickly earned its first Michelin star in 2009. *Prenois, Burgundy; aubergedelacharme.com*

BURGUNDY

beaujolais

As Burgundy's southernmost region, Beaujolais is distinctly different from its neighbors to the north. To begin with, red wines here are made exclusively with the Gamay grape (instead of Pinot Noir), and the region has its own ranking system for quality. Beaujolais produces an abundance of inexpensive, simple-but-satisfying red wines, as well as a number of high-quality bottles that can satisfy the palate of a Burgundy lover at a mere fraction of the cost. A very small amount of Chardonnay-based white wine is also made here, and it can be good.

• **BEAUJOLAIS NOUVEAU** Designed for consumption within weeks of harvest, Beaujolais Nouveau is as light and simple as red wine gets. By law, it is released the third Thursday of every November, conveniently coinciding with the start of the American holiday season.

• **BEAUJOLAIS** Wines made from grapes grown anywhere within the designated region earn the moniker *Beaujolais.* These reds are marked by distinctive light, fruity flavors and are a bit more substantial than Beaujolais Nouveau.

• **BEAUJOLAIS VILLAGES** The title *Beaujolais Villages* is given to any wine made from grapes grown within the 39 villages occupying the rolling hills at the center of the region. These wines are typically made with more care and precision, producing bright fruit flavors as well as an added depth of mineral and spice.

• **CRU BEAUJOLAIS** The region's greatest wines come from ten hillside villages in the northern part of Beaujolais. Called *Cru Beaujolais,* these wines show an even heavier concentration of berry, mineral and spice flavors than Beaujolais Villages, plus ample tannins, which allow them to age, unlike other Beaujolais. Cru Beaujolais labels often do not include the name *Beaujolais,* but rather the name of the village where the grapes were grown: Brouilly, Chénas, Chiroubles, Côte de Brouilly, Fleurie, Juliénas, Morgon, Moulin-à-Vent, Régnié or St-Amour.

beaujolais recommendations

REDS

Clos de la Roilette | 2008 | FLEURIE
★★ $ $ Before the 1920s this wine was classified as a Moulin-à-Vent, and its vineyards still border its former appellation. It features a delicious mix of baking spice and ripe berry flavors wrapped around firm, chewy tannins that give it a medium-length finish.

Domaine Pral Cuvée Terroir | 2008 | BEAUJOLAIS
★★ $ This well-crafted Gamay is fermented with its stems for ten full days, which adds a welcome complexity to the ample blackberry and stony mineral flavors.

star producers
burgundy

Bouchard Père & Fils
A rarity among Burgundy *négociants,* Bouchard actually owns 321 acres, including the famous Vigne de l'Enfant Jésus.

Domaine d'Auvenay
D'Auvenay's proprietor, Lalou Bize-Leroy, was instrumental in making the wines of Domaine de la Romanée-Conti so sought after before striking out to craft her own superior wines.

Domaine de la Romanée-Conti
So well known it can be abbreviated, DRC produces some of Burgundy's most prized, distinctive and expensive wines from its Grand Cru vineyards.

Domaine Georges Roumier
High achiever Christophe Roumier is the third generation of his winemaking family to produce some of the most highly coveted wines of Chambolle-Musigny.

Domaine Henri Gouges
This domaine's small Nuits-St-Georges vineyard yields tight, dense wines that take years to soften—but are worth the wait.

Domaine Leflaive
With top-notch vineyards, biodynamic practices and Anne-Claude Leflaive's talented hand, Domaine Leflaive produces some of the best dry white wines in the region.

Georges Duboeuf Domaine de la Tour du Bief | 2009 |
MOULIN-À-VENT
★★ $ $ Dusty tannins are up-front in this earthy Cru Beaujolais;
wild berry and tobacco notes round them out.

Guy Breton Vieilles Vignes | 2007 | MORGON
★★★ $ $ One of Beaujolais' best producers, Breton employs a
"non-interventionist" approach when making his wines. The result is
a balanced, elegant red that displays a mélange of berry aromas and
a purity of flavor unusual for Beaujolais.

Jean-Claude Lapalu Cuvée Vieilles Vignes | 2007 | BROUILLY
★★★ $ $ This fantastic Brouilly illustrates how closely Gamay can
resemble Pinot Noir in style when made with care. It's intensely
earthy, with complex layers of barnyard and cherry, a medium body
and approachable tannins.

Jean-Paul Brun Terres Dorées | 2008 | CÔTE DE BROUILLY
★★ $ $ An inviting nose of blueberry is followed by ripe plum flavors, soft tannins and juicy acidity in this fleshy red.

Potel-Aviron | 2008 | BEAUJOLAIS VILLAGES
★ $ Bright berry flavors define this charming Beaujolais Villages.
Gentle tannins and a light body make it a perfect picnic wine.

loire valley

Stretching some 300 miles along the Loire River, the fertile
Loire Valley is one of the largest and most diverse wine
regions of France—and one of its most underappreciated.
The wines made here range from dry, still reds, whites and
rosés to sparklers and dessert bottles. Almost all Loire
wines, however, possess relatively high acidity.

Loire Valley Grapes & Styles

The Loire Valley is home to a vast array of grapes. Muscadet, made from the Melon de Bourgogne grape, is crisp and
dry, while Chenin Blanc is used for dry, sweet and sparkling
wines. Sauvignon Blanc is responsible for the whites of
Sancerre and Pouilly-Fumé, and Chardonnay is used for
sparkling wine and a few blends, like those of Valençay. The
valley's dominant red grape is Cabernet Franc, although it
also grows Pinot Noir, Gamay, Malbec and others.

Loire Valley Wine Labels

Because there is no broad Loire appellation for still wines, only the pink Rosé de Loire and the sparkling Crémant de Loire actually bear the name "Loire" on their labels. Most Loire wines are identified by more precise appellations, and since blending of grapes is quite rare, the appellation name is usually enough to determine the variety. Wines made from grapes not tied to a region will list both the grape and the region name.

loire valley whites

The Loire Valley's broad range of white wines, from simple aperitifs to profoundly earthy, complex wines designed for aging, are made from three primary grapes: Melon de Bourgogne, Sauvignon Blanc and Chenin Blanc. Melon de Bourgogne is the only grape used for Muscadet, a relatively light-bodied and simple white wine that is a favorite with fresh shellfish. The best come from the subappellation of Muscadet Sèvre et Maine, where many wines develop slightly richer flavors because they are aged *sur lie*—given prolonged contact with the lees, a sediment consisting mostly of spent yeast cells.

Sauvignon Blanc in the Loire Valley yields white wines filled with ripe grapefruit, gooseberry and grass flavors, as well as refreshing acidity and distinctive flinty aromatics. The benchmark examples hail from the eastern reaches of the valley in Sancerre and Pouilly-Fumé, with the former fuller-bodied and the latter lighter and more perfumed. Nearby Menetou-Salon, Quincy and Reuilly offer more affordable alternatives.

The Loire's most distinctive and versatile grape is surely Chenin Blanc, capable of creating dry to exquisitely sweet still wines, as well as sparkling wines, all featuring bright acidity. Vouvray offers both off-dry and dry versions of Chenin Blanc; Montlouis-sur-Loire, across the river, is a tiny up-and-comer. The Chenin Blancs labeled Savennières, Saumur or Anjou have the potential to age, developing marvelous honey, citrus, truffle and smoke flavors.

loire valley white recommendations

Baumard | 2006 | SAVENNIÈRES
★★ $ $ Vanilla and marshmallow notes infuse the ripe melon and nectarine flavors in this finely balanced, unoaked wine; almond and butter touches fill out the finish.

Clos des Briords Cuvée Vieilles Vignes Sur Lie | 2008 | MUSCADET SÈVRE ET MAINE
★★★ $ $ Crafted from very old vines, this single-vineyard Muscadet offers a combination of white peach, nectarine and chalky mineral flavors. There's a nice spritzy quality on the palate, along with tons of acidity and a stony finish. It's an amazing value for a wine that is so fresh and appealing.

Domaine Alexandre Bain Mademoiselle M | 2008 | POUILLY-FUMÉ
★★★ $ $ This shows lovely notes of caramel and nutty praline amid flavors of honeyed fruit, candied orange peel and pear that explode in the mouth. Organic and biodynamic, with a creamy texture and spicy acidity, it's an exceptional and distinctive wine.

Domaine de la Perrière | 2008 | SANCERRE
★★ $ $ Thanks to stainless steel fermentation, this well-built Sancerre displays fresh grass, gooseberry and chalky minerals in perfect balance. Tart berry and green apple notes mark the mineral-laden, ultradry finish.

Domaine La Haute Févrie Sur Lie | 2008 | MUSCADET SÈVRE ET MAINE
★★ $ This lemony fresh Muscadet is light and crisp, with wet stone aromas, a fierce acidity and loads of peach flavors. Its medium-weight body and solid structure give it some substance.

François Chidaine Clos Habert | 2007 | MONTLOUIS-SUR-LOIRE
★★★ $ $ Crafted in a demi-sec style from grapes grown on old vines, this white features gorgeous apricot and peach flavors layered with minerals and a delicate honeyed sweetness. The palate is rich, with nuances of lemon oil and juicy pineapple.

François Pinon Sec | 2004 | VOUVRAY
★★★ $ $ Although the fruit aromas in this Vouvray are somewhat restrained, there is an incredible mineral intensity to it that is both intriguing and delicious. Oyster shell, chalk and crushed stones, interwoven with subtle notes of lean white peach, carry through on the mineral-rich, dry finish.

Les Cailloux du Paradis Quartz | 2007 | VIN DE TABLE
★ ★ $ $ For a Sauvignon Blanc, this is rather full-bodied, with pronounced chalky minerals on the nose. Flavors of peach, nectarine and herbs abound on the palate, which has a somewhat oxidized quality, due to time spent aging in old barrels.

Les Clissages d'Or sur Lie | 2008 | MUSCADET SÈVRE ET MAINE
★ ★ $ $ In this lively white made by Guy Saget, pretty white peach, mineral and floral aromas waft from the glass and are followed by ripe fruit flavors. A refreshing touch of natural carbon dioxide and vibrant acidity nicely balance the creamy texture and medium-bodied palate.

Pascal Jolivet | 2009 | SANCERRE
★ ★ ★ $ $ Despite a warmer vintage, this Sancerre practically vibrates with acidity, which enlivens guava and lime flavors. Complete with flint and limestone notes, this is a classic example of the region.

where to go next
paris, france

Alfred
Across the street from the 17th-century Palais Royal, one of the loveliest spots in Paris, Alfred serves deliciously inspired but unpretentious French food paired with wines like the fresh and fruity Provence rosé L'Apostrophe, a charming blend of Cinsault, Grenache and Carignan.
52 rue de Richelieu, 1st Arr.

Cavestève
Bright, modern Cavestève is a wineshop first and a place to eat second. So the wine list is relatively large—about 300 labels—with choices extending beyond France to California, Chile and New Zealand. Chef Anne Coquet prepares plates of Spanish sausages and cheeses aged by Bernard Antony.
15 rue de Longchamp, 16th Arr; cavesteve.com

Racines
Located in a 19th-century shopping arcade, Racines specializes in natural wines and offers an impressive selection from about 20 different French producers. The talented chef Nicolas Gauduin prepares homespun dishes like chicken *a la plancha* with fresh vegetables to accompany the wines. *8 Passage des Panoramas, 2nd Arr.*

loire valley reds

Cabernet Franc, with its tolerance for cooler climates, is the preferred red in the Loire. The grape has impressive range, producing youthful, fruity, peppery wines, as well as full-bodied, smoky, tannic reds meant for long aging. The wines of Chinon, Bourgueil and Saumur-Champigny are especially noteworthy. In Sancerre and Menetou-Salon, small amounts of red and rosé are made from Pinot Noir.

loire valley red recommendations

Clos Cristal Hospices de Saumur | 2008 |
SAUMUR-CHAMPIGNY

★★ $ $ Made from 45-year-old Cabernet Franc vines owned by the Saumur hospital, this light-bodied red features herb, sage and berry flavors, bold acidity and some firm, tea-like tannins.

Domaine du Mortier Graviers | 2008 |
ST-NICOLAS-DE-BOURGUEIL

★★★ $ $ This outstanding red was produced using natural wine-making practices on a small, 22-acre estate, and it beautifully expresses its origins with earthy, funky mushroom aromas mingled with dark fruit. On the supple palate, black cherry and herbs come into play before the earthy finish.

La Grapperie Adonis | NV | VIN DE TABLE

★★★ $ $ Pineau d'Aunis, a traditional red grape of the Loire, is responsible for effusive aromas of menthol, herbs, cedar and graphite in this light-bodied red. Spritzy acidity and bright berry flavors laced with alpine herbs and fine tannins create a refreshing palate.

Les Sablonnettes Les Copines Aussi Gamay | 2008 |
VIN DE TABLE

★★★ $ $ This biodynamic Gamay has twice the stuffing of most Beaujolais at this price. With vivid red fruit flavors woven with baking spice and barnyard notes and upheld by bracing acidity, it achieves great balance, complexity and a rare purity.

Noëlla Morantin Mon Cher Gamay | 2008 | TOURAINE

★★★ $ $ Winemaker Noëlla Morantin's first vintage captivates with bright raspberry and spicy white pepper flavors and subtle green undercurrents; a bit of time reveals juicy lingonberry jam notes and a terrific spiciness.

rhône valley

The Rhône Valley of France has ascended to viticultural greatness relatively recently. Its wines, once dismissed as sturdy, coarse and second-class, have the potential to express unbridled power, intense spiciness and an appealing earthy character that makes them distinctive among all the fine wines of France. While Côtes du Rhône are simple, easy-drinking reds, many single-vineyard Rhône Valley reds are world-class wines, as profound as the best Burgundies or Bordeaux, with prices that reflect their rarity.

Rhône Valley: An Overview

The Rhône River flows from the Swiss Alps down into France's Jura mountains and on to the Mediterranean. The Rhône Valley wine region is divided into northern and southern parts, which differ greatly in terms of grapes, wine philosophies, soils and microclimates. The Rhône Valley ranks second in total wine production among major French regions, and while every style of wine is made here, red wines represent approximately 90 percent of the region's AOC production.

RHÔNE VALLEY

northern rhône

The northern Rhône is a narrow 50-mile or so stretch of steep, terraced hills bookended by the appellations of Côte Rôtie in the north and Cornas and St-Péray in the south. The total output of this region is small, accounting for less than 5 percent of all Rhône Valley wine production. Some of the area's most coveted wines hail from its steepest vineyard sites. The northern Rhône is located between cooler-climate Burgundy to the north and the warm, sunny Mediterranean-influenced southern Rhône region, and its wines, both reds and whites, reflect this geographical and climatic diversity in their alluring combination of elegance and robust flavors.

Northern Rhône Grapes & Styles

Though Viognier produces the Rhône Valley's most celebrated white wines in the appellation of Condrieu, two other white grapes play significant roles in the north: Marsanne and Roussanne, which are often blended together to create the full-bodied, nutty, baked pear–scented whites of Hermitage, Crozes-Hermitage, St-Péray and St-Joseph. These

■ Principal Wine Region

Côte Rôtie
Condrieu
• Vienne

Northern Rhône

St-Joseph

Crozes-Hermitage
Hermitage — • Tain-L'Hermitage

Cornas
St-Péray • Valence

Montélimar • Coteaux du Tricastin

Côtes du Rhône & Côtes
du Rhône Villages
• Orange — Gigondas
— Beaumes de Venise
Lirac
Vacqueyras
Tavel
Châteauneuf-du-Pape
• Avignon
Southern Rhône

Rhône River

wines are not especially high in acidity, yet many have the ability to age for a decade or more. The only red grape variety permitted in the production of northern Rhône red wines is Syrah, which can achieve great power and complexity, often displaying signature qualities of black pepper, meat and game. Most northern Rhône red wines are allowed to include regional white grapes, except Cornas, where Syrah must stand alone. Crozes-Hermitage is responsible for about half of the region's wine, mostly everyday reds and whites, while the smaller Hermitage appellation produces more powerful renditions.

Northern Rhône Wine Labels

Very little basic Côtes du Rhône comes from the northern Rhône; most northern Rhône wines meet higher standards and are entitled to label their wines with one of the region's eight crus. Labels generally include the cru and a producer or *négociant*. In the crus that produce red and white wines, like Crozes-Hermitage, the label might say *rouge* or *blanc,* as grape varieties are not given. The top wines from important Rhône producers, such as M. Chapoutier and E. Guigal, often bear a specific vineyard name in addition to the cru.

northern rhône recommendations

WHITES

Christophe Pichon | 2007 | **CONDRIEU**
★★★ **$ $ $** This fresh and lively white has a satisfying weight that is classic Viognier. Melon, apricot and orange blossoms are amplified by fresh acidity.

Delas La Galopine | 2007 | **CONDRIEU**
★★★ **$ $ $** *Galopine* is the local, somewhat archaic name for the Viognier grape. This version is floral and tropical, filled out with notes of figs and stone fruit. The plush, mouth-coating texture lingers on the finish, which is marked by flower and fennel.

Nicolas Jaboulet Perrin Frères | 2008 | **HERMITAGE**
★★★ **$ $ $ $** A typical Hermitage blend of Marsanne and Roussanne, this wine is brawny, yet elegant, with rich, full flavors of peach and apricot and tropical nuances.

REDS

Domaine Courbis | 2007 | ST-JOSEPH
★★★ **$ $** This distinctly mineral-laden St-Joseph, 35 percent aged in tanks and 65 percent in oak barrels, features ripe blackberry flavors layered with an intriguing white pepper quality. It's spicy and wonderfully supple, with a dry, fiery pepper and cinnamon finish.

E. Guigal | 2006 | CROZES-HERMITAGE
★★ **$ $** Guigal is one of the most reliable Rhône producers, and this well-priced Crozes-Hermitage is effusive with berry, cherry and dried flower flavors underscored by earth and animal notes. The very dry finish is framed by light tannins.

star producers
northern rhône

Auguste Clape
The leading estate in Cornas for decades, Auguste Clape makes some wines from 100-year-old vines.

Domaine Jean-Louis Chave
Since he owns parcels in most Hermitage vineyards, J-L Chave can be selective, making good wines in bad growing years and excellent wines in good years.

Domaines Paul Jaboulet Aîné
The extensive Jaboulet range includes wines made all over the Rhône, but its northern Rhône wines, particularly the iconic Hermitage La Chapelle, are the real standouts.

Domaine Yves Cuilleron
Winemaker Yves Cuilleron has spent the last 25 years improving his ancestral family winery, and today his property is responsible for arguably the best Condrieu available.

E. Guigal
The Guigal estate was the first to make single-vineyard "micro-crus" in Côte Rôtie and remains the most influential *négociant* in the Rhône.

M. Chapoutier
An early adopter of biodynamic winemaking, superstar Michel Chapoutier creates a wide range of wines that all have a distinctive sense of place.

Jean-Luc Colombo Les Ruchets Syrah | 2007 | CORNAS

★★★★ $ $ $ $ Brawny, dark, spicy and meaty, this is a particularly savory Cornas. Mushroom, peppercorn and smoke infuse a base of currants and figs on the full-bodied palate; smooth tannins support the power and the fruit.

M. Chapoutier Monier de la Sizeranne | 2006 | HERMITAGE

★★★ $ $ $ $ Deep black fruit flavors meet licorice, mocha and black pepper on the nose of this massive red. Classic Hermitage, with licorice, dried fruit and roast fig notes woven throughout, it has firm, smoky tannins that could use time to soften.

Paul Jaboulet Aîné Les Jalets | 2007 | CROZES-HERMITAGE

★★ $ $ Jaboulet's nicely built Crozes-Hermitage is both fresh and intense, presenting a nose of strawberry jam, earth and smoked sausage. The palate reveals juicy berries laced with peppery spice, stony minerals and light tannins.

RHÔNE VALLEY

southern rhône

About 30 miles south of the northern Rhône, the milder, sunnier southern Rhône begins. Its rolling hills and wide-open vistas are home to vineyards that yield about 95 percent of the entire Rhône Valley's production.

Southern Rhône Grapes & Styles

A large variety of grapes are permitted in various appellations across the southern Rhône, most selected for their ability to withstand the hotter Mediterranean climate—in Châteauneuf-du-Pape, for example, 13 varieties are allowed. The most important white grapes include Grenache Blanc, Clairette and Bourboulenc, plus the classic northern Rhône varieties Marsanne, Roussanne and Viognier. They are typically blended and result in medium-bodied wines ranging in flavor from ripe peach and citrus to herbal and nutty. Of the permitted grape varieties used to make the southern Rhône's dark, fruity, earth-driven red wines, the principal one is Grenache, usually blended with Cinsault, Syrah, Mourvèdre and/or Carignan. Rosés and good sweet wines are also made here.

Southern Rhône Wine Labels

Southern Rhône wines are labeled by appellation. Côtes du Rhône is the most basic category, and represents the vast majority of wines made here. Most Côtes du Rhône wines come from the south, although the entire Rhône Valley is permitted to use the designation. Wines made in the dozens of designated villages that satisfy stricter requirements are labeled *Côtes du Rhône Villages*. Eighteen villages that make wines of consistently high quality have earned the right to add their name to the wine label, such as Côtes du Rhône Villages Cairanne. The best villages—including Gigondas, Vacqueyras and Châteauneuf-du-Pape—have their own appellations. Satellite regions such as Luberon, Ventoux, Coteaux du Tricastin and Costières de Nîmes produce wines that are similar in style and taste profile to the basic Côtes du Rhône, while Lirac and Tavel are best known for their rosé wines.

southern rhône recommendations

WHITES

Château Mont-Redon | 2008 | CHÂTEAUNEUF-DU-PAPE
★★★ $ $ Châteauneuf-du-Pape is undeniably red wine territory, yet stellar whites like this are well worth hunting for. Pink grapefruit and lemon flavors are punctuated by notes of minerals and flowers, and a racy acidity perfectly offsets the medium-full body.

In Fine | 2008 | VENTOUX
★★ $ This Ventoux white, composed of 80 percent Clairette and 20 percent Bourboulenc, yields lovely flavors of minerals, waxy apple and flowers on an oily-textured, dry palate.

Le Plan Vermeersch Classic | 2008 | CÔTES DU RHÔNE
★★ $ $ Race car driver–turned–vintner Dirk Vermeersch is behind this lively white displaying nectarine and citrus flavors with a touch of green almond, a generous body and a rush of acidity.

Perrin & Fils Les Sinards | 2006 | CHÂTEAUNEUF-DU-PAPE
★★★ $ $ $ This vivacious, medium-bodied wine offers tantalizing aromas of honey, beeswax and herbs that are layered with peach and pear and echoed on the slightly oily palate. Mouthwatering acidity makes for a bright finish.

ROSÉS

Château de Campuget Tradition de Campuget | 2009 | COSTIÈRES DE NÎMES

★★ $ At around $10, this blend of 70 percent Syrah and 30 percent Grenache is a steal for its bright strawberry and cherry flavors, jolt of citrusy acidity and ultrafresh finish.

La Vieille Ferme | 2009 | CÔTES DU VENTOUX

★★ $ A dark pink hue hints at the tart berry and currant flavors to come in this rich rosé. Notes of caramel, a weighty body and a very dry finish complete the well-priced package.

REDS

Bastide de Beauvert | 2007 | CÔTES DU RHÔNE

★★ $ This highly aromatic red unfurls plums, violets, cloves and cinnamon with a savory undercurrent of meat. Chewy ripe raspberry flavors are held up by nicely mellowed tannins.

Brotte La Grivelière | 2008 | CÔTES DU RHÔNE

★ $ This light-bodied red is a great party wine, packed with simple berry flavors, rustic tannins and charming minty herb notes.

Campuget 1753 | 2007 | COSTIÈRES DE NÎMES

★★ $ There were vineyards on this estate as long ago as 1753. Campuget's 2007 is a highly likable red, with tobacco, plum, and herb flavors marking a medium-bodied, berry-infused palate.

Château de Beaucastel | 2007 | CHÂTEAUNEUF-DU-PAPE

★★★★ $ $ $ $ A showstopper of a wine for its perfect balance of grace and immense power, Château de Beaucastel offers aromas of figs, grilled fruit and roasted coffee beans that pave the way for flavors of thick berry syrup, black currant and plum. Powdery-fine tannins provide the support.

Château Lamargue Les Grandes Cabanes Syrah | 2008 | COSTIÈRES DE NÎMES

★★ $ Owned by Italian beverage giant Gruppo Campari, this 100 percent Syrah is dark and plush, with abundant black fruit and licorice. It shows surprising power and great structure, with a firm tannic grip on the finish.

Delas Saint-Esprit | 2008 | CÔTES DU RHÔNE

★ $ Bright, fresh and spicy, with peppercorn and red fruit flavors, this quaffable summer red is lean in body and has interesting notes of leather and drying tannins.

Domaine Bahourat | 2008 | COSTIÈRES DE NÎMES
★ ★ $ Another great value from Costières de Nîmes, this impressively polished blend of 80 percent Syrah and 20 percent Grenache delivers dried berry flavors, spice nuances and fine tannins.

Domaine de Cascavel Leonor | 2007 | CÔTES DU VENTOUX
★ ★ $ $ Proprietor Raphaël Trouiller used grapes from his biodynamic estate for this full-bodied, opaque red. Herbs and kirsch dominate the nose, while the palate features dark fruit, licorice, leather and spice, with a minerally edge.

star producers
southern rhône

Château de Beaucastel
Beaucastel produces complex Châteauneuf-du-Pape wines that incorporate all 13 of the appellation's permitted grapes.

Domaine de la Mordorée
Brothers Christophe and Fabrice Delorme get lots of attention for their Châteauneuf-du-Pape, yet they also make some excellent Tavel and Lirac just across the Rhône.

Domaine du Pegau
In 1987, the Feraud family winery was renamed Pegau (an ancient word for a type of papal wine jug) in honor of its commitment to superior Châteauneuf-du-Pape.

Domaine La Garrigue
The talented Bernard family has owned this great property since 1850; they named their famous Cuvée Romaine in honor of the land's early Roman presence.

Domaine Les Cailloux
The renowned André Brunel of Domaine Les Cailloux is one of the most talented winemakers in the entire Châteauneuf-du-Pape region.

Perrin & Fils
Founded in the early 1900s, Perrin & Fils makes stellar wines across the price spectrum that are widely available and always top-notch.

Domaine Grès St. Vincent | 2007 |
CÔTES DU RHÔNE VILLAGES SIGNARGUES

★★ $ $ Grenache takes center stage here, filled out with Syrah, Mourvèdre and Carignan. The result is a floral- and caramel-scented wine with an appealing stony edge to its cherry, mocha and spice flavors and a finish that's very long and delicious.

Domaine la Soumade | 2007 |
CÔTES DU RHÔNE VILLAGES RASTEAU

★★★ $ $ One of the finest wines the village Rasteau has to offer, this dark, juicy red is defined by bold fig and bright berry flavors with lead, coffee and stone nuances. It shows impressive power and fortitude for a Grenache-based wine, with powerful tannins holding up the ripe berry richness.

E. Guigal | 2006 | GIGONDAS

★★★ $ $ Graphite and iron nuances provide a firm mineral edge to the gorgeous flavors of flowers, dense black cherry and plums in this stellar Gigondas. Red pepper flavors and peppery spice are present on the concentrated, black fruit–infused finish.

Jean-Luc Colombo Les Abeilles | 2007 | CÔTES DU RHÔNE

★ $ A classic Grenache-Syrah-Mourvèdre blend from 25-year-old vines, this easy-drinking Côtes du Rhône offers pleasant berry, herb and licorice notes. Light in body, with a medium-length finish, it shows some dusty tannins.

Maison Bouachon La Tiare du Pape | 2007 |
CHÂTEAUNEUF-DU-PAPE

★★★ $ $ $ An enticing Châteauneuf-du-Pape, this weaves lovely flinty, gravel notes with ripe morello cherry aromas. There's a mineral, herbal edge to the palate as well, with sage, bay leaf and vanilla permeating dense berry flavors; cedary spice, mocha and smooth tannins round out the finish.

M. Chapoutier Belleruche | 2007 | CÔTES DU RHÔNE

★★ $ Chapoutier crafts this medium-bodied red in a somewhat New World style. Its ripe cherry and blackberry flavors are layered with mocha, toast and spice. Bright acidity and modest tannins make it immensely drinkable.

Perrin & Fils Les Sinards | 2006 | CHÂTEAUNEUF-DU-PAPE

★★★ $ $ $ Perrin is made by the family behind the legendary Beaucastel. This red is a classic Châteauneuf-du-Pape, with notes of tar, herbs and smoke on the nose, and a red fruit–drenched palate revealing highlights of kirsch, spice and sweet tea.

southern france

The appellations of France's southern coast (Provence, Languedoc and Roussillon) and of the Southwest region were long known primarily for the quantity, not quality, of their wine production. But ongoing global demand for affordable wines has brought the area renewed attention, and the wines are improving dramatically.

Southern France: An Overview

Le Midi, the storied south of France, includes the regions of Languedoc, Roussillon and Provence (the first two are often referred to as a single hyphenated entity, Languedoc-Roussillon, or as just Languedoc). This area is blessed with so much Mediterranean sunlight that it's possible to make wines of every imaginable style here. The lands of the French Southwest, le Sud-Ouest, are under the combined influences of the Pyrenees mountains and the Atlantic.

SOUTHERN FRANCE

languedoc-roussillon

In addition to being France's most prolific region, turning out by some estimates more wine than the entire U.S., Languedoc-Roussillon has also become the most dynamic. In the last decade, vintners here have aggressively pursued quality winemaking, often by ignoring rigid government regulations on grape-growing and vinification processes. The resulting wines are widely regarded as some of the finest ever from the region, even though they must still be classified as merely Vins de Pays or Vins de Table.

Languedoc Grapes & Styles

The formidable Languedoc grows a wide range of grapes, some indigenous to the region, others (such as Cabernet Sauvignon) from different French regions. Red grapes dominate, especially Carignan, which is capable of delicious berry- and spice-flavored wines; excellent examples can be found in Corbières. Syrah, Grenache and Mourvèdre are typically blended to create the hearty, often rustic wines of Minervois and Fitou, as well as those of the Roussillon appellation Collioure near Spain. Cabernet Sauvignon and Merlot—imported from Bordeaux and increasingly planted here—are used mostly for inexpensive wines destined for export (the coveted wines from Cabernet Sauvignon champion Mas de Daumas Gassac are a notable exception). White grape varieties Grenache Blanc, Maccabéo, Muscat, Picpoul Blanc and Rolle create fresh, interesting wines, while Viognier yields richer, more complex whites similar in some cases to examples from the northern Rhône, yet available at a fraction of the cost. Chardonnays from Limoux are worth exploring, too. Roussillon is also famed for its dessert wines (see p. 265).

Languedoc Wine Labels

Languedoc labels list region and sometimes grape. Most of the simplest wines are designated *Vins de Pays d'Oc* and can be made from grapes grown anywhere in Languedoc. Vins de Pays made in specific areas will indicate this on their labels and are subject to greater restrictions. The Languedoc-Roussillon region encompasses a number of smaller appellations. Among them, Minervois, Fitou and Corbières often produce high-quality wines showing distinctive characteristics, as do Faugères, St-Chinian, Montpeyroux, Pic-St-Loup and Collioure.

languedoc recommendations

WHITES

Bourgeois Family Cuvée Stéphi Chardonnay | 2008 |
VIN DE PAYS D'OC
★★ $ This lively Chardonnay sees no oak and achieves some nice complexity in the form of nutty, caramel-tinged citrus and apple flavors and a slightly oily yet bright palate.

Domaine de Sérame Réserve Viognier | 2008 |
VIN DE PAYS D'OC
★★ $ Aromas of apricot, clove and flowers and hints of petrol make this a great example of the Viognier grape. A healthy dose of acidity keeps the spicy, rich stone-fruit flavors balanced.

La Poule Blanche | 2008 | VIN DE PAYS D'OC
★★ $ Chardonnay, Sauvignon Blanc and Viognier come together to create a terrific crowd-pleaser of a wine. Tropical fruit flavors are laced with vanilla and a touch of earthy rusticity, which keep it unmistakably Old World.

Les Costières de Pomerols Picpoul de Pinet | 2009 |
COTEAUX DU LANGUEDOC
★★ $ By macerating this Picpoul with its skins, Les Costières has created a truly complex wine for the price. Ripe pear aromas are followed by lively grapefruit and lime flavors and a sharp acidity.

ROSÉS

Château de Lancyre Pic St-Loup | 2009 |
LANGUEDOC PIC-ST-LOUP
★★ $$ Fresh and highly aromatic, this pale pink wine offers lovely strawberry, floral, banana and bubble gum notes. There's a vivid beam of acidity and loads of strawberry flavors on the ultradry palate.

Le Jaja de Jau Syrah | 2008 | VIN DE PAYS D'OC
★★ $ The juicy blackberry and black cherry flavors in this beautiful rosé taste slightly grilled. There's great length to the dry finish.

Les Vignerons de Pomerols Beauvignac Syrah | 2009 |
VIN DE PAYS D'OC
★★ $ The magenta color here hints at the ripe red fruit flavors to come—strawberry, cherry, rhubarb and watermelon—and an electrifying rush of acidity perfectly balances the hint of sweetness.

Villa des Anges Old Vines | 2009 | VIN DE PAYS D'OC
★ $ Fresh, simple and straightforward, this light-bodied Cinsault-based rosé is the perfect summer sipper for its tasty strawberry and Bing cherry flavors and affordable price tag.

REDS

Château la Bouscade Les Sept Vents Syrah | 2006 |
MINERVOIS
★★ $$ David and Jo Cowderoy acquired this estate in 2005, and have since transformed it into a quality-focused winery. Their 2006 is ripe and refreshing, with loads of spice and hints of leather.

Chemin de Moscou | 2006 | VIN DE PAYS D'OC
★★ $$$ Black fruit aromas meet cedar and spice and merge on the palate with licorice and more blackberries. All flavors are woven seamlessly and framed by supple, peppery tannins.

Domaine Cabirau Malgré les Fonctionnaires | 2008 |
CÔTES DU ROUSSILLON

★★★ $ $ This blend of 70 percent Grenache, 20 percent Syrah and 10 percent Carignan shows dark fruit intertwined with hints of fennel, white pepper and violets. The palate demonstrates an intensity of black cherry and wild berry flavors, an amazing silky texture and a lively, spicy finish.

Domaine de Nidolères La Pierroune | 2008 |
CÔTES DU ROUSSILLON

★★ $ $ A blend of 80 percent Syrah, 10 percent Grenache and 10 percent Mourvèdre, this gutsy wine is filled with dark, brooding fruit flavors underscored by animal nuances and firm tannins that may require time to soften.

Domaine des 2 Ânes Fontanilles | 2006 | CORBIÈRES
★★ $ $ A pronounced earthy, mushroom quality on the nose of this well-made wine infuses a base of dense black and red berry flavors. It's fresh and firm, thanks to powerful tannins.

Domaine Rimbert Le Mas au Schiste | 2007 | ST-CHINIAN
★★ $ $ Aged for 12 months in old barrels, this red retains high-toned red fruit aromas and notes of violets and barnyard. The bright, medium-bodied palate shows up-front ripe cherry flavors coupled with hints of cinnamon and mocha.

Hecht & Bannier | 2006 | MINERVOIS
★★ $ $ Exotic, peppery spice permeates the red fruit–dominated palate of this captivating, medium-bodied Minervois. Smoky herbs and grilled plums make a big first impression, and fine, chalky-textured tannins mark the finish.

Le Loup Blanc Le Régal du Loup | 2008 | MINERVOIS
★★★ $ $ Inky dark and opaque, this tightly wound red takes some time to unfold. Slowly, aromas of black olives, herbs, minerals and black fruit emerge; firm tannins mark the well-knit palate.

Les Deux Rives | 2008 | CORBIÈRES
★ $ Simple berry-cherry fruit punch aromas abound in this Grenache-Syrah-Mourvèdre-Carignan blend. It's a great house wine—affordable, refreshing and immensely drinkable.

L'Ostal Cazes | 2004 | MINERVOIS–LA LIVINIÈRE
★★★ $ $ $ This red is impressive for its creamy, velvety texture as well as its unusual mix of flavors—resin, sage, ginger, star anise and black fruits. Charred wood and spice notes complete the package.

Mont Tauch Carignan/Grenache/Syrah | 2007 | FITOU

★ $ Another wonderfully affordable red blend, this combination of Carignan, Grenache and Syrah yields abundant bright cherry and raspberry flavors that are laced with spice and minerals.

Moulin de Gassac Guilhem | 2008 |
VIN DE PAYS DE L'HÉRAULT

★ $ Incredibly fresh and jammy, this light-bodied basic red is food-friendly, thanks to its great, mouthwatering acidity.

Puydeval "Chevalier" Syrah | 2008 |
VIN DE PAYS DES COTEAUX DE PEYRIAC

★ ★ $ With no oak aging, this ripe red—a blend of 85 percent Syrah and 15 percent Grenache—smells of pure fruit pleasure. Its dark blackberry and boysenberry flavors meet some pepper and earth on the medium-bodied palate.

SOUTHERN FRANCE

provence

Provence is home to one of the world's oldest winemaking traditions, but over the years the region became known only for bulk wine. Thanks to technological innovations and winemaking expertise from other parts of France and abroad, however, Provence wines have never been better.

Provence Grapes & Styles

Provence is best-known for its delicious, dry rosés. Typically made from a blend of Cinsault, Grenache and Mourvèdre, they are meant to be consumed young and with food. Those from Bandol are considered the finest, but rosés from Côtes de Provence and Coteaux d'Aix-en-Provence are also well made. Provence's bright, citrusy whites are usually blends of local grapes Bourboulenc, Rolle, Clairette, Grenache Blanc and/or Ugni Blanc; the best come from the seaside village of Cassis. Bandol's mineral-laden whites are full-bodied, as are its more famous, robust reds made primarily from Mourvèdre. Grenache, Carignan, Cabernet Sauvignon, Cinsault and Syrah are also grown in Provence. The best examples of Provence reds are from Les Baux de Provence and Coteaux d'Aix-en-Provence.

provence recommendations

WHITES

Domaine de la Tour du Bon | 2008 | BANDOL
★★★ $ $ Heady spice aromas are followed by luscious tropical flavors—mango, papaya and pineapple—on the palate of this outstanding Bandol white. A rich nutty finish rounds it out.

Mas de la Dame Coin Caché Blanc | 2007 |
VIN DE PAYS DES ALPILLES
★★★ $ $ $ French for "farm of the woman," the Mas de la Dame winery has been run by a pair of sisters since 1995. Their blended white has aromas of slate and spice, while quince, pear and apricot take over in the mouth before a plush finish.

ROSÉS

Bieler Père et Fils Sabine | 2009 |
COTEAUX D'AIX-EN-PROVENCE
★★★ $ This great value offers delicate floral aromas that shift to wild strawberry and watermelon flavors. An underlying spiciness on the palate carries through into a broad and crisp finish.

Commanderie de la Bargemone | 2009 |
COTEAUX D'AIX-EN-PROVENCE
★★ $ $ Wild strawberries abound in this blend of Syrah, Grenache, Cinsault and Cabernet Sauvignon; vibrant acidity ensures that it's balanced and crisp.

Les Domaniers de Puits Mouret | 2009 | CÔTES DE PROVENCE
★★ $ $ With flavors of bold, sweet cherries and a clean finish, this wine from the renowned Domaines Ott is a formidable mouthful that almost seems more like a red than a rosé.

REDS

Les Comptoirs de Magdala Escapade | 2008 |
CÔTES DE PROVENCE
★★★ $ $ Antoine Pouponneau is the winemaker behind Tour du Bon Bandol as well as this standout wine. With a distinctive earthy, animal quality, it opens with pungent aromas of barnyard that lead into flavors of rich, red fruit.

Les Comptoirs de Magdala L'Amourvedre | 2007 |
VIN DE PAYS DU MONT CAUME
★★ $ $ Another fine wine from Les Comptoirs de Magdala, this rustic Mourvèdre boasts earth and cherry flavors and huge tannins.

Pinot Evil Pinot Noir | NV | VIN DE PAYS DE L'ÎLE DE BEAUTÉ
★ $ Convinced that great Pinot Noir can be cheap, Pinot Evil's wine-making team has crafted an easy-drinking bargain red with delicious notes of bright cherry and chalk. This appellation is located on the nearby island of Corsica.

Routas Cyrano Syrah | 2007 | VIN DE PAYS DE MÉDITERRANÉE
★★ $ $ This Rhône-style Syrah is rich with aromas of violets and plums, and shows a very ripe palate with a violet-candy chalkiness.

SOUTHERN FRANCE

the southwest

The French region known as the Southwest, or le Sud-Ouest, borders the rugged Pyrenees mountains, which separate France from Spain, and is outshone by its formidable neighbor to the northwest, Bordeaux. As a result, the wines of the Southwest remain little known in the U.S., although that is changing. Three appellations in particular are worth exploring: Bergerac, for its wines of distinctly Bordeaux-like finesse; Cahors, for its prestigious reds of massive ruggedness and power; and Monbazillac, for its excellent Sauternes-like sweet wines that cost a fraction as much as the famed sweet wines of Bordeaux.

The Southwest Grapes & Styles

The red wines of Bergerac are made with the same grapes as those in Bordeaux—Cabernet Sauvignon, Merlot, Malbec and Cabernet Franc. The full-bodied reds of Cahors are based on the grape known elsewhere as Malbec or Côt but here called Auxerrois. In Madiran, vintners use the Tannat grape to craft wines that are even darker, fuller-bodied and more tannic. The hearty wines from the Basque Country are made from a blend of hard-to-pronounce local grapes. One example, Jurançon, is a full-bodied, spicy white wine produced from Petit and Gros Manseng grapes in two styles: dry (labeled *Jurançon Sec*) and sweet. Monbazillac and Gaillac are similar wines with both dry and sweet versions. Vins de Pays des Côtes de Gascogne are light- to medium-bodied wines from local and international grapes.

southwest recommendations

WHITES

Colombelle | 2009 | VIN DE PAYS DES CÔTES DE GASCOGNE

★ $ Made from Colombard and Ugni Blanc, the two most common grapes in Cognac, Colombelle is an interesting and refreshing white, with tasty pear flavors and bright acidity. It's also a great value.

François Lurton l'Herré Chardonnay/Gros Manseng | 2009 | VIN DE PAYS DES CÔTES DE GASCOGNE

★ $ Sweet, juicy peach and melon are on display here, which almost makes this Chardonnay–Gros Manseng blend taste like Muscat. It's food-friendly and balanced, with a snappy finish.

Robert & Bernard Plageoles Ondenc | 2008 | GAILLAC

★★ $ $ The Plageoles are well known for using the region's more obscure indigenous grapes to make their wines. Made from the Ondenc grape, this 2008 has dry, mineral aromas, flavors of crisp Granny Smith apples and nuts and a soft, chalky texture.

REDS

Château Lagrézette Cru d'Exception Malbec | 2005 | CAHORS

★★★ $ $ Most people think of Argentina when they hear Malbec, but the grape's ancestral home is here, in the Cahors region. This version shows off its rustic side. Brimming with black currant and blackberry flavors laced with a chalky minerality, it is a testament to its southwestern terroir.

Clos Siguier | 2007 | CAHORS

★★★ $ With its gorgeous dark eggplant color and aromas of violet and wild berry, this wine seems custom-made for a cured meat feast. It's also a magnificent value, offering the power and complexity of a bottle three times its price.

Domaine du Crampilh l'Originel | 2006 | MADIRAN

★★ $ $ This wine is made from Madiran's Tannat grape. Although it's loaded with firm tannins, it turns silky smooth and nicely spicy when paired with food.

Laffont Erigone | 2007 | MADIRAN

★★ $ $ Named for Erigone, Dionysus's Athenian paramour (at least according to many versions of the myth), this wine is seductive and bold. Spice aromas are followed by ample black fruit flavors that linger impressively on the palate.

italy

The quality of Italy's wines has been improving steadily. Once-pallid Chiantis have become more flavorful and are imported today alongside a growing number of esteemed Barolos, Super-Tuscans and Pinot Grigios. Southern Italy's wine regions are among the most dynamic anywhere.

Lombardy
Trentino–Alto Adige
Valle d'Aosta
Friuli–Venezia Giulia
Veneto
• Milan
Venice
Piedmont
• Genoa
Emilia-Romagna
Liguria
Florence •
Adriatic Sea
Le Marche
Tuscany —————— Umbria
Abruzzo
Lazio
Molise
Rome ☆
Campania
Apulia
Naples •
Sardinia
Basilicata ———
Tyrrhenian Sea
Calabria
Palermo •
Pantelleria
Sicily

▨ Principal
Wine Region

Italy: An Overview

From the foothills of the Alps in the north to the island of Sicily in the south, almost every region in Italy makes wine. Italian vintners succeed throughout their country's varied terrains and climate zones by utilizing a wide array of indigenous and French grapes as well as cutting-edge winemaking styles. Consequently, Italy contains over 300 DOC and DOCG zones (see Italian Wine Labels, below). Two regions stand out: Piedmont, in the northwest, where the Nebbiolo grape yields powerful, long-lived Barolo and lighter Barbaresco; and Tuscany, home of the cherry-scented Sangiovese grape, responsible for two of Italy's most recognized wines—Chianti and Brunello di Montalcino. From the crisp whites of Friuli and Trentino–Alto Adige to Umbria's dark Sagrantino di Montefalco and the bold reds of Sicily, Italy makes wines for all tastes, budgets and seasons.

Italian Wine Labels

Italian wines are traditionally labeled by their place of origin, though some labels list the grape if it defines a region, such as Montepulciano d'Abruzzo, made from the Montepulciano grape in Abruzzo. Grape names commonly appear on wines from the northeastern regions of Alto Adige and Friuli–Venezia Giulia. Italy's regulatory system is the *Denominazione di Origine Controllata* (DOC), which delineates basic standards; more rigorous standards apply to wines with the DOCG (*Denominazione di Origine Controllata e Garantita*) imprimatur. The term *Classico* on a label indicates a prestigious subregion. For much of the system's history, wines not adhering to DOC or DOCG standards were given the humble title *Vino da Tavola* (table wine). Since the 1994 vintage, the *Indicazione Geografica Tipica* (IGT) classification has been used for many regional table wines. It is also used for more prestigious wines that ironically don't qualify for higher designations due to the use of unorthodox grape varieties or production methods.

piedmont

Located in northwestern Italy, Piedmont is home to the Nebbiolo grape, which yields some of the world's most outstanding reds. Chief among them are Barolo and, of lesser import, Barbaresco; both draw comparisons to Burgundies for their elegance and ability to age. The region is also known for light, fruity, everyday wines, such as Barbera and Dolcetto, and the popular sparkling white Asti.

piedmont whites

Piedmont's reputation is based upon its reds, but there are still a handful of interesting whites worth seeking out. Gavi di Gavi, from the Cortese grape, is perhaps Piedmont's most famous still white, although Arneis, particularly from the subregion of Roero, is more substantial and compelling. Piedmont's Chardonnays can be wonderfully balanced. Sweeter sparkling wines are also prevalent, with the well-known, though rarely exciting, Asti Spumante leading the way. The superior Moscato d'Asti (see p. 253) is unusually delicate, fragrant and refreshing.

piedmont white recommendations

Casa Vinicola Bruno Giacosa | 2009 | **ROERO ARNEIS**
★★★ $ $ Bruno Giacosa was one of only a few producers crafting Arneis in the 1970s and remains dedicated to the variety today. Floral, fruity and briny, the 2009 kicks off with lots of opulent fruit flavors layered with honey, minerals and a whisper of vanilla.

Cascina Bongiovanni Arneis | 2008 | **LANGHE**
★★ $ $ Brimming with slate, chalk and mineral aromas, this Bongiovanni retains its bright character on the palate, with citrus notes and a touch of honey marking the finish.

Cascina Chicco Anterisio | 2008 | **ROERO ARNEIS**
★★ $ $ For many years, the Arneis grape was used primarily to soften the reds of Piedmont, but it can make beautiful wines on its own as well. This version boasts spicy tropical notes and a chalky minerality rounded out with soft apple and pear flavors.

Ceretto Blangé Arneis | 2008 | LANGHE
★ ★ ★ $ $ The Ceretto family is serious about the Arneis grape. Their 2008 is exceptionally delicious, with its apple, pear and mineral flavors upheld by bright acidity.

Marchesi di Grésy Chardonnay | 2008 | LANGHE
★ ★ $ $ Creamy and plush in texture, this Chardonnay is loaded with vanilla, toast and oak flavors; crisp apple, spice and citrus notes provide nice highlights throughout the rich finish.

Villa Sparina | 2008 | GAVI
★ ★ $ $ Believed to be native to Piedmont, the Cortese grape tends to display delicate aromas, perhaps due to Piedmont's proximity to the moderating Ligurian coast. This version offers flavors of apples, minerals and citrus woven with hints of honey and subtle spice.

piedmont reds

The Nebbiolo grape is responsible for Piedmont's greatest reds: Barolo and Barbaresco. Also called Spanna, Nebbiolo produces the less familiar wines of Gattinara, Ghemme and Langhe as well. Piedmont's most prolific grape, though, is Barbera, a highly acidic chameleon that can yield powerful, ageworthy wines as well as young, light reds. Dolcetto produces a large amount of the region's simpler reds. Cabernet Sauvignon, Pinot Noir and Syrah are also grown here, but the wines generally aren't worth seeking out.

PIEDMONT REDS

barolo & barbaresco

These two renowned reds are among the world's greatest wines. Although both are Nebbiolo-based, Barolo tends to be heartier, Barbaresco lighter and more subtle. While both improve with age, regulations require Barolo to be aged three years, two in barrel, before release, whereas Barbaresco must be aged two years, one in barrel. Vintners tend to make these wines in one of two styles: Traditionalists craft austere, earthy wines that may age for decades; modern-minded producers opt for a more fruit-forward style that typically shows the use of new oak barrels.

barolo & barbaresco recommendations

Castello di Verduno | 2005 | **BARBARESCO**
★ ★ ★ **$ $ $** This lovely, medium-bodied wine has tart strawberry and cherry flavors and loads of great regional character. Aged in large oak casks and steel tanks, it has power that builds through the medium-long finish.

Ceretto Asij | 2006 | **BARBARESCO**
★ ★ ★ **$ $ $** Some of the grapes used in this wine are from the same vineyards as the winery's famous (and much more expensive) Bricco Asili Barbaresco. Dark red berry flavors laced with toast, flowers and oak come together on a silky-textured palate with formidable tannins.

star producers
barolo & barbaresco

Bruno Giacosa
Some make great Barolos, others fine Barbarescos. In his 60-plus years of winemaking, Piedmont legend Bruno Giacosa has consistently made the very best of both.

Ceretto
Brothers Bruno and Marcello are the Piedmont region's dynamic duo, producing legendary single-vineyard Barolos and Barbarescos since the late 1960s.

Domenico Clerico
Considered a Piedmont innovator by many, the talented Domenico Clerico is best known for his ready-to-drink, modern-style Barolos.

Gaja
For nearly half a century, the single-vineyard Nebbiolos of Angelo Gaja—most notably Sorì Tildìn and Sorì San Lorenzo—have been among Piedmont's best.

Massolino
The Massolinos are revered in Piedmont and around the world as much for their traditional Vigna Rionda as for their potent single-vineyard Margheria and Parafada.

Vietti
A champion of terroir, Luca Currado carries on his family's custom of making beautifully focused wines that offer both quality and value.

Conterno Fantino Sorì Ginestra | 2006 | BAROLO

★★★★ $ $ $ $ Crafted in a somewhat old-fashioned, traditional style, this full-bodied Barolo offers dusty, rich cherry and berry flavors woven with classic spice and floral notes. Powerful yet supple tannins ensure that it will age remarkably well, although it is wonderfully approachable right now.

Gaja Dagromis | 2004 | BAROLO

★★★★ $ $ $ $ This magnificent wine is named for the Gromis family, who in the 19th century owned one of the two Gaja vineyards that still provide its grapes. Equal parts traditional and modern, this shows a perfect marriage between earthy tar, leaf and floral flavors and a pronounced ripe fruit character—blackberries and plum jam.

Manzone Castelletto | 2005 | BAROLO

★★★ $ $ $ While featuring plenty of up-front ripe fruit, this red retains its Barolo identity. There's a spicy and earthy edge to the generous black fruit flavors. Its texture is silky, and the mouthwatering finish lingers long after the last sip.

taste here now

LA REI Sommelier Matteo Toso's stellar wine list at La Rei, inside the luxurious Il Boscareto resort and spa, offers a huge selection of Barolos from nearly 50 of the greatest producers in the region. To pair with the wines are chef Chen Shiqin's delicious renditions of the traditional dishes of Piedmont. *Serralunga d'Alba, Piedmont; ilboscaretoresort.com*

Massolino | 2006 | BAROLO

★★★ $ $ $ This is Massolino's entry-level Barolo, introduced a century ago, in 1911, but made today in a considerably more modern style. In this polished 2006, streamlined blackberry and raspberry flavors display hints of cherry and earth, and silky tannins give structure to the generous body.

Piazzo | 2006 | BARBARESCO

★★★ $ $ $ As Piazzo's Barbaresco beautifully illustrates, 2006 was a standout year for Piedmont. Modest cherry and dusty herb flavors give the wine a traditional feel, while the soft palate culminates in a big, spicy finish.

Pio Cesare | 2005 | BAROLO

★★★ $ $ $ $ As usual, Pio Cesare delivers a fairly old-fashioned red wine, with tea leaf, tart cherry, leather and dried flower aromas. The full-bodied palate exudes dark fruit and wood, with fine tannins providing plenty of grip.

other piedmont reds

Nebbiolo reaches its apex in the highly desirable, often very expensive wines from the renowned Barolo and Barbaresco regions. But other Nebbiolo-based reds, such as those of Gattinara, Ghemme, Langhe and Nebbiolo d'Alba, can offer a taste of the noble grape variety at a fraction of the cost of Barolos and Barbarescos. A step down from Nebbiolos are wines made with the Barbera and Dolcetto grapes. Barberas are slightly more aromatic and complex, yet both make wines that are smooth, crowd-pleasing and generally affordable. Blends of these red varieties may be labeled simply *Piemonte DOC* or *Langhe DOC*.

other piedmont red recommendations

Cascina Bruciata Rian | 2008 | DOLCETTO D'ALBA
★★★ **$** Renowned winemaker Federico Curtaz, former viticulturist for Angelo Gaja, consulted for Cascina Bruciata, too. Full-bodied, luscious and balanced, this great-value Dolcetto seduces with its plum, licorice and cocoa powder aromas.

Domenico Clerico Trevigne | 2006 | BARBERA D'ALBA
★★ **$ $** Clerico brings out Barbera's powerful side in this New World–style wine. The palate oozes dark chocolate and ripe cherries, while a solid streak of acidity and fine tannins provide balance.

Elio Altare | 2008 | DOLCETTO D'ALBA
★★ **$ $** Elio Altare is a pioneer of modern winemaking in Piedmont. His 2008 Dolcetto is a great everyday red, offering dark mocha, roasted coffee, earth, violet and ripe red cherry flavors layered with an appealing chalkiness.

Fontanafredda Briccotondo Barbera | 2008 | PIEDMONT
★★ **$** Made with grapes grown in Monferrato and Langhe, this rich red features bright red cherry, earth and spice. Vibrant acidity carries it through the soft finish.

Manzone | 2008 | BARBERA D'ALBA
★★★ **$ $** The Barbera grape rarely yields wines that are this concentrated or intense. Manzone has crafted a terrific version, with equal parts citrusy acidity and dense black fruit flavors and a dried fruit–infused finish.

Marziano Abbona Rinaldi | 2007 | **BARBERA D'ALBA**
★★★ $ $ Dense and rich, this opens with an enticing animal quality, woven with blackberry and spice flavors on the palate. With intriguing notes of meat and licorice, it's a complex and tasty wine.

Parusso Ornati | 2008 | **BARBERA D'ALBA**
★★★ $ $ $ Impressively fruit-forward and bright, this Barbera offers a lovely chalky texture and plenty of bold red cherry flavors to offset the ample toasted oak.

Poderi Luigi Einaudi | 2009 | **DOLCETTO DI DOGLIANI**
★★ $ $ Old World charm abounds in this wine, as violet, tar and dried fruit aromas lead to soft berry flavors. It's quite full-bodied, with creamy minerals and flower and plum nuances on the clean finish.

Prinsi San Cristoforo | 2008 | **DOLCETTO D'ALBA**
★★ $ $ Made with grapes from 40-year-old vines, this fruit-driven Dolcetto was aged in stainless steel, which preserves the freshness of the blackberry and cherry flavors. A vivid acidity keeps it refreshing.

Renato Ratti Ochetti | 2008 | **NEBBIOLO D'ALBA**
★★★ $ $ This wine is truly Barolo-like, brimming with gorgeous chocolate-covered cherry aromas that are echoed on the palate, alongside rich and creamy cocoa and earth flavors.

Seghesio | 2007 | **BARBERA D'ALBA**
★★ $ $ Spicy *salumi*, animal and cocoa aromas come together on the nose of this terrific Barbera and are joined on the palate by berries and a chalky minerality. While not powerful, it's indisputably delicious.

Travaglini | 2004 | **GATTINARA**
★★★ $ $ Spice and flowers jump out of the glass in this standout Nebbiolo. Filled out with black plum and oak flavors, it's fruity and powerful, with firm tannins and a spicy finish.

Vietti Tre Vigne | 2007 | **BARBERA D'ASTI**
★★★ $ $ Sourced from 10-year-old vineyards, this youthful red shows concentrated blackberry and plum flavors interspersed with chalky minerals, vanilla and oak, all held aloft by invigorating acidity.

Vigne Regali L'Ardì | 2008 | **DOLCETTO D'ACQUI**
★★ $ An outstanding value, this Dolcetto delivers plum flavors wrapped in a pleasing minerality, a creamy texture and a juicy finish.

Volpi Vobis Tua | 2007 | **BARBERA D'ASTI**
★★ $ Cocoa and berry flavors, a medium body, a plummy finish and a great price make this likable Barbera worth stocking up on.

other northern italian regions

Northeastern Italy's most productive wine region by far is the Veneto, which makes popular but inconsistent wines like red Valpolicella and Bardolino and white Soave and Pinot Grigio. But throughout Italy's northeast, a growing number of winemakers are concentrating on quality over quantity and producing some excellent wines using a unique array of indigenous grapes.

• **TRENTINO–ALTO ADIGE & FRIULI–VENEZIA GIULIA**
Bordering Austria, the Trentino–Alto Adige area comprises two separate regions grouped together because of their proximity. Perhaps due to Trentino–Alto Adige's Austro-Hungarian background (the northern parts of the area are primarily German-speaking), many wines here are labeled by grape variety, such as Gewürztraminer (often called Tra-miner here), Sylvaner and Müller-Thurgau. Friuli–Venezia Giulia boasts many unusual grape varieties, such as Refosco, Tazzelenghe, Schioppettino and the recently revived Pignolo. Though Friuli is more famous for white wines, its subregion Colli Orientali del Friuli also produces a handful of reds. Even the apparently desolate hill region of Carso makes some noteworthy wines.

• **VENETO** In spite of its reputation for uninteresting bulk production, the Veneto is responsible for many high-quality wines. The best bottles come from the Soave and Valpoli-cella zones, especially the hilly Classico regions. Another important wine of note is the popular sparkling white Prosecco (see p. 253).

• **LOMBARDY** The most famous wine region in Lombardy is Franciacorta, which makes Italy's highest-quality sparkling wines (see p. 253). Lombardy also encompasses Valtellina, located near the Swiss border, which is responsible for the well-regarded red Sforzato wine from the Chiavennasca (Nebbiolo) grape.

other northern italian whites

White-wine lovers will find many inspired choices in Italy's northern regions. From Trentino–Alto Adige come such Austrian-influenced wines as Pinot Bianco, Müller-Thurgau, Riesling and the weighty, aromatic Gewürztraminer, as well as wines from international grapes such as Chardonnay, Pinot Grigio and Sauvignon Blanc (referred to here as just "Sauvignon"). Veneto offers the Garganega-based Soave. Much Soave is poorly crafted, but good wines can be found in the Classico zones spanning the hills outside Verona. Indigenous white grapes in the Friuli region include Friulano, Ribolla Gialla and Picolit, yet the region is perhaps more renowned for its superb Pinot Grigio, Pinot Bianco and Sauvignon. The white Prosecco grape flourishes in Veneto, where it is used to make a refreshingly light, sparkling wine of the same name. The wine was recently given DOCG status, and the grape renamed "Glera" (its name before it became associated with the town of Prosecco).

other northern italian white recommendations

Alois Lageder Beta Delta Chardonnay/Pinot Grigio | 2008 | VIGNETI DELLE DOLOMITI

★★ $ $ A 50-50 blend of Chardonnay and Pinot Grigio, this biodynamic wine offers enchanting aromas of peach, citrus and quince with herb nuances. Medium-bodied, sleek and round on the palate, it shows a mineral finish.

Anselmi San Vincenzo | 2009 | VENETO

★★ $ Expressive melon, pineapple and spiced pear aromas are echoed on this wine's plush palate, where they are filled out with warm ginger and clove notes and a succulent peachy core.

Eugenio Collavini Broy | 2007 | COLLIO

★★★ $ $ Slightly oily and viscous in texture, this white starts off with fragrant cantaloupe, nettle and alpine herbs and takes a juicy turn on the full-bodied palate, with waves of pear and peach flavors. It shows impressive depth and balance.

Girlan Indra Sauvignon | 2009 | ALTO ADIGE

★★ $$ A winery cooperative made up of more than 240 members produces this full-flavored Sauvignon from Alto Adige. It's packed with expressive tropical fruit and grapefruit flavors highlighted by notes of grass and herbs.

Kellerei Cantina Andrian Pinot Grigio | 2009 | ALTO ADIGE

★★ $$ From one of Alto Adige's finest cooperative wineries comes this pretty Pinot Grigio, offering peach, spiced apple and juicy tangerine aromas. Underlying minerality and strong acidity offset the full-bodied style, keeping the wine firm and steely.

Kris Pinot Grigio | 2008 | DELLE VENEZIE

★★ $ Bright and airy, with aromas of flowers, almond and lime, this is a crisp and medium-bodied wine. Its zesty citrus flavors are rich, ripe and elegant.

Livon Braide Grande Pinot Grigio | 2008 | COLLIO

★★ $$ Livon gives this Pinot Grigio some oak treatment (30 percent of it is fermented and aged in French barrels), which imparts well-integrated toast, vanilla and spice notes to flavors of bright grapefruit and apple.

Muri-Gries Müller Thurgau | 2009 | ALTO ADIGE

★★ $$ Produced in the ancient Muri-Gries monastery, this Müller-Thurgau smells like a handful of fresh herbs—basil, thyme and oregano. It delivers supple flavors of apple and ripe peach woven with more herbs and vivid acidity.

Niedermayr Pinot Bianco | 2008 | ALTO ADIGE

★★ $$ This unoaked Pinot Bianco, marked by white peach, green almond, mixed herbs and a touch of yeasty lees on the nose, is wonderfully crisp and refreshing. The bright citrus flavors show intriguing hints of menthol.

Peter Zemmer Cortinie Bianco | 2008 |
VIGNETI DELLE DOLOMITI

★★ $$ This well-crafted blend of Chardonnay, Pinot Grigio, Gewürztraminer and Sauvignon Blanc is lean, fresh and mineral-laden, with a pleasing earthy quality alongside flavors of ripe orchard fruit and subtle oak.

Rocca Sveva | 2008 | SOAVE CLASSICO

★ $ Delicate aromas of acacia flower and lemon icing precede a clean, light-bodied palate full of slightly sweet citrus flavors in this charming quaffer.

St. Magdalena Dellago Weissburgunder (Pinot Bianco)
| 2009 | **ALTO ADIGE**

★★ $ $ This well-built white displays distinctive notes of ginger-snap, lemon, clove and citrus on the nose, followed by mandarin orange flavors. Undertones of herbs and menthol give the wine an intriguing savory quality.

St. Michael-Eppan Gewürztraminer | 2009 | **ALTO ADIGE**

★★ $ $ Spice and roses, woven with peaches and banana notes, come on strong on the nose of this beautiful Gewürztraminer. Flavors of peaches, ginger and anise round out the peppery palate.

Tamellini | 2008 | **SOAVE**

★★ $ The classic Soave elements—stone fruit, spice, dried flowers and earth—are showcased in this harmonious wine. Its medium-bodied palate has fine acidity, which carries through on the bracing mineral- and citrus-laden finish.

eat here now

ANTICO FOLEDOR CONTE LOVARIA Chef Antonia Klugmann likes to update the traditional dishes that recall her childhood in the seaport city of Trieste in northeastern Italy. Her favorite dish: venison with cabbage, persimmon and chocolate. Sommelier Romano De Feo collaborates on her tasting menus, offering many local wine selections. *Pavia di Udine, Friuli; villalovaria.it*

other northern italian reds

The north of Italy is a wellspring of fascinating reds beyond Barolo and Barbaresco. In the Veneto, there are more and more well-made Valpolicellas, crafted mainly from the Corvina grape, and these can be bright, floral and inspired. The best, labeled *Superiore,* come from the Classico zone. Two other notable types of Valpolicella are Amarone and Ripasso. Amarone is a rich wine made from grapes that traditionally have been air-dried for several months before pressing, which concentrates their flavor; Recioto (see p. 267) is a sweet version of Amarone. Ripasso seeks a middle ground by infusing Valpolicella wine with leftover pressed Amarone grapes. Other native grapes include Friuli's rustic Refosco; sharp Pignolo and Schioppettino; and softer Lagrein and Schiava from Alto Adige. Vintners blend these local grapes with Bordeaux varieties to add structure and complexity.

other northern italian red recommendations

Allegrini Palazzo della Torre | 2006 | VERONESE

★★★ $ $ With bold fruit flavors—prune, cassis, black currant— brassy tannins and a formidable finish, this wine from Allegrini's Palazzo della Torre vineyard is practically chewy in texture. It delivers tremendous power for a fair price.

Bertani | 2001 | AMARONE DELLA VALPOLICELLA CLASSICO

★★★★ $ $ $ $ Established in 1857, the Bertani family winery has experience with Amarone—and it is on display here. Chianti-like aromas of tea and dried cherry mingle with tobacco and spice flavors supported by mouthwatering acidity and a big finish.

Corte Rugolin Crosara de la Strìe | 2005 | AMARONE DELLA VALPOLICELLA CLASSICO

★★★ $ $ $ The Coati family's meticulous attention to detail—low yields, judicious use of oak—results in wines like this well-structured Amarone. Rich, black and balanced, it shows ripe fruit, chalky minerals and fine-grained tannins.

J. Hofstätter Meczan Pinot Nero | 2008 | ALTO ADIGE

★★★ $ $ Martin Foradori's Pinot Neros are among the best in Alto Adige. This juicy, light-bodied version starts off with ripe fruit and minerals, evolving on the palate to reveal nice black cherry flavors and vanilla nuances.

Kellerei Cantina Terlan Montigl Riserva Pinot Noir | 2007 | ALTO ADIGE

★★★ $ $ $ The combination of a northern climate and warm, south-facing vineyard slopes yields this gorgeous, silky Pinot Noir. It's fragrant with red berries and spice, while vibrant acidity and fine tannins contribute great structure.

Laimburg Lago di Caldaro Scelto Ölleiten | 2008 | ALTO ADIGE

★★ $ $ A great example of Schiava—a grape variety that thrives in Alto Adige—this wine has a signature of bright cherries, minerality and a silky, svelte texture.

La Roncaia Il Fusco | 2005 | COLLI ORIENTALI DEL FRIULI

★★★ $ $ $ A complex fragrance of dried figs, dates and blackberries introduces this blend of Tazzelenghe, Refosco, Cabernet Franc and Merlot, while plum and chalk dominate the palate. It's medium-bodied, with smooth, fine tannins and a juicy finish.

Mezzacorona Riserva | 2005 | **TEROLDEGO ROTALIANO**
★★ **$ $** The Teroldego grape is native to Trentino and known for making easy-drinking reds. This juicy rendition boasts flowers, cherries and a whiff of gravel.

Nino Negri Sfursat | 2006 | **SFORZATO DI VALTELLINA**
★★★ **$ $ $** North of Lake Como in a sun-drenched Alpine valley, Nino Negri crafts plush, powerful wines. This shows black cherry and raisin notes balanced by a spicy finish.

Zenato | 2007 | **VALPOLICELLA CLASSICO SUPERIORE**
★ **$** Valpolicella deserves more attention—because so often the grape yields affordable, food-friendly wines like this one. Zippy acidity enlivens tasty fruit and earth flavors.

news from italy

Vintage Notes
Heat spikes throughout Italy during the 2009 harvest could make it an uneven vintage, especially since Sangiovese is so sensitive to heat. Southern regions like Campania fare better in hot years, as grapes such as Aglianico are sturdier. The 2007 vintage was excellent in both Piedmont and Tuscany. Some winemakers are calling it the vintage of a lifetime.

Regions to Watch
Sicily is increasingly becoming an interesting wine region, especially in the Mount Etna area, where producers like Tenuta delle Terre Nere and Il Cantante are leading the way with indigenous grapes such as Nerello, Catarratto and Nero d'Avola. Piedmont's Roero region, long known for its white wine Arneis, is beginning to emerge as a great region for Nebbiolo reds; Matteo Correggia is producing terrific examples. And a relatively new appellation in Tuscany, Orcia, is capable of producing spectacular Sangiovese wines; these are hard to find in the U.S. but worth searching out.

Great-Value Regions
Abruzzo and Le Marche offer some of the best values in all of Italy. Wineries like Illuminati and Cataldi Madonna make excellent Montepulciano d'Abruzzos that are food-friendly and very affordable.

tuscany

Tuscany lies at the heart of Italy's wine heritage. Home to the versatile red Sangiovese grape, Tuscany is responsible for what could be considered Italy's most popular wine, Chianti, as well as one of its most esteemed, Brunello di Montalcino. Tuscany's creative winemakers also craft many outstanding red blends, such as the innovative, modern-style Super-Tuscans (see p. 90).

tuscan whites

Although Tuscany is much more famous for its red wines, the region does produce a decent amount of white wine, most of it based on the rather bland Trebbiano grape and somewhat overpriced. Two of Tuscany's white wines, however, are definitely worth seeking out: Vernaccia from San Gimignano, which is light-bodied and crisp on its own but has more weight and texture when blended with Chardonnay; and Vermentino, a wine full of minerals and refreshing, zesty lime flavors.

tuscan white recommendations

Banfi Centine | 2008 | TUSCANY

★★ $ Banfi tries its hand at something new with this interesting blend of Sauvignon Blanc, Chardonnay and Pinot Grigio. The result is a lovely wine with notes of apple and pear, a refreshing acidity and hints of minerals.

Castello ColleMassari Melacce Vermentino | 2008 | MONTECUCCO

★★ $ $ From a young winery in the relatively new Montecucco appellation, this wine comes on strong with an intense nose of Granny Smith apples and fresh mint; it turns toward ripe fruit on the medium-bodied, brightly acidic palate.

Il Monticello di Davide Neri Groppolo Vermentino | 2008 | COLLI DI LUNI

★★★ $ $ This is from a Tuscan-Ligurian DOC. Apricot aromas and flavors meet crisp minerals and near-effervescent acidity in an utterly refreshing wine that's as drinkable as lemonade.

Palagetto | 2009 | VERNACCIA DI SAN GIMIGNANO
★ $ Crafted entirely from Vernaccia, this wine was made with the help of veteran winemaker Giacomo Tachis. It presents a clean, crisp palate full of green apple and mineral flavors.

Poggio al Tesoro Solosole Vermentino | 2008 | TUSCANY
★ ★ ★ $ $ This well-priced Vermentino is an exceptional wine, bursting with citrus zest, chamomile and petrol on the nose, much like an Alsace Riesling. In the mouth, there's a great minerality throughout.

tuscan reds

Tuscany's reds are almost entirely based on Sangiovese. Though the grape's characteristics include high acidity and bright fruit flavors, the wines it yields range from simple to bold and complex. There are also many great blends crafted with other grapes, including relative newcomers Cabernet Sauvignon, Merlot and Syrah, all grown in the Bolgheri and Maremma regions. Other native grapes such as Canaiolo, Mammolo and Colorino are used in blends.

TUSCAN REDS

chianti

Until 1996, Chianti producers were required to blend white grapes with their Sangiovese-based reds and to age them in large old casks. Those regulations have been overhauled, and since the 2006 vintage, white grapes have been prohibited in Chianti Classico. Most wineries use 100 percent Sangiovese, or blend it with up to 20 percent (in Chianti Classico; more is allowed in basic Chianti) Cabernet Sauvignon, Merlot or native grapes like Canaiolo and Colorino. Generic Chianti, with no subzone on the label, is the simplest. Wines labeled *Riserva* require at least two years of aging, and are more powerful as a result. Chianti encompasses seven subzones, which are noted on labels; Chianti Rùfina is one of the finest. Chianti Classico, the historic heart of Chianti and home to the highest-quality wines from *all* of Chianti, was elevated from a subzone to an independent DOCG within Chianti about 15 years ago.

chianti recommendations

Agricola Querciabella Querciabella | 2007 |
CHIANTI CLASSICO

★★★ $ $ Powerful juicy cherry and dusty spice flavors are on display in this Sangiovese-dominated red (blended with 5 percent Cabernet Sauvignon). It spent up to 14 months aging in French oak, which added a supple quality and helped soften the tight tannins.

Antinori Marchese Antinori Riserva | 2005 |
CHIANTI CLASSICO

★★★ $ $ $ Grapes from Antinori's Santa Cristina, Pèppoli and Badia a Passignano estates make up this terrific Chianti. Violet and cherry aromas abound, followed by a rich, dark fruitiness that is beautifully balanced with elegant, cherry-infused acidity.

Badia a Coltibuono | 2007 | CHIANTI CLASSICO

★★★ $ $ This thousand-year-old estate is run by the Stucchi Prinetti family, who made the switch to organic, biodynamic farming. Ripe and luscious red fruit flavors dominate in this polished, velvety, medium-bodied red; the finish is long and savory.

Borgo Scopeto | 2006 | CHIANTI CLASSICO

★★ $ $ The cherries, berries and earthy floral notes that define this medium-bodied Chianti are offset by a mouthwatering kiss of acidity.

Carpineto | 2008 | CHIANTI CLASSICO

★★ $ $ Carpineto skillfully weaves vanilla bean sweetness with tart red and black cherry flavors in this charming, supple red framed by just the right amount of soft tannins.

Conti Capponi Villa Calcinaia | 2006 | CHIANTI CLASSICO

★★ $ $ Piquant cherry and violet aromas, a zippy acidity and subtle notes of tea leaves characterize this great Chianti, which emphasizes aromatics over power.

Dievole Novecento Riserva | 2005 | CHIANTI CLASSICO

★★★ $ $ $ The coin motif on this bottle refers to the six *denari lucchesi* that the first owners paid for the property back in 1090. The estate's 2005 is rich and full-bodied, brimming with violets and blackberries held together with silky tannins.

Losi Millennium Riserva | 2005 | CHIANTI CLASSICO

★★★ $ $ $ Dusty herbs and dried berry aromas introduce Querciavalle's great Classico. Oak barrel aging imparts a brawny quality, which is expertly balanced by the purity of the fruit flavors.

Marchesi de' Frescobaldi Nipozzano Riserva | 2006 |
CHIANTI RÙFINA
★★ $ $ From Frescobaldi's Chianti Rùfina estate comes this elegant, approachable red bearing all the hallmarks of quality Chianti— dark cherries and dusty herbs, plus a streak of licorice that lifts it nicely off the medium-bodied palate.

Mazzei Fonterutoli | 2007 | CHIANTI CLASSICO
★★★ $ $ A solid Chianti Classico priced well for what it delivers, this is deeply concentrated, with flavors of black currant and blackberry and hints of vanilla and flowers on the polished finish.

Melini Borghi d'Elsa | 2008 | CHIANTI
★★ $ This outstanding bargain offers a lot of complexity for the price. Bright cherry and berry aromas are echoed on the palate, and deep notes of cedar emerge toward the finish.

star producers
tuscany

Antinori
Superstar Piero Antinori is among Italy's most dynamic winemakers and important wine ambassadors, instrumental in the development of the Super-Tuscan category.

Barone Ricasoli
Since taking over at Castello di Brolio in 1993, Francesco Ricasoli has modernized the iconic winery while simultaneously taking it back to its more traditional roots.

Case Basse di Soldera
Gianfranco Soldera is master of the fickle Sangiovese grape, making Brunellos that always provide pleasurable drinking.

Marchesi de' Frescobaldi
The Frescobaldis have been in the wine business for 30 generations and have become one of the largest Tuscan producers without sacrificing an ounce of quality.

Querciabella
With biodynamic advocate Sebastiano Castiglioni at the helm, Querciabella has emerged as one of Chianti's most exciting producers.

Tenuta dell'Ornellaia
Established in 1981, Tenuta dell'Ornellaia crafts Sangiovese and Bordeaux-style wines in a Napa-style winery while maintaining its Tuscan soul.

Principe Corsini Don Tommaso | 2006 | **CHIANTI CLASSICO**
★★★ $ $ $ This blend of 85 percent Sangiovese and 15 percent Merlot is perfumed with cherries and wild sage. It was aged in 70 percent new *barriques* for 16 months, which imparted soft waves of vanilla layered with delicious flavors of ripe cherries and black fruit.

Querceto Riserva | 2005 | **CHIANTI CLASSICO**
★★★ $ $ This is a solid, approachable example of Chianti Classico that won't break the bank. Refined aromas of violets and black cherries lead to sweet black fruit flavors and chalky minerals supported by velvety tannins.

Rocca delle Macìe Riserva | 2006 | **CHIANTI CLASSICO**
★★ $ $ Although this is mostly Sangiovese, Cabernet and Merlot contribute 5 percent each to the blend, adding great concentration to this Tuscan wine, which is marked by dense black fruit flavors cut with a sharp acidity.

Villa Trasqua Riserva | 2006 | **CHIANTI CLASSICO**
★★★ $ $ $ Superstar oenologist Stefano Chioccioli had a hand in crafting this 100 percent Sangiovese. It's soft and chalky, yet also quite robust, with cherry, violet and sage flavors that are rich and round on the palate.

Volpaia | 2007 | **CHIANTI CLASSICO**
★★ $ $ True to Volpaia's style, this wine shows loads of aromatics—tea leaves, dusty sage, cherries and dried violets. Medium-bodied and fruit-driven, it offers everything a well-made Tuscan red should.

TUSCAN REDS

montalcino

Brunello di Montalcino is made with 100 percent Sangiovese (called Brunello in Montalcino) and is considered to be among the greatest of Tuscany's traditional wines. Bold, firm and tannic, Brunello requires at least four years of aging before release (five if Riserva), although, as a concession to modern palates, only two of the four years must be spent in oak, which can mask fruit flavors. A lighter, less costly version of Brunello can be found in Rosso di Montalcino (a.k.a. "Baby Brunello"). These wines require only one year of aging before release and usually cost a fraction of the price of Brunello.

montalcino recommendations

Caparzo | 2006 | **ROSSO DI MONTALCINO**

★★ $ $ From a sprawling estate with about 225 acres under vine, this readily available red is a favorite for its berry and floral aromas and vanilla and blackberry flavors carrying the dry palate.

Casanova di Neri Tenuta Nuova | 2005 |
BRUNELLO DI MONTALCINO

★★★★ $ $ $ $ Brunellos don't come much bigger or more power-ful than this magnificent wine. Massive and concentrated, it unfurls layer after layer of blackberries and ripe cassis flavors laced with lico-rice and spice and an invigorating acidity. The solid tannins really need time in the cellar to soften.

Col d'Orcia | 2007 | **ROSSO DI MONTALCINO**

★★ $ $ Tart berries, tea leaves and minerals appear on the nose of this medium-bodied, easy-drinking Rosso di Montalcino. It was aged in large Slavonian oak casks and French barrels, and the combination created a bold yet balanced wine.

Conti Costanti | 2005 | **BRUNELLO DI MONTALCINO**

★★★ $ $ $ $ With family roots in the area reaching back to the 15th century, Andrea Costanti has a long winemaking tradition to draw on and crafts beautifully old-fashioned wines like this richly lay-ered example. Earthy and funky, with solid tannins and notes of roast coffee, it delivers a solid core of sweet berries and plums that makes it plush and irresistible.

Fattoria dei Barbi | 2004 | **BRUNELLO DI MONTALCINO**

★★★ $ $ $ It is evident from the first sip: This is a serious wine. Black cherries come on strong and build in intensity, joined by herbs and big chewy tannins.

Fuligni | 2005 | **BRUNELLO DI MONTALCINO**

★★★★ $ $ $ $ With dusty *herbes de Provence* and luscious, full-bodied flavors of dark fruit, this Brunello superbly balances its tradi-tional and modern influences. Coffee and cocoa notes infuse the fruit intensity all the way through the massive finish. Look also for Fuligni's Super-Tuscan, S.J.

Il Poggione | 2007 | **ROSSO DI MONTALCINO**

★★★ $ $ Aging in large French oak barrels made this wine soft, approachable and incredibly easy to drink. Cocoa-dusted berry fla-vors alternate with bright tart cherry in the mouth, and a nice acidity is woven throughout.

Poggio Antico | 2005 | **BRUNELLO DI MONTALCINO**

★ ★ ★ ★ **$ $ $ $** Wild and effusive at first, with aromas of candied berries, vanilla, citron and coffee, this fine red delivers dark, brooding flavors of prune, coffee and vanilla framed by velvety tannins.

Uccelliera Riserva | 2004 | **BRUNELLO DI MONTALCINO**

★ ★ ★ ★ **$ $ $ $** Those looking for an extraordinary Brunello that is drinkable now should splurge on this standout example. Classic aromas of cherry and tea are followed by dark fruit flavors and a fine dusting of minerals.

Valdicava | 2007 | **ROSSO DI MONTALCINO**

★ ★ ★ **$ $ $** This red begins with a sweet perfume of delicate berries. On the palate it's surprisingly full-bodied, with mineral nuances and firm tannins tempered beautifully by plenty of luscious black fruit. It becomes even more powerful with a bit of time in the glass.

TUSCAN REDS

montepulciano, carmignano, morellino di scansano

Though the wines of Montepulciano are produced less than 30 miles from Montalcino, the two regions are markedly different. Vino Nobile di Montepulciano wines can include small amounts of other varieties along with Sangiovese (known locally as Prugnolo Gentile) and have a minimum aging requirement of two years (three for Riservas). Rosso di Montepulciano requires considerably less aging—only six months—and is lighter, ready to drink upon release and much less expensive. Straddling Montepulciano is Cortona, a relatively new DOC where the Syrah grape has found a comfortable home. Carmignano wines are made of Sangiovese grapes blended with Canaiolo and Cabernet Sauvignon and/or Cabernet Franc; they have lower acidity and firmer tannins than typical Chianti Classico. Morellino di Scansano (the "little cherry of Scansano") is a charming, mainly Sangiovese-based wine that has improved considerably in recent years.

montepulciano recommendations

Avignonesi | 2006 | VINO NOBILE DI MONTEPULCIANO
★★★ $ $ A terrific value, this blend of 85 percent Sangiovese (called Prugnolo Gentile here), 10 percent Canaiolo Nero and 5 percent Mammolo offers a fragrant bouquet of violets and berries that are joined by mouthwatering acidity and soft tannins on the palate.

Boscarelli | 2007 | VINO NOBILE DI MONTEPULCIANO
★★★ $ $ $ Berry compote and chalky minerals—punctuated by notes of dusty herbs and tea leaves—come together beautifully in this Sangiovese-led Montepulciano. It's full-bodied and remarkably dense, with firm tannins and a very dry finish.

Dei | 2006 |
VINO NOBILE DI MONTEPULCIANO
★★★ $ $ This enticing Montepulciano has a distinctive nose of cured meat, citrus zest, cherry and tea notes. Lively acidity, firm tannins and stony minerals deftly offset the abundant ripe fruit flavors.

La Braccesca | 2006 |
VINO NOBILE DI MONTEPULCIANO
★★★ $ $ Made by the prolific and pioneering Antinori family, this stunning wine displays a vibrant berry nose with whiffs of flowers and citrus. Berries mingle with cocoa on the silky palate, which is beautifully balanced and concentrated.

taste here now

LA FORNACE DI MELETO
Surrounded by gorgeous vineyards at the base of Chianti's 13th-century Castello di Meleto, La Fornace di Meleto is run by sommelier Valentina Stiaccini and chef Diego Babboni. The impressive wine list is made up primarily of Tuscan bottles, highlighting selections from the Castello di Meleto winery. *Meleto Gaiole, Tuscany; lafornacedimeleto.com*

Poliziano | 2006 | VINO NOBILE DI MONTEPULCIANO
★★★ $ $ Poliziano's oak regimen includes aging this Sangiovese-dominated red in both French and traditional large oak barrels. The combination works wonderfully, yielding a raspberry-flavored wine that is juicy and ripe, with notes of oak and caramel and tight tannins.

Salcheto | 2005 | VINO NOBILE DI MONTEPULCIANO
★★★★ $ $ $ Salcheto is a relative newcomer, a mere quarter century old, and uses only Sangiovese to craft this scrumptious red. Its aromas are delicate but emerge with time to reveal dark fruit, spice, coffee and leather. The power and depth of this wine are amazing, especially considering the under-$40 price tag.

carmignano & morellino di scansano recommendations

Ambra Santa Cristina in Pilli | 2006 | CARMIGNANO
★★ $ $ Sangiovese dominates here, as evidenced by the chalky berry and violet candy flavors. With a rush of cherry on the medium-weight finish, there's impressive complexity for the modest price.

Capezzana | 2007 | BARCO REALE DI CARMIGNANO
★★ $ Capezzana makes this fruity red with Sangiovese, Cabernet Sauvignon and a bit of Canaiolo. The result is an affordable plum- and violet-flavored wine with a medium-body and soft tannins.

Doga delle Clavule | 2006 | MORELLINO DI SCANSANO
★★ $ $ This medium-bodied blend of Sangiovese with small amounts of Merlot and Alicante offers fleshy berry flavors layered with chocolate-dipped raisins and vanilla; the finish lingers impressively.

Poggio Argentiera Bellamarsilia | 2008 |
MORELLINO DI SCANSANO
★★ $ $ Although this region now has DOCG status, Poggio Argentiera maintains a humble price for this entry-level Morellino. Pure flavors of cherries, berries, violets and chalk are joined by sweet tannins.

TUSCAN REDS

super-tuscans & other tuscan reds

Sangiovese's popularity and propensity for blending has inspired winemakers to combine the grape with international varieties (namely Cabernet Sauvignon, Merlot and Syrah) to create wines that are known colloquially as Super-Tuscans. The moniker stems from an era when these powerful, often world-class wines could be classified only as lowly Vino da Tavola, or table wine, because they broke from any accepted regional regulations. The creation of the IGT designation (see p. 69) offered an alternative classification for these nontraditional wines. The successful approval of the Bolgheri and Bolgheri Sassicaia DOC, established in 1994, was an important step in the acceptance of Super-Tuscans. This coastal region is home to some of the greatest of these wines; the new DOC mandated a maximum of 80 percent Cabernet Sauvignon, 70 percent Merlot and 70 percent Sangiovese for Bolgheri; and 85 percent Cabernet Sauvignon and 15 percent Cabernet Franc for Bolgheri Sassicaia, which is exclusive to the esteemed Tenuta San Guido estate. Super-Tuscans are unique in that they are not a regulated category of wine in Tuscany, but a collection of innovative modern wines, mostly of IGT status. In addition to Super-Tuscans, there are many other Sangiovese-based reds labeled with the Tuscany designation but made in a more traditional style.

super-tuscan recommendations

Banfi Centine | 2007 | **TUSCANY**
★ ★ $ Aged in oak, this well-built Sangiovese-Cabernet-Merlot blend offers a soft texture and lots of delicious blackberry and raisin flavors.

Fattoria Sardi Giustiniani Quinis Rosso | 2007 |
COLLINE LUCCHESI
★ ★ $ $ This lush, plump blend of Sangiovese and Merlot delivers abundant ripe cherry and berry flavors, followed by a chalky finish.

Luce della Vite | 2006 | **TUSCANY**
★ ★ ★ ★ $ $ $ $ This wine, whose name means "light of the vine," was born of a Mondavi-Frescobaldi partnership. Fine-grained tannins temper a heavenly mix of cherry, berry, spice and oak flavors. Full-bodied and concentrated, it drinks well now but will age well for years.

Mazzei Serrata Belguardo | 2007 | **MAREMMA TOSCANA**
★ ★ ★ $ $ $ $ The Mazzei family has been making wine in Tuscany for nearly 600 years. The exceptional 2007 boasts plum and cassis aromas, a fruit-driven palate and a sweetly tannic finish.

Mazzoni Sangiovese/Merlot | 2007 | **TUSCANY**
★ ★ $ $ Tobacco and earth infuse a base of bold cherry and blueberry flavors in this Sangiovese-Merlot blend. Soft tannins round out the palate, making it balanced and easy to drink.

Monte Antico Sangiovese/Merlot/Cabernet Sauvignon
| 2006 | **TUSCANY**
★ ★ ★ $ Though a Super-Tuscan, this is more traditional in style than most. It's made with 85 percent Sangiovese and small additions of Cabernet Sauvignon and Merlot, and features satisfying flavors of cherry and crisp minerals, all for a very low price.

Orma | 2006 | TUSCANY
★★★ $ $ $ $ Orma's nose practically overwhelms with powerful notes of leafy green tobacco, chocolate and licorice. Undeniably a Super-Tuscan in style, it shows loads of black fruit, fine tannins and an ultrasmooth finish.

Palagetto Sottobosco | 2005 | SAN GIMIGNANO
★★ $ $ $ This blend of Sangiovese, Cabernet Sauvignon and Syrah opens with a nose of toasted oak and vanilla, then brims over with blackberries. Hints of spice and a firm tannic finish make it a great choice for roasted meat.

Ruffino Modus | 2006 | TUSCANY
★★★★ $ $ This wine's power is always deceptive, considering its low (for a Super-Tuscan) price tag. Huge, heady aromas and flavors of blackberry and licorice, plus spicy-earthy nuances toward the mid-palate, are balanced by a graceful silkiness on the finish.

Terrabianca Campaccio | 2006 | TUSCANY
★★★ $ $ Cassis, blackberry, tobacco and stewed fruit flavors are woven skillfully in this balanced Sangiovese–Cabernet Sauvignon blend. The palate is at once silky, chewy and wild, and a bright acidity takes over the finish.

other tuscan red recommendations

Carpineto Dogajolo | 2008 | TUSCANY
★ $ With soft tannins, ripe raspberry and blackberry flavors and a juicy finish, this is a great everyday pour.

Jacopo Biondi Santi Sassoalloro | 2006 | TUSCANY
★★★ $ $ From one of the oldest winemaking families in Tuscany comes this appealingly juicy *rosso* oozing sweet blackberry flavors with warm notes of baking spice and wood chips. Silky tannins hold everything together.

Luiano Sangiovese | 2008 | TUSCANY
★ $ Crafted in a youthful, super-fresh style, this well-built Sangiovese makes a great pizza wine for its combination of tea, cherry and berry flavors and juicy finish.

Tenuta di Ghizzano Veneroso | 2005 | TUSCANY
★★★ $ $ $ Made from grapes grown in southwest-facing vineyards in the village of Ghizzano halfway between Florence and Pisa, this earthy, spicy blend abounds with the flavors of plush, ripe blackberry. Chewy tannins and a whiff of cocoa linger on the finish.

other central italian regions

Beyond Tuscany and its many treasures lie other central Italian regions whose wines are well worth exploring. The most notable of these regions is Abruzzo, known primarily for robust, affordable red wines. Other central Italian offerings range from the intensely earthy, smoky Rosso Conero of Le Marche to the popular, slightly sparkling red Lambrusco of Emilia-Romagna.

• **EMILIA-ROMAGNA** Much better known for its food, Emilia-Romagna still produces some interesting wines. The most popular is fizzy red Lambrusco, but whites from Chardonnay and Albana grapes and reds from Sangiovese, Barbera and Cabernet Sauvignon are also made here.

• **LE MARCHE** The distinctively rich white made from the Verdicchio grape is the signature wine of the underestimated Le Marche region. The standout red here is Rosso Conero, a bold, full-bodied wine based primarily on the Montepulciano grape.

• **ABRUZZO** Crisp, lovely Trebbiano d'Abruzzo is a redemption for the otherwise quite dull Trebbiano grape. This is also the most important region for the Montepulciano grape, which yields dark, spicy wines (not to be confused with Tuscany's Sangiovese-based Montepulciano wine, which is named for a town).

• **UMBRIA** Orvieto is the region's most important wine. Simple, less interesting examples of this white wine are made from the Trebbiano grape alone; blends with the lively Grechetto grape are far better. Umbria's Sagrantino grape yields one of Italy's most tannic, powerful and long-lived reds, particularly in the Montefalco district.

• **LAZIO** The region surrounding Rome provides the capital with one of its simpler pleasures—the lightly sparkling white Frascati. Made from a Trebbiano and Malvasia blend, most versions offer delicate, citrusy refreshment.

other central italian whites

Like many Italian wines, Le Marche's Verdicchio was once a simple, mass-produced commodity with little character. Today, as the region's winemakers focus their attention and resources on the variety, more and more interesting expressions are being crafted. Trebbiano d'Abruzzo is another central Italian white wine making a name for itself internationally. The low-acid Albana grape shines particularly brightly in the Emilia-Romagna region, where it yields a variety of compelling styles, both dry and sweet.

other central italian white recommendations

Antinori Cervaro della Sala | 2007 | **UMBRIA**
★★★★ **$ $ $** Antinori blends Chardonnay with 15 percent Grechetto to make this big, buttery, delicious wine. It was aged on its lees in oak barrels for about six months, which lends toast notes to a richly textured palate of banana and melon flavors.

Caldora | 2009 | **TREBBIANO D'ABRUZZO**
★★ **$** Floral and lime aromas dominate the nose of this dry, light-bodied white. Its citrus-driven acidity lingers pleasantly on the finish.

Cataldi Madonna | 2008 | **TREBBIANO D'ABRUZZO**
★ **$ $** Cataldi Madonna's winery is located in Ofena, which has been nicknamed the "oven of Abruzzo." Warm temperatures contribute ripe flavors to this medium-bodied citrus- and mineral-laden white.

Falesco Vitiano | 2008 | **UMBRIA**
★ **$** A stainless steel–fermented blend of equal parts Verdicchio and Vermentino, this crisp white has hints of peach on the nose and copious amounts of citrus on the palate.

Farnese | 2008 | **TREBBIANO D'ABRUZZO**
★ **$** With its light weight, citruslike acidity and mineral core, this clean-cut white is a great alternative to everyday Pinot Grigio.

Palazzone Terre Vineate | 2009 |
ORVIETO CLASSICO SUPERIORE
★★ **$ $** This bright, lemon-colored wine comes from an estate that practices organic agriculture. Tart and tangy, it's medium-bodied and dry, with tasty flavors of soft pear and citrus.

other central italian reds

The Marche region produces two noteworthy Sangiovese-Montepulciano blends: Rosso Conero and Rosso Piceno. Emilia-Romagna, sometimes called the birthplace of Sangiovese, makes a fine, if underappreciated, version of the grape. Umbria's Sagrantino di Montefalco is full-bodied, dark and complex, though small production can lead to high prices. Probably the most popular wine from Italy's other central regions is Montepulciano d'Abruzzo: Though typically a simple wine with nice berry flavors, it can also be remarkably robust and tannic.

other central italian red recommendations

Barone Cornacchia | 2007 | **MONTEPULCIANO D'ABRUZZO**
★★ $ $ There's 10 percent Sangiovese in this Montepulciano, which accounts for its strawberry undertones and rich acidity. Aging in Slavonian oak for 6 to 8 months gives it further depth and spiciness.

Boccadigabbia | 2007 | **ROSSO PICENO**
★★ $ $ Napoleon III owned this estate, and it was during his time that international varieties were planted here—long before the term *Super-Tuscan* was invented. This blend is a traditional one, however—Sangiovese and Montepulciano—and yields a robust, firm wine brimming with flavors of earth, mineral and red cherry.

Di Majo Norante Sangiovese | 2008 | **TERRA DEGLI OSCI**
★★ $ Fine-grained tannins meld with strawberry, cherry and earth aromas in this medium-bodied red from the Molise region; it is all uplifted by juicy acidity.

Enzo Mecella | 2009 | **LACRIMA DI MORRO D'ALBA**
★★ $ $ Elevated to DOC status in 1985, Lacrima di Morro d'Alba tends to yield wines that are extremely perfumed and aromatic. This stellar example is pungent and inviting, with a violet and blueberry bouquet that is followed by a ripe, approachable palate.

Fattoria Le Terrazze Sassi Neri Riserva | 2006 | **CONERO**
★★★ $ $ $ This organic producer got a lot of attention when it made a wine at the request of Bob Dylan and named it Planet Waves after the singer-songwriter's album. Le Terrazze's Riserva offers red berry and barnyard aromas, a medium body and mellow tannins.

Fausti Fausto | 2008 | **ROSSO PICENO**

★ **$** This straightforward, everyday red presents a delightful mix of cherry and blossom; its bright acidity and somewhat firm tannins provide a nice frame.

Lungarotti Fiamme Sangiovese/Merlot | 2008 | **UMBRIA**

★ **$** This Sangiovese-dominated blend entices with aromas and flavors of blackberry and black cherry. Chewy tannins abound, making it an ideal red for summer barbecues.

Nicodemi | 2007 | **MONTEPULCIANO D'ABRUZZO**

★★ **$ $** Utterly delicious, this layered and complex Montepulciano d'Abruzzo priced under $20 is a good example of the great value that central Italy can offer. Dusty tannins and red berry flavors are followed by an earthy finish.

Paolo Bea Pagliaro | 2005 | **MONTEFALCO SAGRANTINO**

★★★★ **$ $ $ $** This dense, extremely concentrated Sagrantino spent 46 days macerating and fermenting, which explains some of its impressive power. Still youthful, the wine delivers flavors of cherry and dust that carry through the very long, structured finish.

Quattro Mani | 2008 | **MONTEPULCIANO D'ABRUZZO**

★ **$** Attilio Pagli, the consulting winemaker at Velenosi, crafts this rich, blackberry-laden red. Smoke, earth and black cherry aromas come on strong and lead to a soft, supple palate with gentle tannins.

southern italy & the islands

While regional names like Barolo and Chianti dominate wine labels in Italy's well-established northern regions, many of the exciting wines emerging from the up-and-coming south use actual grape names on their labels. Varieties like Aglianico, Falanghina and Greco di Tufo, among others, are unfamiliar to many wine drinkers, but that is changing. In Campania, more producers have come to champion these truly ancient varieties, reclaiming wine-making traditions that date back to Roman times. Quality is also soaring in Sicily, where vintners succeed with both traditional and international varieties.

southern italy

Despite its warm climate, Campania produces both excellent red and white wines, largely from native grapes. White wines, including Falanghina, Fiano di Avellino and Greco di Tufo, are similarly crisp, floral and minerally, and usually well priced. Aglianico is the leading red grape, responsible for Campania's robust Taurasi, rivaled by the best Aglianico del Vulture from Basilicata. Increasingly available in the U.S. are the Primitivo wines of Apulia; the grape is related to California's Zinfandel, and exhibits many of the same exuberant, jammy berry flavors.

• **APULIA** Still known primarily for its mass production of wines that will never reach an international market, Apulia (or Puglia in Italian) is home to an increasing number of high-quality red wines. Look for the spicy reds from Salice Salentino and Copertino, both made from the dark-skinned Negroamaro grape, as well as the fruity Primitivo, which tastes similar to a California Zinfandel.

• **BASILICATA** With the menacingly named Monte Vulture volcano looming in the background, the vineyards of Basilicata produce aromatic, spicy, powerful Aglianico-based red wines influenced by the volcanic soils of the region. The more tannic versions of Basilicata's reds can require many years of aging.

• **CALABRIA** This region, located in the toe of Italy's boot, is responsible for a good deal of low-quality wine. One exception is the Gaglioppo-based red wine of Cirò, which is lightly tannic and flush with berry flavors.

• **CAMPANIA** The highlight of southern Italian winemaking is the historic Campania region. Its Aglianico-based red Taurasi, which requires a minimum of three years of aging before it is released, has earned much well-deserved acclaim since it achieved DOCG status in 1993. Both the quality and quantity of Falanghina, the region's principal white wine, are on the rise, while the two other whites particular to Campania, Fiano di Avellino and floral Greco di Tufo, also deserve recognition.

southern italy recommendations

WHITES

Feudi di San Gregorio | 2008 | FIANO DI AVELLINO
★★★ $ $ The volcanic ash–rich soil of the Irpinia region, near Mount Vesuvius, has imparted a luscious, flinty minerality to this white's satisfying apple and pear flavors.

Rivera Preludio Nº 1 Chardonnay | 2008 | CASTEL DEL MONTE
★ $ Packed with sweet vanilla and juicy apricot flavors with just a hint of quince, this classic Chardonnay is tasty and balanced.

Vesevo Falanghina | 2009 | BENEVENTANO
★★ $ Marzipan and peanuts dominate the nose on this Falanghina, while flowers, apricots and minerals turn up on the palate. It's zesty and plush at the same time, with a lovely mouthfeel.

REDS

Antica Masseria del Sigillo Sigillo Primo Primitivo | 2007 | SALENTO
★★★ $ $ In this stellar Primitivo, raisin, tea, dried herbs and black fruit flavors are held together by fine tannins. Like a mini Amarone, it builds in power throughout the mouthwatering finish.

Cantore di Castelforte Donna Maria Primitivo | 2007 | SALENTO
★★★ $ A spectacular bargain from Italy's south, this Primitivo is made in the Salento region—the heel of Italy's boot. Featuring cherry, prune and mocha flavors, this is a lip-smackingly delicious wine.

Castello Monaci Liante | 2008 | SALICE SALENTINO
★ $ This blend of Negroamaro and Malvasia Nera provides easy-drinking pleasure in the form of soft-textured plum and cherry flavors and a hint of spice on the finish.

Feudi di San Gregorio | 2004 | TAURASI
★★★ $ $ $ Mouth-coating and full-bodied, this is a massive wine, dripping with unctuous mocha, dried berry and burnt caramel flavors. Great acidity adds a lovely brightness to the palate.

Layer Cake Primitivo | 2007 | APULIA
★★★★ $ $ California winemaker Jayson Woodbridge created his Layer Cake wine label to showcase quality wines from around the world with surprisingly low prices. His Primitivo—grown in vineyards that date back to Roman times—more than fills the bill, with its delectable waves of black fruit, spice and chalk.

Primaterra Primitivo | 2008 | **APULIA**

★ ★ **$** At less than $10, this Apulian red is a knockout bargain offering juicy, spicy cherry flavors and a charming soft texture.

Terra dei Re Divinus | 2005 | **AGLIANICO DEL VULTURE**

★ ★ **$ $ $** This powerhouse Aglianico balances its dark currant, blackberry and cigar box flavors against a firming acidity. With each sip, bold tannins assert themselves and build in power through the huge finish.

Tormaresca Torcicoda Primitivo | 2006 | **SALENTO**

★ ★ ★ **$ $** *Tormaresca* loosely translates as "tower by the sea," referring to the distinctive watchtowers of Salento. This red boasts a rich, ripe and succulent palate with great body and a nice spicy note on the finish.

eat here now

MORABIANCA Mastroberardino winery owner Piero Mastroberardino spent ten years developing his dream hotel and golf course, Radici. Its restaurant, Morabianca, stocks many vintages of Mastroberardino's wines—some of them available nowhere else— to go with chef Francesco Spagnuolo's updated versions of regional dishes. *Mirabella Eclano, Campania; morabianca.it*

Torre Quarto Bottaccia Uva di Troia | 2007 | **APULIA**

★ ★ **$ $** This Uva di Troia red is spicy and seductive. Black cherry and plum allure on the nose, while chocolate-drizzled dark fruit flavors come on strong in the mouth.

sicily & sardinia

Italy's largest grape grower, the island of Sicily was long known only for bulk production, but a handful of winemakers are now creating laudable wines. The warm climate is best suited to reds, particularly from the local Nero d'Avola grape, which is often blended with international varieties, like Cabernet Sauvignon, Merlot, and Syrah. But the island does produce some bright, citrusy whites, usually with the Catarratto grape, which is often combined with Inzolia. Sardinia has a great diversity of ancient grapes, with the sole DOCG awarded to the white Vermentino di Gallura. Like the wines of Sicily, Sardinian wines are affordable, but they're more challenging to find. Look for the island's spicy, often rustic Cannonau (Grenache), which is appearing more frequently in American wineshops.

sicily & sardinia recommendations

WHITES

Argiolas Costamolino | 2009 | **VERMENTINO DI SARDEGNA**

★ ★ $ In order to maintain high acidity levels, Sardinia's Vermentino growers traditionally pick the grapes very early in the season. This example displays pleasing flavors of clean minerals and light citrus before a mouthwatering finish.

Cusumano Insolia | 2008 | **SICILY**

★ $ Made from 100 percent Inzolia, this medium-bodied white presents flinty mineral and fresh sliced apple on the nose, creamy apple flavors, good acidity and a chalky finish.

Feudo Arancio Grillo | 2008 | **SICILY**

★ $ Vinified from Grillo, an indigenous Sicilian grape, this wine is bone-dry, brisk and intensely mineral, with a lovely peachy quality to the dusty, crisp finish.

REDS

Cantina Santadi Terre Brune | 2004 |
CARIGNANO DEL SULCIS SUPERIORE

★ ★ ★ ★ $ $ $ $ This producer specializes in the Carignano grape and does amazing things with the humble variety. This example boasts gorgeous aromas of cherries, plums, licorice and roses, while the palate highlights black fruit, coffee and leather held together by silky, plush tannins.

Di Giovanna Gerbino | 2008 | **SICILY**

★ ★ $ $ Composed of 35 percent Cabernet Sauvignon, 35 percent Merlot, 15 percent Nero d'Avola and 15 percent Syrah, this red has a wild nose of licorice, sarsaparilla and plum. The palate is funky and earthy, with a smooth, balanced finish.

Feudo Maccari Saia Nero d'Avola | 2007 | **SICILY**

★ ★ ★ $ $ $ *Saia* is the Arabic-derived Sicilian word for "canal." Feudo Maccari's Saia comes from sun-drenched vineyards in Sicily, which require irrigation in the blistering summer. The wine's black cherry, dusty oregano, sage and lavender flavors are woven with vibrant acidity and firm tannins.

MandraRossa Nero d'Avola | 2008 | **SICILY**

★ $ This is a friendly wine with delicate floral, cherry and red plum aromas that are joined on the palate by berry and licorice flavors. The finish is soft, juicy and satisfying.

Mazzei Zisola | 2007 | SICILY
★★★ $ $ Aged for ten months in French oak barrels, this Nero d'Avola offers a complex mélange of citrus zest, plum jam, violet and cocoa flavors and a chocolate-infused finish.

Mirabile Nero d'Avola | 2007 |
SICILY
★★ $ There's a distinct homemade cranberry sauce character to the nose of this gulpable red; delicious flavors of candied plum and berries round out the mouthwatering palate.

Planeta | 2008 |
CERASUOLO DI VITTORIA
★★★ $ $ Cerasuolo di Vittoria is the only Sicilian region that has been granted DOCG status, and Planeta is one of the area's finest producers. A blend of Nero d'Avola and Frappato, this wine offers aromas of red cherry and tea leaf and darker flavors of prune, earth and coffee.

eat here now

CUCINA Just off Palermo's Piazza Politeama, Cucina attracts many high-profile celebrities and politicians with its wonderful *osteria*-style Sicilian cuisine. Cucina's wine list includes just two local wines, which are served in charming flasklike decanters. They pair perfectly with chef Roberto Giannettino's satisfying comfort dishes. *Via Principe di Villafranca 54, Palermo, Sicily*

Sella & Mosca Riserva | 2006 | CANNONAU DI SARDEGNA
★ $ Aged in oak for two years, this pleasing red has developed aromas of dusty sage and tea and soft flavors of ripe red berry.

Tasca d'Almerita Lamùri Nero d'Avola | 2007 | SICILY
★★★ $ $ Named for *l'amuri*—"love" in the Sicilian dialect—Lamùri is a concentrated, delightfully flavorful red marked by cherries, kirsch, chocolate, cinnamon and coffee. Thanks to a beautiful acidity, the chalky finish is bright and refreshing.

Tenuta Rapitalà Nuar Nero d'Avola/Pinot Nero | 2007 | SICILY
★★ $ $ Though an unlikely duo, this Nero d'Avola–Pinot Nero partnership is harmonious. Complete with spice, minerals, loads of cherries and integrated tannins, it's a polished wine for a great price.

Umberto Soletta Corona Majore | 2006 | CANNONAU DI SARDEGNA
★★ $ $ Tenute Soletta's Cannonau starts off with violet aromas that turn to candied violet flavors in the mouth, accompanied by mouthwatering berry, kirsch and spice. A chewy texture makes this red particularly satisfying.

spain

Roughly a third of all of Europe's vineyards are in Spain, which has more land under vine than any other nation. Yet production here is falling—a positive result of Spain's new quality initiatives. Winemakers throughout the country are following the example of famous regions like Rioja, Ribera del Duero and Priorat, making less, but better, wine. The result is that Spain offers more top-quality wines than ever before.

Bay of Biscay

GALICIA
Rías Baixas   Rioja
Bierzo   Navarra
        Cigales   Somontano   CATALONIA
Toro   Ribera del Duero   Barcelona
        CASTILLA Y LEÓN   Priorat   Penedès
        Rueda   Calatayud

Madrid ☆   VALENCIA
                Utiel-
SPAIN   Requena
        La Mancha   • Valencia   Mallorca
Ribera
del   Valdepeñas
Guadiana   Alicante
        Jumilla
                MURCIA   *Mediterranean Sea*
        • Seville
Jerez

PORTUGAL

Málaga

Atlantic Ocean

■ Principal Wine Region

Spain: An Overview

Spain's mountain ranges divide the country into distinct viticultural areas. Albariño-based whites hail from the cool Atlantic region of Rías Baixas in Galicia, while farther east, Rueda produces zippier whites. Catalonia, in the northeast, is home to sparkling Cavas, still wines from Penedès and robust reds from Priorat. Luxurious reds come from Ribera del Duero, while Bierzo is known for fragrant reds. Toro and Jumilla earn praise for their powerful reds. Jerez is famous for its fortified Sherries (see p. 259).

Spanish Wine Labels

Spain's *Denominación de Origen* (DO) board determines a region's permitted grapes, harvest limits and vinification techniques and regulates wine labels. Labels list the region, and sometimes the grape. The *Vino de la Tierra* designation is like the French *Vin de Pays* category; it is used for wines from designated zones that don't qualify for DO status. Terms such as *Joven, Crianza, Reserva* or *Gran Reserva* indicate the amount of time spent aging in barrel and bottle, although these standards vary by region (see Rioja, below). Two regions, Rioja and Priorat, lay claim to the elite status of DOCa (*Denominación de Origen Calificada*).

rioja & navarra

Rioja is Spain's most famous designated wine region. Many of Rioja's traditional reds historically lacked fruitiness, as a result of long oak aging. Contemporary tastes have driven vintners to make their wines differently, and modern Rioja reds display more pronounced fruit flavors augmented by sweet spice and vanilla notes. Rioja whites, too, are now made in a fresher style (though some older-style whites are excellent). Rioja's neighbor Navarra has long been a source for *rosados* (rosé wines), and today makes many great reds.

Rioja & Navarra Grapes & Styles

If one grape is synonymous with Rioja, it is Tempranillo. Traditionally, it is blended with Garnacha (Grenache), Graciano and Mazuelo (the Rioja name for Carignane), and aged in American oak. Cabernet Sauvignon is allowed in some vineyards. Rioja reds are given designations based on aging time in barrel and bottle: Joven wines spend little or no time in barrels; Crianza reds must be aged two years, one in barrel; Reservas require three years total, one in oak; Gran Reservas, five years total, two in oak. A growing number of vintners here, however, are now using subtler French oak barrels and aging their wines for shorter lengths of time. Sometimes referred to as *alta expresión* (high expression), these wines have fresh, bold flavors. Rioja's rosado wines are dry, with orange and berry flavors. Traditional white wines from Rioja, made mostly with Viura (the local name for Macabeo) and some Malvasia and Garnacha Blanca, are richly layered, barrel aged and often intentionally oxidized. While this style still exists, the trend is toward fresher wines. Rioja growers planted nonnative white varieties, including Chardonnay, Sauvignon Blanc and Verdejo, for the first time in 2007, and winemakers are now using them in blends.

In Navarra, Tempranillo has surpassed Garnacha, the traditional regional grape, in total plantings. Cabernet Sauvignon and/or Merlot often join these regional grapes in creative red blends. The region's rosados are excellent and widely exported. White grapes account for only 5 percent of Navarra's vineyards, but plantings continue to increase.

rioja & navarra recommendations

WHITES

Finca Nueva | 2008 | RIOJA
★★ $ $ Fermented in barrel, this $20 white made by Finca Allende resembles a basic white Burgundy in its toasted apple and oak aromas. The palate is round and buttery, with a clean, crisp finish.

Monjardin El Cerezo Unoaked Chardonnay | 2008 | NAVARRA
★ $ This unoaked white is bright and friendly, with loads of big, ripe grapefruit flavors offset by brisk acidity.

Muga | 2009 | RIOJA

★ ★ ★ $ Up-front peach aromas are followed by a perfect balance of ripe stone-fruit flavors and toasted oak notes in this enticing wine. With a long finish and a great price, it's worth stocking up on.

R. López de Heredia Viña Tondonia Viña Gravonia Crianza | 2000 | RIOJA

★ ★ ★ ★ $ $ Produced at the oldest bodega in the town of Haro, this white is astonishingly complex. Mineral-laden and clean, it displays aromas of apple, pear and macadamia nut that lead into a white fruit–drenched palate with hints of petrol.

ROSÉS

Julián Chivite Gran Feudo Rosado | 2009 | NAVARRA

★ $ Though Chivite was founded in the mid-17th century, its existing winery was built in the 1870s. This *saignée*-method rosé—made by using only the runoff juice, mainly from Garnacha—features peach and nectarine flavors.

Marqués de Cáceres | 2008 | RIOJA

★ ★ $ Deep pink in color, this rosé is dry and crisp, with a waxy texture and delicate wildflower and pear flavors.

Señorío de Sarría Viñedo Nº 5 | 2009 | NAVARRA

★ ★ $ Rather full-bodied, this dark-hued rosé is almost like a light-bodied red wine. It's 100 percent old-vine Garnacha and offers layers of rich raspberry and currant flavors.

REDS

Almira Los Dos Old Vines Grenache/Syrah | 2008 | CAMPO DE BORJA

★ $ Campo de Borja is located just south of Navarra and is a go-to region for great-value reds. This simple, unoaked wine is spicy, fruity and wonderfully easy to drink, and comes at a very attractive price.

Alto Moncayo Veraton Garnacha | 2007 | CAMPO DE BORJA

★ ★ ★ $ $ Since its debut vintage in 2004, this wine has been winning fans with its opulent, intense style. Flavors of charred oak, berries, spice and earth are framed by ripe tannins on a very full body.

Barón de Ley 7 Viñas Reserva | 2004 | RIOJA

★ ★ ★ ★ $ $ $ This wine's name refers to its composition of all seven of Rioja's authorized grape varieties. It is complex, distinctive and extremely delicious, with aromas of violet, smoke and spice followed by flavors of strawberry and earth.

Bodega Inurrieta Sur | 2006 | NAVARRA

★★★★ $ $ Inurrieta planted vines only in 1999, but already the wines are showing incredible promise. This outstanding bargain, a blend of 75 percent Garnacha and 25 percent Graciano, has stunning complexity and balance, with flavors of subtle oak, leather and cherry.

Bodegas Marqués de Murrieta Castillo Ygay Gran Reserva Especial | 2001 | RIOJA

★★★★ $ $ $ The flagship wine of Marqués de Murrieta, this red is never released to market earlier than seven years after vintage. It displays great complexity on the nose—strawberry, leather and cigar box—and has a long, wonderfully balanced finish.

El Coto Crianza | 2006 | RIOJA

★ $ This is a textbook Rioja, with simple yet tasty flavors of red cherries and oak laced with smoke, strawberry and earth. Mellow tannins and subtle toast notes round out the package.

Faustino VII | 2007 | RIOJA

★★ $ Fairly robust for an entry-level Rioja, Faustino VII brims with juicy cherry flavors and hints of leather. It's medium-bodied, with fine-grained tannins that ensure a smooth finish.

Finca Allende | 2005 | RIOJA

★★★ $ $ Owner Miguel Ángel de Gregorio learned to make wine from his father, who worked for the esteemed Marqués de Murrieta. This wine is decidedly more modern than Murrieta's, featuring a full body, chewy tannins and mocha, charred oak and sour cherry flavors.

Loriñon Reserva | 2005 | RIOJA

★★★ $ $ Bodegas Bretón makes this wine in their modern, state-of-the-art winery. Featuring Tempranillo, Mazuelo, Garnacha and Graciano, it boasts firm tannins rounded out with classic raspberry and strawberry flavors and highlights of leather and coffee.

Monte Oton Garnacha | 2008 | CAMPO DE BORJA

★ $ A super value from Bodegas Borsao, this vibrant, unoaked red is all about pure fruit flavors—raspberry, plum and cherry—with a little spice and tannic structure.

Pago de Larrainzar | 2005 | NAVARRA

★★★★ $ $ $ This is Pago de Larrainzar's second vintage, and the winery has already achieved true excellence. This stunning blend of 45 percent Merlot, 40 percent Cabernet Sauvignon and 15 percent Tempranillo shows fragrant charred oak and strawberry, which follow through on the palate alongside cherry flavors and beautiful acidity.

Príncipe de Viana 1432 Reserva | 2004 | NAVARRA
★★★ $ $ This red blend—Tempranillo, Cabernet and Merlot—is hearty, full and ripe. Smooth tannins add structure and finesse to wild berry and vanilla flavors.

Solnia Tempranillo/Graciano | 2008 | RIOJA
★ $ Though Graciano accounts for only about 1 percent of vineyard plantings in Rioja, it makes up half the blend in this wine. It's fresh and fruity, with abundant mocha and dark cherry notes.

Vega Sindoa Cabernet Sauvignon/Tempranillo | 2007 |
NAVARRA
★★ $ Bodega Nekeas makes this wine, and it displays all the benchmark features of Cabernet—black currant and oak, a full body and firm tannins. The Tempranillo adds notes of spice, leather and earth.

galicia

Galicia is located in Spain's northwestern corner, north of Portugal on the Atlantic Ocean. In the region's star DO, Rías Baixas, fronting both the Atlantic and the Miño River, white wine accounts for 99 percent of production. Since the denomination was officially created in 1988, Rías Baixas has made rapid international inroads, earning Galicia its well-deserved reputation as a source for fresh, lively whites. The warmer subregions of Valdeorras and Ribeira Sacra produce a small amount of interesting red wine.

Galicia Grapes & Styles

Galacia's finest grape is Albariño, the white grape of Rías Baixas. Albariño is usually fresh and crisp, showing peach, mineral and melon flavors. Although generally bottled on its own, it may be blended with other local grapes, such as Treixadura or Loureira. The Ribeiro region makes Albariño blends, although Treixadura is the leading white grape there. Winemaking is rapidly improving In Galicia's inland regions of Valdeorras and Ribeira Sacra, where the Godello grape yields fuller-bodied whites and the Mencía grape produces fruity young reds. The Monterrei region, along the Portugal border, produces mainly whites from the Doña Blanca grape, as well as Treixadura and Godello.

galicia recommendations

WHITES

Avanthia Godello | 2008 | VALDEORRAS

★★ **$ $** Despite generous oak, this white delivers loads of fresh fruit flavors, with tangerine, pear and melon at the forefront. There are toasted marshmallow nuances throughout, and though rich, the wine remains refreshing and crisp.

Condes de Albarei Albariño | 2009 | RÍAS BAIXAS

★★ **$** Made by a cooperative of 400-plus producers that is responsible for 1.5 million bottles of Albariño each year, this fresh white is a great bargain for its stone-fruit, flower and mineral flavors.

Don Olegario Albariño | 2009 | RÍAS BAIXAS

★★★ **$ $** Bold and aromatic, with effusive grapefruit and mango, this solidly built white is intensely citrusy on the palate. There's a lovely minerality coursing throughout, as well as spiced pear, lemon oil and lanolin notes.

Fillaboa Albariño | 2008 | RÍAS BAIXAS

★★ **$ $** Albariño displays a rich, decadent side in this wine. The plush palate oozes melon, apricot, green almond and citrus flavors and contains plenty of acidity to balance the slightly oily texture.

Granbazán Etiqueta Ámbar Albariño | 2008 | RÍAS BAIXAS

★★ **$ $** Although this displays a light body, it's incredibly rich in flavor. Pineapple, grapefruit and pear dominate the lemony fresh palate, with a hint of mineral and orange peel coming in at the end.

Lícia Albariño | 2008 | RÍAS BAIXAS

★★ **$** Zesty, clean and bright, this mineral-laden Albariño offers apple, peach and Asian pear aromas joined by honeysuckle and thyme on the palate, along with a fresh burst of acidity.

Martín Códax Albariño | 2008 | RÍAS BAIXAS

★★ **$** With more than 550 member wineries, this cooperative is quite large, yet its wines are thoughtfully made. Vibrant and peachy, this delicious example is underscored by nuances of nectarines, lemons, pine and herbs.

Pazo Serantellos Albariño | 2009 | RÍAS BAIXAS

★★ **$** An outstanding value, this well-built Albariño combines juicy apple, nectarine and citrus flavors with hints of honeysuckle and herbs. Thanks to a process known as malolactic fermentation, it has a generous, fleshy texture, while retaining its freshness.

Salneval Albariño | 2009 | RÍAS BAIXAS
★ ★ **$** Savory notes of thyme and fennel infuse this crisp white; they are filled out with peach and golden apple flavors that linger on the palate and finish with a limestone kick.

Zárate Albariño | 2008 | RÍAS BAIXAS
★ ★ **$ $** Sourced from vineyards averaging 35 years of age, this invigorating white was aged six months on its lees. It's pure, bold and fresh, showcasing gorgeous flavors of lemon oil, herbs and seashells.

REDS

Finca Míllara | 2007 |
RIBEIRA SACRA
★ ★ **$ $ $** This estate encompasses the entire village of Míllara overlooking the Miño River. Its well-built red, made with the Mencía grape, offers flavors of cassis, cherry and licorice, with muscular tannins and minerals rounding out the very dry finish.

Viña do Campo Mencía | 2007 |
RIBEIRO
★ ★ **$ $** It's hard not to like this drinkable wine for its soft, sweet red berry flavors tinged with fresh herbs and sweet vanilla.

visit here now

PONTEVEDRA Before visiting the Albariño producers of Rías Baixas, make a tapas crawl through this port city. At Jaqueyvi (*Rúa de Doña Tareixa 1*), *jamón* is the specialty. El Bocaíto (*Calle de Paio Gómez Chariño 2*) is a local's hangout, with soccer on TV and an excellent tortilla. For more upscale food, and an extensive local wine list, try Eirado da Leña (*Praza da Leña 3*).

southeastern spain

The regions of Valencia and Murcia occupy much of Spain's southeast; offshore lie the Balearic Islands, of which only Mallorca produces a significant amount of wine. Long a source of olives, almonds, citrus and bulk wine, this area is still developing as a quality wine region. Vineyards in Murcia's Jumilla region were destroyed by phylloxera in 1989, a full century after most of Europe's vineyards recovered. The plague was something of a blessing, however, as it spurred necessary replanting.

Southeastern Spain Grapes & Styles

Though still a source of bulk wine, the Jumilla region is getting deserved attention for its inky, ripe reds based on the Monastrell (Mourvèdre) grape. Monastrell also stars in the quality wines of the adjacent Murcia DO Yecla, a small area of just 11 wineries. The larger DO of Valencia utilizes a vast mix of grapes to make wine, yet little is high quality. The primary white grape of Valencia is Merseguera, while Tempranillo is becoming a more important red. Bobal is the region's most distinctive native grape, used mainly for dark, brooding red wines. Utiel-Requena is the finest denomination for the grape—Bobal accounts for 80 percent of its total production. The DOs Binissalem Mallorca and Pla i Llevant are the best regions on Mallorca, although in 2007 the entire island became eligible for the quality designation *Vino de la Tierra de Mallorca.* While white wine is produced throughout southeastern Spain, most of it is unremarkable, and very little of it is imported to the U.S.

southeastern spain recommendations

REDS

Altos del Cuco Monastrell/Syrah/Tempranillo | 2008 | YECLA
★ $ Plum and blackberry jump to the forefront in this nice blend, and are joined by more berries and vanilla on the palate.

Casa de la Ermita Crianza Monastrell/Petit Verdot | 2006 | JUMILLA
★★ $ $ Enticing dark fruit flavors meet cigar box, pine forest, nutmeg, clove and toasted oak in this beautiful red. The plush red berry and plum palate is full-bodied and well structured.

Enrique Mendoza La Tremenda Monastrell | 2007 | ALICANTE
★★ $ This Monastrell is particularly fleshy in texture, revealing layers of strawberry jam and plum flavors. It has an herbal side, too—eucalyptus, thyme and licorice—and a dense finish.

Finca Sandoval | 2007 | MANCHUELA
★★★ $ $ $ Sandoval fashions this red in a decadent style, with oozing flavors of cinnamon, coffee and dark chocolate infusing a base of raisins and ripe, chewy berries. Silky in texture, it displays a lovely smokiness throughout.

Juan Gil Monastrell | 2007 | JUMILLA

★ ★ ★ ★ **$ $** Made from 45-year-old estate vines, this Monastrell offers an array of gorgeous spices—clove, cinnamon, caraway and ginger—alongside juicy cherry flavors. Its ripe tannins are well integrated, and hints of licorice and tobacco mark the long finish.

La Aldea | 2008 | JUMILLA

★ ★ **$** Plum pudding meets earth and licorice in this inviting red made with 100 percent Monastrell. Ripe blackberry and raspberry flavors come through on the spicy palate.

Tarima Monastrell | 2009 | JUMILLA

★ ★ **$** Made from 25- to 35-year-old vines, this red is Zinfandel-like in its intensely fruit-driven character. Ripe, jammy and peppery, it's easy to like and crowd-pleasing.

star producers
spain

Alvaro Palacios

One of nine Palacios children, Alvaro left his family's respected winery in Rioja and, after a stint at Château Pétrus, went on to become a leader in the Priorat quality revolution.

Bodegas Alejandro Fernández Tinto Pesquera

Alejandro Fernández's full-bodied, concentrated reds helped earn Ribera del Duero its DO classification in 1982.

Bodegas Muga

Presiding over one of Rioja's better-known wineries, talented vintner Jorge Muga takes a decidedly modern approach in his winemaking.

Do Ferreiro

Proprietor Gerardo Mendez uses indigenous yeasts and organic methods to make his complex Albariños, standouts in the Rías Baixas region.

R. López de Heredia Viña Tondonia

The most tradition-bound among their contemporaries, the three López de Heredia siblings craft outstanding white and red Rioja wines that have an impressive ability to age.

Vega Sicilia

Vega Sicilia built its reputation as one of Spain's best wineries centuries before Ribera del Duero acquired its DO status.

catalonia

The region of Catalonia (Catalunya in the Catalan language) is located in the northeastern corner of Spain. Production of sparkling Cava, one of Spain's best-known wines, is centered in Penedès (see p. 254). The vast regional DO of Catalonia serves as the generic designation for wines of the region. Priorat, which joins the ranks of Rioja with a superior DOCa (in Catalan, DOQ) designation, gets international attention for its reds.

Catalonia Grapes & Styles

Catalonia is largely planted with Garnacha; many old vines date back as far as a century. Cariñena (Carignane) and Garnacha compose the heart of Priorat's full-bodied red wines. These Mediterranean grapes are often blended with such varieties as Cabernet Sauvignon or Syrah. Encircling Priorat is the DO of Montsant, formally established in 2001, which produces slightly softer reds using the same grapes. Spain's sparkling wine DO Cava encompasses several regions across the country. Of these, the largest and most significant is Penedès in Catalonia, where the traditional Cava grapes, Macabeo, Parellada and Xarel-lo, as well as Chardonnay, are also used to make fresh and affordable still whites. Penedès reds are often blends of Catalonia's leading red grapes along with Tempranillo or Monastrell.

catalonia recommendations

WHITES

Marqués de Alella Pansa Blanca | 2008 | ALELLA
★ $ Made from the Pansa Blanca grape—a local name for Xarel-lo—this is brimming with fresh golden apples, citrus and banana aromas that take a juicy turn on the palate. It's light-bodied yet plump, with a refreshing peppery quality and a bone-dry finish.

Segura Viudas Creu de Lavit Xarel-lo | 2007 | PENEDÈS
★★ $ Xarel-lo is a native grape of Catalonia, better known for its role in Cava. Here it reveals flavors of apricot, apple and pear, augmented by hints of spice and nutty oak.

Torres Viña Esmeralda Moscato/Gewürztraminer | 2009 | CATALONIA

★ ★ ★ $ Torres blends 85 percent Moscatel with 15 percent Gewürztraminer to highly aromatic effect. Orange blossom, passion fruit and lychee jump out of the glass, followed by a palate dominated by pink grapefruit and citrus peel. The kick of spice and bright acidity keep it balanced and immensely enjoyable.

ROSÉS

1+1=3 Cabernet Sauvignon Rosé | 2009 | PENEDÈS

★ ★ $ $ Reminiscent—in a good way—of a juice box, this fruity, punchlike rosé offers fun refreshment. Strawberry candy flavors are offset by a touch of tannins, acidity and a refreshing herbal quality.

René Barbier Mediterranean Rosé | NV | CATALONIA

★ $ This affordable non-vintage wine displays a slightly rustic edge to its dried cherry flavors and a surprising dose of tannins. This is a quaffable wine with a good amount of character for its very low price.

REDS

Albet i Noya Petit Albet | 2008 | CATALONIA

★ ★ $ An organic blend of about half-and-half Tempranillo and Garnatxa (Garnacha), this unoaked red is light-bodied and juicy, with loads of black cherry flavors, leather nuances and soft tannins.

Can Blau | 2008 | MONTSANT

★ ★ $ $ A blend of 40 percent Mazuelo (a local name for Carignane), 40 percent Syrah and 20 percent Garnacha, this red displays a smoky, meaty touch to its blueberry and raspberry flavors. Plenty of toasted oak, peppery spice and dusty herbs come through at the end.

Celler Piñol Portal Roble | 2007 | TERRA ALTA

★ ★ $ $ Spanish and international varieties make up this tasty blend, full of mixed berries, dark espresso, mocha and peppery spice balanced by bright acidity.

Cellers Capafons-Ossó Sirsell | 2005 | PRIORAT

★ ★ ★ $ $ This is convincingly Bordeaux-like, with gorgeous aromas of plum, cedar and earth. A blend of Garnacha, Cabernet Sauvignon, Merlot, Cariñena and Syrah, it has a complex palate marked by red fruit and supple tannins.

Cellers Unió Clos del Pinell Negre | 2009 | TERRA ALTA

★ $ Youthful and simple, this pleasant quaffer delivers juicy flavors of cherry and blueberry woven with notes of tobacco and mocha.

Heredad Soliterra Carignan/Grenache/Shiraz | 2006 | PRIORAT

★ ★ $ $ In this dry blend, blueberry and raspberry aromas lead to a medium-bodied, mouthwatering palate with subtle oak influences.

Pinord Clos de Torribas Tempranillo Crianza | 2005 | PENEDÈS

★ ★ $ Hints of leather and earth add sophistication to this red berry–flavored Crianza. There's a chalky texture to the palate, where bright berries are supported by supple, mouthwatering tannins.

Vall Llach Embruix | 2006 | PRIORAT

★ ★ $ $ This is a standout Priorat. Its enticing aromas of coffee, plum and mocha are echoed on the full palate, which is framed by substantial tannins.

Venus La Universal Dido | 2007 | MONTSANT

★ ★ ★ $ $ Fans of funky, intensely earthy wines will appreciate this complex red, a blend of Garnacha, Merlot and Cabernet Sauvignon. It is defined by barnyard on the nose, while flavors of tart red fruit, strawberries, spice and pepper are nicely offset by a vibrant acidity.

castilla y león

Castilla y León, in north-central Spain, comprises several diverse wine regions around the capital city of Valladolid. Foremost is Ribera del Duero, named for the Duero River. This region owes much of its original fame to one pioneering producer, Vega Sicilia, whose legendary Unico (a blend of Tempranillo and Cabernet) is famous for its longevity—and exorbitant price. Not until the debut in the 1980s of Alejandro Fernández's Pesquera—a bargain by comparison—did interest in Ribera del Duero increase in a significant way. Now Castilla y León has many new wineries, and if there is a prevailing winemaking style, it is an emphasis on sheer power, particularly evident in the wines of the Ribera del Duero and Toro denominations. The Cigales DO traditionally produces rosados, which have recently become better and fresher, but the region is also making more bold red wines. Long underrated, Rueda shines as a producer of crisp white wines, and red wine production is newly permitted there.

Castilla y León Grapes & Styles

Tempranillo (known locally as Tinto Fino or Tinta del País) is the star grape of Castilla y León. In Ribera del Duero, most wines are 100 percent Tempranillo, although small amounts of Cabernet, Merlot and Malbec are permitted. The aging regulations for reds are the same as in Rioja (see p. 104). Rueda is an anomaly in this red wine–dominated region, creating wonderfully crisp, citrusy whites, the best of which use the local Verdejo grape, although Viura and recently introduced Sauvignon Blanc are often added. The pure Tempranillo wines of Toro (where the grape is known as Tinta de Toro) are full-bodied and concentrated, usually made to be consumed at a younger age than those of Ribera. The northerly Bierzo DO makes mostly reds from the Mencía grape and a handful of whites from Godello.

news from spain

Vintage Notes

Spain experienced a very warm 2009 season, with temperatures rivaling the hot summer of 2003. Growers in the south were forced to pick early and lost about 30 percent of their grapes to drought. The north, however, had a great year despite the heat, thanks to a wet September, which pushed the harvest back. Vintners in Rioja, Ribera del Duero and Toro report that 2009 is one of the best vintages they've ever seen.

Regions to Watch

Spain's northwestern Ribeira Sacra region has been getting a lot of press in the U.S. for its fragrant red wines made from the Mencía grape. Unfortunately, these wines are hard to find, largely because not very much is made—grape growing is extremely difficult on the region's precipitous slopes. The neighboring region of Bierzo also produces some excellent Mencías, which tend to be a bit more powerful than those in Ribeira Sacra and are somewhat easier to track down. Rising star winemaker Gregory Pérez, a native of Bordeaux, is definitely a producer to watch: Look for the rich, concentrated old-vine bottlings from his Mengoba winery.

castilla y león recommendations

WHITES

Castelo de Medina Verdejo | 2009 | RUEDA

★ ★ **$** Effusively aromatic, this brims with gooseberry and guava, leading to a palate of baked pear, spice and lime, with grapefruit-infused acidity. It's refreshing and distinctive, thanks to notes of mushroom and blue cheese at the end.

Condesa Eylo Verdejo | 2008 | RUEDA

★ **$** There's a touch of Sauvignon Blanc in this somewhat full-bodied Verdejo, which is marked by crisp green and golden apple flavors woven with grapefruit zest and Bartlett pear.

Javier Sanz Viticultor Villa Narcisa Verdejo | 2009 | RUEDA

★ ★ **$ $** Fans of Sauvignon Blanc will especially enjoy this sweet-savory white. Citrus and peanut candy aromas layered with aspara-gus, grass and chive notes precede the tropical fruit–laden palate packed with flinty minerals; there is a kiss of citrus on the finish.

Palacio de Bornos Verdejo | 2009 | RUEDA

★ ★ **$** Fresh, fragrant white peach, nettle and gooseberry lead to papaya, guava and pineapple flavors—this would be decadent if not for the jolt of firming acidity.

Shaya Old Vines Verdejo | 2009 | RUEDA

★ ★ ★ **$** A great value, this Verdejo was sourced partially from vines between 75 and 112 years old. It's classic and pure, with quince, ginger and citrus flavors, tons of lemony fresh acidity and chalky minerals.

REDS

Albaliza Tempranillo/Garnacha | 2007 |
VINO DE LA TIERRA DE CASTILLA

★ ★ **$** Made with 65 percent Tempranillo and 35 percent Garnacha, this bargain is crafted in a fresh, jammy style, with juicy cherry and spice flavors and plenty of rustic tannins to provide structure.

Auroch | 2008 | TORO

★ ★ **$** A hint of beef underscores the cherry aromas in this dense red; it has great acidity and fine tannins—all for a low price.

Cepa 21 | 2007 | RIBERA DEL DUERO

★ ★ ★ **$ $** This 100 percent Tempranillo wine, a project of the vener-able Emilio Moro family, shows chocolate-covered cherry and straw-berry aromas, more red fruit flavors, fresh acidity and solid tannins with earthy, tobacco nuances on the finish.

Dominio de Tares Baltos Mencía | 2007 | BIERZO

★ ★ ★ $ $ Made with the Mencía grape, this red offers a mélange of licorice, spice and cherry flavors, with some notes of animal, tobacco and earth adding balance and intrigue. At under $20, it's a very good value for its complexity and polish.

Emilio Moro Finca Resalso | 2008 |
RIBERA DEL DUERO

★ ★ $ The Finca Resalso vineyard was planted in 1932—the year that Emilio Moro was born. It yields this bold wine characterized by raspberry ganache and cassis flavors, underscored by touches of caramel, pine resin and toasted oak.

Montecastro | 2006 | RIBERA DEL DUERO

★ ★ ★ $ $ This standout red has a very New World style, with its up-front smoky blackberry flavors and ample vanilla. It was aged in a combination of French, American and Eastern European barrels, which added weight and complexity. Notes of graphite, dill and herbs shine through the ripe fruit and oak.

Museum Crianza | 2005 | CIGALES

★ ★ $ $ Cigales was once known only for rosé, but today it creates terrific reds like this one. Loads of dark fruit are offset by shiitake mushroom and earth flavors, while fine tannins provide structure.

Nuestro Crianza | 2006 | RIBERA DEL DUERO

★ ★ $ $ Produced by Bodega Díaz Bayo, this ripe, supple red shows equal parts cherry and earth, with notes of cigar, cocoa and dust on the lovely finish.

O. Fournier Urban | 2007 | RIBERA DEL DUERO

★ ★ $ Generous red fruit competes with chocolate and spice on the nose of this well-built red. Clove, nutmeg and jammy strawberries emerge on the palate, followed by a kick of black pepper and soft tannins on the finish.

Pazo de Arribi Mencía | 2007 | BIERZO

★ ★ $ $ Kirsch, dark chocolate and toasted oak aromas introduce this brawny, full-bodied red, which finishes with flavors of vanilla, pine resin and grilled sage.

Tinto Pesquera Crianza | 2007 | RIBERA DEL DUERO

★ ★ ★ ★ $ $ $ A superb effort from a classic producer, this Crianza is distinctive, with its profound barnyard aromas mingled with black fruit and roasted herbs. Good acidity and rustic tannins hold the ripe cherry and licorice flavors together.

portugal

The nonfortified wines of Portugal have not gotten the attention they deserve, given the enduring fame of the country's long-lived fortified wine, Port. But with each passing year, Portugal's increasingly well-made, sultry, spicy reds—and a handful of sprightly whites—recruit more fans.

Portugal: An Overview

For decades Portugal's non-Port wine production was dominated by large cooperatives that prioritized quantity over quality. This began to change in 1986, when Portugal entered the European Union, and outside investment enabled vintners to vastly improve their wines. Results have been particularly dramatic in the Douro—home of the country's famed sweet, fortified Port wines (see p. 261)— where producers began making quality strides with their dry reds. While traditional Douro Ports and the new generation of dry reds are distinctly different types of wine, they are typically crafted with the same grape varieties and thus share a similar flavor profile. Other regions of note in this small yet geographically diverse country include Alentejo, Bairrada and Dão, where structured, spicy reds are produced. Look to Estremadura, Ribatejo (now known as "Tejo" on labels) and Terras do Sado near Lisbon for value reds.

Portuguese Grapes & Styles

Though relatively small in size, Portugal is home to many diverse regions where dozens of indigenous grapes thrive. Largely unknown to many wine drinkers, Vinho Verde could take the title of official white wine of summer. It is one of the most refreshing whites made anywhere, thanks to a bracing acidity, slight effervescence and low alcohol. Fuller-bodied examples are made from Alvarinho (called Albariño in Spain) and Loureiro grapes, which are often identified on the label. Whites from other regions such as Alentejo, Dão, Douro, Bairrada and Bucelas are worth seeking out, too. Not surprisingly, Cabernet Sauvignon, Merlot and Syrah have been planted in Portugal, but the country's most compelling reds remain wines made from local varieties, such as Baga, Touriga Franca, Touriga Nacional and Tinta Roriz (Tempranillo), appearing in blends or on their own. Baga is especially important in Bairrada, where winemakers use it to make dry and tannic red wines with berry flavors.

Portuguese Wine Labels

Most Portuguese wines are labeled by their region and adhere to requirements set up by the country's wine regulatory system, the *Denominação de Origem Controlada* (DOC). Wines labeled *Reserva* must be at least half a percent higher in alcohol than the DOC-established minimum. Wines labeled by grape variety must be made from at least 85 percent of the specified grape.

portuguese whites

Portugal's enviably long Atlantic coastline is ideal for producing crisp white wines. The wine regions here yield a lovely range of fish-friendly whites, from the north's simple, tart Vinho Verde to the long-lived, relatively full-bodied whites from Alentejo in the south.

portuguese white recommendations

Aveleda Alvarinho | 2009 | **MINHO**
★★ **$** Made from one of Portugal's signature grapes, Alvarinho, this delicious wine shows notes of peaches, cream, pear and melon and a wonderfully plush finish.

Broadbent | NV | **VINHO VERDE**
★ **$** Thanks to a low, 9 percent alcohol content and sweet and sour citrus flavors, this zippy white provides perfect summer refreshment, at a great price, too.

Campolargo Arinto | 2007 | **BAIRRADA**
★★ **$ $** The third generation is now at the helm at the family-owned Campolargo in Bairrada. This Arinto is spicy and herbaceous, with a pronounced minerality; the rich and mouthwatering finish also hints at a stony quality.

Casa de Vila Verde Alvarinho | 2008 | **MINHO**
★ **$** This estate has been owned by the same family for centuries. The 2008 Alvarinho is juicy and supple, with spice and mineral flavors.

Foral de Évora | 2008 | **ALENTEJO**
★ **$** Produced by Cartuxa, this soft, intensely floral wine is delicate and finely balanced, with a lovely core of minerals. The winery occupies a former Jesuit house that was declared a national treasure two and a half centuries ago.

Lagoalva Espírito | 2008 | TEJO
★★ $ A scrumptious blend of Sauvignon Blanc, Alvarinho, Verdelho, Fernão Pires and Arinto, this white is an exceptional value, offering a mix of apricot, citrus and quince flavors that finish crisp.

Touquinheiras Alvarinho | 2008 | MONÇÃO
★★ $ $ From a Vinho Verde subregion, Alvarinho is opulent and lush here, producing peaches and cream aromas and the sweet-tart flavors of pear and quince paste.

Ventozelo | 2008 | DOURO
★★ $ $ This centuries-old *quinta* is known primarily for its contribution of bulk wines to some of the finest Port houses, but this Douro white is worth hunting for. Clean, peachy aromas meet notes of crisp green apple and Asian pear on the spicy palate.

portuguese reds

Although international interest in Portugal's red wines is growing, even most of those from the acclaimed Douro region remain underappreciated. There are many wines to consider here, and most offer tremendous value. Made primarily with distinctive local grape varieties, the simpler examples have a charming rustic quality and a unique array of flavors, while others have the complexity and grace of some of the world's best reds.

portuguese red recommendations

Aliança Garrida | 2007 | DÃO
★★ $ This affordable red table wine is brimming with fragrant blackberry, plum and cherry. Notes of spice and meat add a distinctive accent, and the finish is tinged with minerals.

Churchill's Estates | 2007 | DOURO
★★★★ $ $ This nonfortified red wine from the legendary Port house is every bit as rich, dark and powerful as its Port sibling, offering waves of ripe plum and cherry flavors. A whiff of cocoa complements notes of cigar box on the finish.

Domaines François Lurton Barco Negro | 2008 | DOURO
★★ $ This decidedly smooth Douro red is dominated by soft raspberry and strawberry flavors nicely balanced by cocoa and dried plum accents on the creamy finish.

Dominios François Lurton Pilheiros | 2007 | **DOURO**

★★ **$ $** A tasty blend of eight different grapes, this red offers dense flavors of stewed strawberries and fruit jam. It's very ripe and smoky, with notes of spice and caramel.

Frei João | 2006 | **BAIRRADA**

★★ **$** Bold aromas of cured meat come on strong at first, giving way to flavors of dark plum and dried cherry in this mineral-laden wine. Firming acidity provides great balance.

José Maria da Fonseca Periquita Reserva | 2005 |
TERRAS DO SADO

★★ **$ $** First exported in the mid-19th century, Periquita has always been a hearty red wine that withstands long journeys with its delicious flavors intact. Inviting aromas of cherries and dark berries, hints of oak and a rich mouthfeel are supported by plush tannins through the long finish.

news from portugal

Vintage Notes

It's worth stocking up on Portugal's remarkable 2007 vintage before it sells out. The 2008 vintage, which recently hit store shelves, is also very good. Producers can't agree which vintage is better. The 2009 harvest in the Douro was a little tricky due to exceptional heat, which led to wines with cooked notes rather than the usual vibrant aromatics.

Region to Watch

The Alentejo is very exciting now, producing fruit-driven, ripe, concentrated wines; producers Herdade do Mouchão and Quinta do Mouro are leading the way. Since the Alentejo's Júlio Bastos sold his remaining stake in Quinta do Carmo to Domaines Barons de Rothschild (Lafite), he has been working on his own again, and his Quinta Dona Maria is turning out stunning wines from some of the region's best vineyards.

Travel News

In the past, travel in Portugal's wine country has been limited by a shortage of great hotels, but that has changed in recent years. New to the scene is a luxury resort in the Porto area called the Yeatman, owned by the Fladgate Partnership, the high-end Port giant.

Marquês de Borba | 2008 | ALENTEJO

★★ $ Ripe plum and red cherry aromas immediately emerge from the glass here, slowly making way for notes of dark fruit and mocha. A ribbon of minerality ties it all together through a soft, chalky finish.

Porta dos Cavaleiros | 2006 | DÃO

★★★ $ This is easily among the best-tasting bargains out of Portugal. Part of the Caves São João portfolio, it is marked by aromas of prune and meat pâté leading to mouth-coating black plum and cherry flavors that are supple and utterly enjoyable.

Quinta de la Rosa | 2007 | DOURO

★★ $$ Produced from the main grape varieties used to make Port—Tinta Roriz, Touriga Nacional, Tinta Cão and Touriga Franca—this wine bears the aromas and flavors of bright red fruit. Earthy overtones peek out mid-palate, and chalky minerals pave the finish.

Quinta de Roriz Prazo de Roriz | 2007 | DOURO

★★★ $$ Up-front cherry and raspberry flavors are joined by hints of stewed prune in this standout red, which shows distinct cocoa and spice flavors on the balanced finish.

Quinta do Crasto Old Vines Reserva | 2007 | DOURO

★★★★ $$$ Though slightly more expensive than many Portuguese reds, this is still a tremendous bargain when compared to wines from many regions around the world. For under $50, you get a wonderful mélange of plum, black and red cherry and blueberry flavors woven with notes of peppery spice, cocoa and espresso. The finish is seemingly endless.

Quinta do Vallado | 2007 | DOURO

★★★★ $$ Definitive proof that Portugal is a land of unbelievable wine values, this spectacular wine is easily worth twice what it costs. Meat aromas meld with prunes, dried cherries, tobacco and mushrooms, while chocolate and slate come together on the refined palate.

Ramos Pinto Duas Quintas Reserva | 2004 | DOURO

★★★ $$$ Owned by the French Champagne house Roederer since 1990, Ramos Pinto has deep Portuguese roots. The red is made with grapes from two vineyards and yields dense plum, black raspberry and mocha flavors that are chalky and powerful.

Tâmara | 2008 | RIBATEJANO

★★ $ A blend of Castelão, Alicante Bouschet and Trincadeira, this nicely balanced wine is equal parts ripe plums and juicy grapes leading to a mouthwatering finish.

germany & austria

The wines of Germany and Austria are sommelier darlings. One sip of a juicy, off-dry German Riesling or a zesty Austrian Grüner Veltliner reveals why: These white wines are perfect with food, especially spicy dishes and vegetables.

germany

It's ironic that Americans—who often love sugary White Zinfandel—malign German wines as "too sweet." It's true that the fruity character of German Riesling does seem to benefit from a touch of residual sugar, but that sweetness is inevitably balanced with ample fresh acidity. And German wines come in an array of styles from dry to sweet; the best display equal parts lean, mineral qualities and pure, expressive fruit flavors.

Germany: An Overview

Even white grapes can struggle to ripen in Germany's cool climate, and that is why the country became a beer power-house. Yet Germany also produces terrific wine, by and large. Thankfully, the days when sweet Liebfraumilch was the only German wine in U.S. wineshops are long gone.

To make the most of the chilly climate, many of the best vineyards cling to steep, south-facing slopes along the river valleys of the Rhine and Mosel and the Mosel's Saar and

Principal
Wine Region

Ruwer tributaries. It is here that the noble Riesling grape thrives. Rieslings from the Mosel tend to be delicate and mineral-laden; those from the Rheingau are usually drier and fuller-bodied. The hilly terrain of the Rheinhessen yields many low-quality sweet wines, the sort that have besmirched Germany's reputation for years and fueled the common perception that all German wines are sweet (though the region does yield some wonderful wines, particularly from the subregion Rheinterrasse). The relatively warmer Pfalz (Palatinate), Nahe and Baden regions produce lusher Rieslings, as well as a range of interesting wines from other grape varieties such as Gewürztraminer, Grauburgunder and Weissburgunder.

German Grapes & Styles

Unlike most other Old World countries, Germany is famous for its white wines. The Riesling grape arguably performs better here than anywhere else, thriving in spite of the cold and producing wines of rare delicacy and refinement. Thanks to high levels of residual sugar tempered by equally high acidity, Germany's best Rieslings achieve impressive balance and a range that extends from crisp and dry to concentrated sweet nectars, with many styles in between.

Germany's second most widely planted grape is the white Müller-Thurgau, which is used mostly for uninspired blends, with the exception of some compelling yields from Franken (Franconia). Germany's other noteworthy grapes include Gewürztraminer, Grauburgunder (Pinot Gris) and Weissburgunder (Pinot Blanc), which particularly excel in the regions of Baden and Pfalz. Centuries of tradition have given German vintners an acute understanding—culled, of course, from experimentation—of their country's *terroir,* which has helped them transform often hard-to-ripen red grapes such as Spätburgunder (Pinot Noir) and Dornfelder into respectable wines.

German Wine Labels

Although they may appear difficult to decipher, German wine labels offer more information than most, including not just producer and geographic origin but also winemaking details like grape ripeness. Labels usually list grapes, though in regions like the Rheingau, Riesling is assumed.

While Germany makes small amounts of pedestrian table wine (*Tafelwein*), the vast majority of German wine qualifies for one of two "quality" designations. The first category— which represents the majority of the country's production— is *Qualitätswein bestimmter Anbaugebiete* (QbA), or simply "Qualitätswein." This guarantees that the grapes came from a quality region and reached a mandated level of ripeness at harvest time. *Qualitätswein mit Prädikat* (QmP) wines are held to higher standards; they are ranked by grape ripeness at harvest, from *Kabinett* to *Spätlese, Auslese, Beerenauslese* (BA) and *Trockenbeerenauslese* (TBA), in ascending order of ripeness. In theory, riper grapes have the potential to make sweeter wines. Yet in actual practice, perceived sweetness depends more on the balance between acidity and sugar or the amount of natural grape sugar allowed to ferment into alcohol. A Kabinett wine is usually drier than an Auslese wine, but there are no guarantees. Some wineries list *trocken* (dry) or *halbtrocken* (off-dry) on their labels as indicators of style. *Spätlese trocken,* for example, means that the wine is dry in style and made from grapes picked at Spätlese levels of ripeness.

Classic and *Selection* on labels denote wines that are dry and high in quality. Classic wines are almost always made with a single grape variety and bear the name of the producer but not the vineyard. Selection wines are higher in quality; they must be made from hand-harvested grapes and list both the producer's name and the vineyard.

The recent trend for German producers has been to add more consumer-friendly proprietary names to some quality wines, such as Dr. Loosen's "Blue Slate" Riesling.

german whites

Whether made from Riesling or one of the country's many second-tier grapes, like Müller-Thurgau or Silvaner, German wines fill a distinctive niche in the world of white wines. With few exceptions, German whites are unoaked, aromatic, fruity and low in alcohol, often with some degree of sweetness to balance their generous acidity. International white varieties such as Chardonnay and Sauvignon Blanc do exist in Germany but are of little importance.

GERMAN WHITES

riesling

This is Germany's most highly regarded and widely planted grape. Like Chardonnay, Riesling makes white wines with potential for cellaring, and the best can age for decades, a process that brings out appealing flavors often identified as smoky or petrol. However, in contrast to Chardonnay,

Riesling is a highly aromatic grape that needs no oak aging. It is also very versatile in the hands of the winemaker, and can be made in a full range of styles (see "German Wine Labels," p. 126). The driest styles often reveal a mineral character beneath crisp apple, while off-dry and sweet versions can deliver dense, even unctuous tropical and stone-fruit flavors that are best when balanced with Riesling's natural acidity. Many of the top Rieslings come from the Mosel-Saar-Ruwer and Rheingau regions, where slate soils express themselves in the wines' mineral-tinged aromatics. Riesling is also the leading grape in the Pfalz and Nahe regions, where the wines are less minerally, exhibiting riper tropical fruit flavors instead.

riesling recommendations

August Kesseler R | 2008 | RHEINGAU
★ ★ $ $ Light-bodied and bright, with a subtle spritz, this refreshing Riesling shows intense ripe nectarine flavors laced with slate notes and an electric acidity.

C.H. Berres Impulse | 2008 | MOSEL
★ ★ $ $ A blend of fruit from three different vineyard sites, this Riesling is light-bodied and lean, marked by firm stone-fruit and yellow apple flavors along with mouthwatering acidity.

Darting Dürkheimer Hochbenn Kabinett | 2008 | PFALZ
★ ★ $ $ This is unexpectedly rich and ripe for a Kabinett, full of upfront guava and passion fruit flavors with accents of honey, bubble gum, banana and spice.

Dr. H. Thanisch Bernkasteler Badstube Kabinett
| 2008 | MOSEL
★ ★ ★ $ $ Sourced from sustainably farmed vineyards, this elegant, distinctive wine shows a lovely mix of mineral, rose petals and apple aromas. The palate offers juicy stone fruit, citrus and spicy pear.

Dr. Loosen Blue Slate Kabinett | 2008 | MOSEL
★ ★ ★ $ $ An excellent value, Dr. Loosen's charming Riesling reveals aromas of iced lemon cookie and succulent nectarine that follow through on the juicy, fresh palate, where they are complemented by peach notes and minerals. This is a superbly fresh and balanced wine, with a finish that lingers.

Dr. Pauly-Bergweiler Noble House | 2009 | MOSEL
★ $ Minerals and acidity offset the slight sweetness in this well-made, everyday Riesling. Flint, honey and stone fruit are woven with apples and quince paste on the generous, medium-bodied palate.

Fritz Hasselbach Fritz's | 2008 | RHEINHESSEN
★ $ Named after Fritz Hasselbach, owner of the Gunderloch estate, this entry-level QbA wine offers flint, apricot and concentrated peach flavors woven with grapefruit throughout.

Gunderloch Jean-Baptiste Kabinett | 2008 | RHEINHESSEN
★★★ $ $ Here is another standout Kabinett that overdelivers for the price. Bright and alluring, it offers floral and stone-fruit aromas followed by nectarine and almond flavors. The sweet, nutty palate has a distinct wet stone minerality that adds balance to the long finish.

star producers
german riesling

Dr. Loosen
Ernst Loosen revitalized his 200-year-old family estate when he took over in the 1980s, and the wines have never tasted better.

Gunderloch
Today, this high-achieving estate is managed by Agnes Hasselbach-Usinger and her husband, celebrated wine-maker Fritz Hasselbach.

Joh. Jos. Christoffel
This minuscule and elite Mosel estate has been in the family for 400 years. For the past decade, it has been run by the talented Robert Eymael, who owns Weingut Mönchhof.

Prinz von Hessen
The von Hessens, members of the 800-year-old Hessian dynasty, founded this estate in the 1950s. Today, it's recognized as one of the finest Riesling producers in Germany.

Reichsrat von Buhl
Founded in 1849, this winery has been beautifully modern-ized under its lessee, a Japanese management company.

S.A. Prüm
Riesling accounts for 90 percent of Prüm's vineyards, and the stellar producer can be credited with popularizing the grape in America.

Gutzler Auslese | 2008 | RHEINHESSEN

★★ $ $ Well priced for Auslese, this is a ripe and interesting one, with enticing tea notes and rich, juicy tropical fruit flavors. Honey and guava paste nuances round out the mouthwatering finish.

Joh. Jos. Christoffel Erben Erdener Treppchen Spätlese
| 2008 | MOSEL

★★★ $ $ $ There is a mature quality to this Riesling's fruit flavors, as petrol and honeycomb aromas infuse a base of white flowers and peaches. It has a waxy texture, a richly layered, round palate and nice toasted almond and mineral nuances throughout the finish.

Joh. Jos. Prüm Graacher Himmelreich Spätlese | 2008 |
MOSEL-SAAR-RUWER

★★★ $ $ $ This expressive Riesling shows apple, pineapple and acacia flower aromas. While it is surprisingly delicate on the palate, it builds in creaminess and complexity, with an alluring minerality and a formidable finish.

Kruger-Rumpf Münsterer Rheinberg Kabinett | 2008 |
NAHE

★★ $ $ For its modest 8.5 percent alcohol, this wine packs a good punch of red and golden apple flavors laced with lemon curd. It has a lot of character for a Kabinett, with juicy fruit and intense minerals that linger on the palate.

Leitz Eins Zwei Dry 3 | 2008 | RHEINGAU

★★ $ $ True to its label, this is bone-dry, with a vivid burst of lemony acidity coursing throughout. Yet, with peach, berry and apricot flavors and a lovely minerality, it's far from austere.

Melsheimer Rieler Mullay-Hofberg #34 Auslese | 2007 |
MOSEL-SAAR-RUWER

★★★ $ $ $ $ There's a dark yellow hue to this Auslese, which hints at the concentrated apricot compote and honey flavors within. As mouth-coating, and nearly as sweet, as a dessert wine, it is reminiscent of peach nectar, with rich notes of caramel and malt; all is balanced by a touch of slate and fine acidity.

Mönchhof Mosel Slate Spätlese | 2008 |
MOSEL-SAAR-RUWER

★★ $ $ Aromas of honey, slate and apple jelly ooze from this terrific wine, followed by a generous palate of rich quince paste and sticky honey. The bracing acidity and green tea–infused finish add a wonderful refreshing quality.

Prinz von Hessen | 2007 | RHEINGAU

★★ $ $ Located on the edge of Johannisberg in Rheingau, this estate is dedicated solely to Riesling. Its focus pays off in well-priced gems like this one, filled with crisp green apple, citrus and mineral flavors that are woven with white peaches and minerals.

Reichsgraf von Kesselstatt Josephshöfer Kabinett | 2008 | MOSEL

★★★★ $ $ A supremely elegant Riesling, this offers aromas of apple, quince, marmalade and flowers and a palate marked by green tea, honey and dense apricot. The ripe fruit makes this wine richer than one would expect for a Kabinett, and there are just enough minerals and acidity to add refinement.

Reichsrat von Buhl Armand Kabinett | 2008 | PFALZ

★★ $ $ Shortbread and lemon dominate the nose of this enticing wine, while stone-fruit and red berry flavors round out the palate. Vivacious and robust, it's nicely offset by bright acidity and notes of Asian pear on the finish.

S.A. Prüm Essence | 2008 | MOSEL

★★★ $ A standout every year, Prüm's Riesling is a stunning wine for the price. Equal parts ripe, citrusy tropical fruit and flinty minerals, it has layers and layers of pineapple and tangerine flavors.

Strub Soil to Soul Kabinett | 2008 | RHEINHESSEN

★★ $ $ Crafted from the red-soil vineyards of Brückchen and Paterberg, this Riesling displays solid structure: taut flavors of apricots and citrus held together with stony minerals and mouthwatering acidity.

Theo Minges Burrweiler Schlossgarten Spätlese | 2007 | PFALZ

★★★ $ $ Following extended contact with grape skins, this wine emerges effusively aromatic, with a dense, chewy palate of candied pear, dried apricot and honey flavors. The fruity intensity is matched by spicy acidity and a touch of drying tannins.

Weingut Blees Ferber Piesporter Gärtchen Feinherb Spätlese | 2008 | MOSEL

★★ $ $ A beam of racy acidity balances the touch of sweetness in the apple, citrus and star fruit flavors in this brisk, off-dry white.

Weingut Dr. Heyden Oppenheimer Kabinett | 2008 | RHEINHESSEN

★★ $ This would be a perfect aperitif or picnic wine for its light style, freshness and key lime, Granny Smith apple and mineral flavors.

Weingut Gysler Weinheimer Kabinett | 2008 |
RHEINHESSEN

★ ★ **$ $** With just 7.5 percent alcohol, this tastes like a delicious wine spritzer. It's simple, fruity and very satisfying, complete with lemon icing flavors and citrusy acidity.

Weingut Hans Lang Charta | 2007 | RHEINGAU

★ ★ **$ $** Made in a very dry yet fully ripe style, this wine reveals bright lime, white peach and bitter orange peel flavors. Flinty smoke, minerals and an underlying racy acidity keep it balanced.

Weingut Johannishof Charta | 2008 | RHEINGAU

★ ★ **$ $** Tart green apples and flowers introduce this wine and are joined on the palate by orange blossom, candied apple and hints of banana. It's distinctive and fresh, with a fleshy, round texture.

other german whites

The Pfalz and Baden regions benefit from their proximity to France's Alsace, with which they share many of the same white grapes in addition to Riesling. Grauburgunder (Pinot Gris) and Weissburgunder (Pinot Blanc) compare well to their French counterparts. Scheurebe from the Rheinhessen region is intriguing for it currant flavors and strong acidity. Kerner resembles Riesling, while Bacchus and Huxelrebe are similar to Muscat. Muskateller (Muscat) and Gewürztraminer make intensely fragrant wines. Müller-Thurgau and Silvaner are used mainly in dull blends, though both can yield lovely whites, especially in Franken.

other german white recommendations

Fitz-Ritter Gewürztraminer Spätlese | 2008 | PFALZ

★ ★ **$ $** Located just a short drive from Alsace, this German estate balances Riesling's ripeness with impressive restraint. Rose petal and lychee aromas lead to a deliciously spicy palate of ripe apple, tart citrus and zesty grapefruit and then to a dry, mineral-tinged finish.

Kruger-Rumpf Scheurebe Kabinett | 2008 | NAHE

★ ★ **$ $** This highly aromatic white is reminiscent of elderflower liqueur and tropical fruit thanks to the expressive nature of the Scheurebe grape. It's intensely fruity and ripe with mild acidity: a perfect summer quaffer.

Schloss Grünhaus Weissburgunder | 2008 | **MOSEL**
★ ★ ★ $ $ $ Weissburgunder (Pinot Blanc) shows its exotic side in this fascinating wine. Nuances of graham cracker, gingersnap, citrus and nutmeg are woven with ripe melon flavors on a medium-bodied palate. The finish has an intriguing salt-and-peppery mineral quality.

Weingut G & M Machmer Bechtheimer Stein Gewürztraminer Spätlese | 2008 | **RHEINHESSEN**
★ $ $ Fragrant honeyed peaches reverberate on the nose and palate of this generously sweet wine; there's just enough acidity and spice to keep it balanced—and make it a perfect partner for Asian cuisine.

german reds

It isn't easy to grow red grapes in Germany, yet plantings soared in the 1990s, and today red wine accounts for 37 percent of production. Restricted mainly to the southern regions, red wine is most important in Baden, where Spät-burgunder (Pinot Noir) dominates. Dornfelder, a relatively new grape first cultivated in 1979, holds great promise in Rheinhessen and Pfalz, where it yields deep-colored wines. These two leading reds are followed by Portugieser, which makes fairly light reds, Trollinger, Schwarzriesling (Pinot Meunier), Regent and Blaufränkisch (Lemberger).

german red recommendations

Becker Estate Pinot Noir | 2007 | **PFALZ**
★ ★ ★ $ $ About 70 percent of Becker's production is red, including this wonderfully light, fresh, Burgundy-style Pinot Noir. Ripe and tart cherries are met with delicate spice, sassafras, earth and hints of smoke, all framed by bracing acidity.

Weingut Bernhard Huber Pinot Noir | 2007 | **BADEN**
★ ★ $ $ $ Huber's interesting Pinot Noir shows pine forest and Asian spice aromas. On the palate, generous cherry and plum flavors are underscored by peppery spice, supple tannins and acidic verve.

Weingut Binz Nackenheimer Dornfelder | 2007 |
RHEINHESSEN
★ $ Opaque and inky in the glass, this simple red has cherry and grape aromas with touches of herbs and anise. The palate offers lots of black fruit leading to a dry finish with very soft tannins.

austria

Austria uses many more grape varieties than Germany and produces only a quarter as much wine, but the wine industries of the two countries share an important similarity: While most of the wine production is high-quality white, red wines are gaining ground. Now that Austrian winemakers have distanced themselves from the scandal of 1985 (when a portion of the country's wine was tainted with diethylene glycol, an ingredient in antifreeze), Austria has succeeded in building a new reputation, particularly with its leading white wine—Grüner Veltliner.

Austrian Grapes & Styles

Austria's most popular and most planted grape is the spicy, citrusy Grüner Veltliner. Riesling is the other high-quality white grape grown in Austria, although Welschriesling and Müller-Thurgau vines are planted more extensively. Bur-

■ Principal
Wine Region

gundy grapes of importance include Chardonnay (called Morillon here) and Pinot Blanc (known as Weissburgunder). Austrian reds that have come to the forefront in recent years include spicy, peppery Blaufränkisch (Lemberger), juicy Zweigelt, elegant Blauburgunder (Pinot Noir) and intensely smoky St. Laurent.

Austrian Wine Labels

Most Austrian wines list grape variety and region on the bottle and use a quality system similar to Germany's *Qualitätswein* (see p. 126), although Austrian standards are often considerably higher. Austria's premier area for white wines, Wachau, uses its own classification: *Steinfeder* are light wines, *Federspiel* are heavier and *Smaragd* are rich and capable of long aging.

austrian whites

High in minerals and acidity and bursting with expressive fruit flavors, Austrian whites are among the world's most exciting wines. Grüner Veltliner and Riesling are responsible for most of the finest, though 21 other varieties produce wines worthy of consideration.

AUSTRIAN WHITES

grüner veltliner & riesling

Grüner Veltliner, which represents more than a third of Austria's vineyards, has in recent years been embraced by Americans for its light-bodied, crisp and often peppery taste profile. Most often made in a youthful, vibrant style, Grüner (or "GrüVee," as marketers have dubbed it) also produces ageworthy wines that gradually reveal mineral, smoke and honeyed nuances. Austrian Rieslings tend to be drier than those of Germany, with the riper and often sweeter Spätlese and Auslese versions quite rare. In general, Austrian Rieslings are also richer and fuller-bodied than German examples, yet express more fruit flavors than versions from Alsace.

grüner veltliner recommendations

Domäne Wachau Terrassen Federspiel | 2008 | WACHAU
★★★ $ $ Federspiel is a designation of quality between Steinfeder and Smaragd, but this wine exceeds all expectations, with distinctive white pepper and stone-fruit aromas leading to a silky, citrus-laden palate. There are touches of nettle and nuts on the crisp finish.

Forstreiter Schiefer | 2008 | KREMSTAL
★★★ $ $ Grüner Veltliner reveals its rich and creamy side in this stellar wine. Honeyed citrus peel, ripe melon and juicy apple flavors are laced with intriguing white pepper, watercress and arugula notes on the lively palate.

Franz Hirtzberger Rotes Tor Federspiel | 2008 | WACHAU
★★★ $ $ $ The Wachau is Austria's westernmost wine region, and its proximity to the moderating Danube River makes it an ideal place for crafting flavorful yet refreshing wines. There's an up-front vegetal, peppery quality to this Grüner. It's fresh and inviting, layered with citrus, herbs and minerals, and finishes on a salty, dry note.

Fritsch Steinberg | 2008 | WAGRAM
★★ $ $ White flower and jasmine tea aromas meet apple and pear flavors in this vibrant and focused white. Minerals and citrus mark the zippy, saline-accented finish.

Grooner | 2009 | NIEDERÖSTERREICH
★★ $ Meinhard Forstreiter is the acclaimed winemaker behind this terrific Grüner Veltliner. Invigorating and fresh, thanks to electric acidity and a slight spritz, it's loaded with pink grapefruit and tart gooseberry flavors.

GV | 2008 | WEINLAND
★ $ (1 L) This wonderful bargain (a full liter for less than $15) is light-bodied and quaffable, with juicy green and yellow apple flavors, notes of bread and minerals and zesty acidity.

Hirsch Veltliner #1 | 2008 | NIEDERÖSTERREICH
★★ $ $ Tart green apple and lime are woven with undercurrents of grapefruit and minerals in this snappy white.

Neumayer Engelberg | 2008 | TRAISENTAL
★★★ $ $ Earth and burnt citrus peel characterize the nose of this unusual Grüner, which follows up with toasted nut, fresh herb and intense grapefruit flavors in the mouth. It's very dry, with minerals and powerful acidity.

R&A Pfaffl Haidviertel | 2008 | **WEINVIERTEL**
★★ $ $ This Grüner has a banana bread quality—nuts, spice, sweet fruit—woven with apple and orange flavors, a soft, rounded palate and nicely balanced acidity.

Salomon Undhof Hochterrassen | 2009 |
NIEDERÖSTERREICH
★★ $ $ *Hochterrassen* refers to the high terraces that grow the grapes for this fruity Grüner. Rich flavors of stone fruit, green apple, grapefruit, pineapple and guava are laced with a minerality that's reminiscent of seashells.

Weingut Schwarzböck Kirchberg | 2008 |
NIEDERÖSTERREICH
★★ $ $ Rather generous and full in body for a Grüner Veltliner, this highly aromatic wine displays golden apple, bright citrus and berry flavors uplifted by lively acidity throughout the slightly bitter, citrus rind–infused finish.

riesling recommendations

Brandl Heiligenstein | 2008 | **KAMPTAL**
★★★ $ $ Kamptal is defined by steep, south-facing vineyards and hot sun, which result in particularly expressive wines. This shows pretty floral, mineral and peach aromas and flavors of crisp green apple with a fine saline streak. Lean and tight, without an abundance of fruit, it captivates with a bright acidity and slatelike minerality.

Gobelsburger | 2009 | **KAMPTAL**
★★ $ $ Banana and bubble gum aromas turn to ripe orange and grapefruit flavors on the palate of this well-made Riesling. After a bit of time in the glass, tart red berries and gooseberries begin to emerge, adding intrigue and refreshment.

Graf Hardegg vom Schloss | 2008 | **NIEDERÖSTERREICH**
★★★ $ $ Graf Hardegg makes wine the old-fashioned way, such as aging Riesling in large oak barrels. The result is an outstanding, very dry wine displaying complex layers of flower, peach, apricot, pear and petrol flavors with a mineral edge.

Weingut Johann Donabaum Bergterrassen Federspiel
| 2008 | **WACHAU**
★★ $ $ This is classic Austrian Riesling, with its super-dry, mineral-laden, flinty style and well-structured palate full of firm white peach, green apple, pepper and slate flavors.

other austrian whites

Austrian vintners produce an impressive range of other wonderfully expressive white wines, most notably Welschriesling and Gelber Muskateller, as well as a small amount of Weissburgunder, Grauburgunder (Pinot Gris), Morillon and Muskat-Sylvaner (Sauvignon Blanc). This last grape variety comes predominantly from the Styria (Steiermark) region, where most of the grapes are hand-picked and the wines well crafted.

other austrian white recommendations

Lackner-Tinnacher Gamitz Gelber Muskateller | 2007 | SÜDSTEIERMARK

★★★ $ $ Tea, flowers and jasmine jump out of the glass of this beautiful white. The palate offers slightly bitter green tea and firm peach flavors that are flecked with minerals, banana and melon on the very dry finish.

Neumeister Sauvignon Blanc Steirische Klassik | 2008 | SÜD-OSTSTEIERMARK

★★★ $ $ Neumeister specializes in Sauvignon Blanc and grows more of it than any other variety. This version is somewhat Sancerre-like, with tart currant, gooseberry and herbal aromas and a lovely undercurrent of minerals beneath grapefruit, berry and lime flavors.

Stift Kloster Neuburg Wiener Nussberg Gemischter Satz | 2009 | VIENNA

★★ $ Produced by a 900-year-old monastic order, this bargain white is a field blend—a mix of many grapes grown in the same vineyard. Fresh, delicious citrus flavors have a touch of herbs and pepper and end on a melon note.

austrian reds

Austria's most popular red grape is Zweigelt; it yields light-bodied wines with juicy red cherry flavors. Blaufränkisch (Lemberger) is decidedly spicier and has firmer tannins. It is responsible for some of the most interesting Austrian reds today, though they can be hard to find in the U.S. Blauburgunder (Pinot Noir) and St. Laurent (which is similar to Pinot Noir) can also yield some great wines.

austrian red recommendations

Glatzer Blaufränkisch | 2007 | CARNUNTUM
★★ $ $ Glatzer is known for well-priced red wines. Silky and inviting, with a medium-bodied, Pinot Noir–like palate, this terrific red
features earth, dark cherry and peppery spice flavors with some
toasted oak notes.

Heinrich Red | 2008 | BURGENLAND
★★ $ $ This combination of Zweigelt, Blaufränkisch and St. Laurent
shows greatly balanced dried cherries, roasted red fruits and smoke.

Moric Blaufränkisch | 2008 | BURGENLAND
★★★ $ $ Winemaker Roland Velich crafts this ultraserious Blaufränkisch layered with aromas of prunes, berries, meat and smoke.
The body remains light and refreshing; fresh pine and herbs are
woven among black cherry, earth and leather flavors, which finish
with good acidic verve.

Prieler Johanneshöhe Blaufränkisch | 2007 | BURGENLAND
★★ $ $ Soft, round and plush on the palate, with very fine tannins,
this is a supremely well-balanced red, marked by flavors of earth, peppery spice and dusty cherry.

Rosi Schuster Sankt Laurent | 2008 | BURGENLAND
★★ $ $ Ripe blackberry meets pine, juniper and smoke on the nose
of this nice red, turning to vanilla-tinged cherry-berry flavors on the
palate. A strong acidic backbone and extremely light tannins make
this a supple, elegant wine.

Umathum Zweigelt | 2008 | BURGENLAND
★★ $ $ Ample dark fruit, cocoa and plum flavors come on strong in
this very dry yet plush Zweigelt, which concludes with a final burst of
black pepper and spice.

Zantho Zweigelt | 2008 | BURGENLAND
★★ $ Joseph Umathum and the Andau winegrowers' cooperative
craft this line of modern-style wines from traditional grapes. Round
and soft, with some floral, meaty and red fruit aromas, this shows
fleshy berry flavors tinged with oak and vanilla on the finish.

greece

Greece is certainly not one of Europe's largest producers (Spain turns out about ten times as much wine), but it is one of the most diverse. With more than 300 native grapes to choose from, Greek winemakers use international varieties sparingly. Recently they have been producing fewer grapes in order to create better wines. While Greece's hard-to-pronounce wines can be difficult to find in the U.S., they are well worth hunting for.

Greece: An Overview

As Greek winemakers look to their peers abroad for advice, they're focusing on native grape varieties, and on figuring out the best vineyard sites. Some have determined, for instance, that north-facing, high-altitude slopes are key to tempering extreme summer heat.

There are four main viticultural zones in Greece: north, central, the Peloponnese and the islands. The northern zone encompasses the mountainous regions of Macedonia and Thrace; Naoussa is one of the area's most famous appellations. Central Greece features some of the country's highest-elevation vineyards. The warm valleys and cooler slopes of the Peloponnese peninsula, including the important subregions of Mantinia, Nemea and Patras, have the most appellations. Of the islands, Crete is responsible for a large quantity of wine, while the Aegean islands of Santorini and Samos offer some of the country's finest wines.

Greek Grapes & Styles

Chardonnay, Merlot and Cabernet Sauvignon appear in Greece, but winemakers typically use these international grapes only in blends along with their prized indigenous varieties. Savatiano, used to make Greece's well-known pine resin–flavored wine, Retsina, is the most common grape grown in Greece, but not the most important in terms of quality wine production. The white Assyrtiko grape is used to make crisp, bone-dry wines with pronounced mineral and bright citrus flavors; the best of these come from the beautiful island of Santorini. Pink-skinned, spicy Moschofilero is produced as a dry white as well as a dry rosé, both of which tend to be high in acidity, low in alcohol and wonderfully aromatic. Agiorgitiko—sometimes listed on wine labels as St. George—is one of Greece's most widely planted red grape varieties; its wines draw comparisons to spicy, robust Cabernet Francs. In the Macedonia region of northern Greece, the Xynomavro grape yields red wines that are reminiscent of Piedmont's Nebbiolo-based wines, with high acidity, heavy tannins and an impressive ability to age. Honorable mentions go to Roditis, which is responsible for the light-bodied, citrus-flavored white wines of Patras; and Mavrodaphne, a red grape that is vinified in both dry and sweet styles and often used by winemakers as a blending grape as well.

Greek Wine Labels

In the European tradition, wine regions take priority over the names of grape varieties on the majority of Greek wine labels. Red wines from Naoussa are required by law to be made from the Xynomavro grape, while those from Nemea are produced with Agiorgitiko. Mantinia wines must be made from at least 85 percent Moschofilero, while wines from Santorini are dominated by Assyrtiko. Grape varieties that are not traditional to particular areas, however, are usually noted on labels.

greek whites

Greek whites are as distinctive and varied as the appellations that produce them. The volcanic soils on the island of Santorini yield bold, mineral-laden whites. Peloponnesian Moschofilero possesses the spiciness of Gewürztraminer. Floral Roditis from Patras, Robola from the Ionian island Cephalonia (Kefalonia) and Assyrtiko from Santorini are universally crisp, mineral-laden and dry.

greek white recommendations

Argyros Atlantis | 2009 | SANTORINI
★★ $ $ Exhilarating and bright, this Assyrtiko-dominated white from Santorini has a mineral verve all the way through its zippy finish. The nose hints at lemon rind and subtle floral notes, while the palate offers juicy citrus flavors.

Boutari Moschofilero | 2009 | MANTINIA
★★ $ $ Boutari's take on the Moschofilero grape is light and perfumed, with bright lemon and melon flavors laden with minerals. This is one of the more well-distributed Greek whites.

Costa Lazaridi Amethystos | 2009 | DRAMA
★★ $ $ This well-crafted blend of Sauvignon Blanc, Assyrtiko and Sémillon hails from one of the oldest wineries in the Drama region. Made without oak aging, it's crisp and pleasingly grassy, with generous grapefruit flavors.

Domaine Gerovassiliou Malagousia | 2008 | EPANOMI
★★★ $ $ Like springtime in a glass, this white offers aromas of orange blossom and apricot, followed by fresh peach and nectarine flavors that have an impressively long finish.

Domaine Porto Carras Assyrtiko | 2009 | SITHONIA
★★ $ Famed French oenologist Emile Peynaud helped establish this vineyard in the late 1960s. Today, it's Greece's largest organic vineyard, yielding bright, citrusy whites like this Assyrtiko.

Domaine Spiropoulos Astála | 2008 | MANTINIA
★★★ $ $ Moschofilero is the specialty of this estate—it produces several versions, including a sparkling one. This organically grown example is elegant and medium-bodied, with floral aromas and citrus flavors that are crisp yet bold.

Emery Wines Rhodos | 2008 | RHODES
★ $ In this fruity, tangy white, fragrant lemon and peach are echoed on the palate by loads more citrus and stone fruit. A nutty, savory quality comes through at the end.

Gai'a Wild Ferment Assyrtiko | 2009 | SANTORINI
★★★ $ $ Made from 80-year-old ungrafted grapevines and fermented naturally, this wine carries significant weight on the palate. The generous citrus flavors are layered with smoke notes and a strong minerality that makes it especially satisfying to drink.

Ktima Biblia Chora Chardonnay | 2008 | PANGEON
★★ $ $ $ Acclaimed Greek winemakers Evangelos Gerovassilou and Vassilis Tsaktsarlis jointly established this winery in 2001. Their solid, international-style Chardonnay has oak-influenced aromas of smoke, sweet vanilla and ripe apple and a medium-bodied palate that is nutty and rich.

Ktima Pavlidis Thema | 2009 | DRAMA
★★ $ $ Situated at the base of Mount Falakro in northern Greece, Ktima Pavlidis produces lively, delicious wines like this blend. Sauvignon Blanc provides the grapefruit and grassy flavors, while Assyrtiko contributes a backbone of steely acidity.

Mercouri Estate Folói | 2009 | PISATIS
★★★ $ Founded in 1870, the Mercouri estate lay dormant between 1955 and the late 1980s, but today it is better than ever. This well-priced blend of Roditis and Viognier is full of citrusy acidity and richly textured tropical flavors.

Moraitis Sillogi Moraiti Assyrtiko/Malagouzia | 2008 | PAROS
★★ $ $ This zippy organic blend is more than the sum of its parts. Intense aromas of grapefruit and flowers marry with flavors of tangy citrus fruit on the palate, and the long finish is crisp and clean.

Oenoforos Asprolithi Roditis | 2009 | PATRAS
★ $ Fermented and aged without oak, this well-crafted Roditis is reminiscent of Sauvignon Blanc, displaying fragrant citrus and melon and lively acidity.

Semeli Mountain Sun White | 2009 | PELOPONNESE
★ $ Mostly Moschofilero, blended with 15 percent Roditis, this hand-harvested, stainless steel–fermented white pleases with melon, mineral and citrus flavors. A relatively low level of alcohol—11.5 percent—makes it particularly refreshing.

Sigalas Asirtiko/Athiri | 2009 | SANTORINI
★★ $$ A mathematician by training, Paris Sigalas has helped to establish Santorini's reputation as a world-class wine region since starting this winery in 1991. A blend of 75 percent Assyrtiko and 25 percent Athiri, this is well built and vibrant, with ripe citrus flavors.

Tsantali Assyrtiko/Sauvignon Blanc | 2009 | HALKIDIKI
★ $ Tsantali was already an established distillery when Evangelos Tsantalis founded the family's winery in 1970. Marked by gooseberry, grapefruit and green apple flavors, this modern-style blend is equal parts Assyrtiko and Sauvignon Blanc.

Tselepos Moschofilero | 2008 | MANTINIA
★★ $$ This dry, vibrant, medium-bodied white wafts honeysuckle and spring flower aromas, followed by citrus flavors and an intriguing bitter almond finish.

greek reds

Greek red wines range from simple and light to complex and rich. The best wines of Naoussa and nearby Amyndeon, which tend to be oak-aged reds made with Xynomavro, are often comparable to quality Barbarescos. Some reds from Nemea possess a Bordeaux-like elegance; others display a chewy richness and depth of fruit.

greek red recommendations

Alpha Estate Xinomavro | 2007 | AMYNDEON
★★ $$ This big, robust red will benefit from a bit of time in the cellar. In its youth, it is packed with baked dark fruit flavors supported by very firm tannins.

Evangelo | 2005 | EPANOMI
★★★★ $$$$ Evangelo's magnificent blend of 92 percent Syrah and 8 percent Viognier is made in a New World style. Though the nose is a bit floral, the palate is broad-shouldered and much fuller-bodied than most Greek reds; dense flavors of dark berry, fresh herbs and smoked meat abound.

Harlaftis | 2008 | NEMEA
★ $ Bright ripe plum flavors, good acidity, a medium-weight body and a surprisingly long finish make this a great introduction to the lovely Agiorgitiko grape.

Kir-Yianni Ramnista | 2006 | NAOUSSA
★★ $ This youthful, assertive red is Syrah-like in its flavor and structure; the palate is all cherry, plum and peppery spice.

Ktima Papaioannou Microclima Agiorgitiko | 2001 | NEMEA
★★ $ $ Having spent 20 months in new oak casks, this wine displays a nose of assertive cedar, red currant and pencil lead that carries through on the long, tannic finish.

Lyrarakis Symbolo Grand Cuvee | 2005 | CRETE
★★★ $ $ $ Though the Lyrarakis family has grown grapes since the 1960s, they didn't start making their own wine until 1992. This red shows developed aromas of barnyard and dried leaves, while the richly tannic palate is a mouthful of blackberry jam.

Semeli Mountain Sun Agiorgitiko | 2008 | PELOPONNESE
★ $ Named for Dionysus's mother, Semeli, this is a straightforward red with a nose of dusty spice and red fruit. Medium-bodied, with mild tannins, it offers up-front flavors of red cherry and plum.

Skouras Grande Cuvée | 2006 | NEMEA
★★★ $ $ Winemaker George Skouras excels at international as well as indigenous Greek grape varieties. His Agiorgitiko shows perfect balance, with concentrated red currant and spice flavors leading to a juicy finish.

Strofilia | 2007 | PELOPONNESE
★ $ This blend of Agiorgitiko, Cabernet Sauvignon and Syrah sees 12 months in oak, which adds weight and concentration to flavors of blackberries and spice.

Tsantali Kanenas Maronia Vineyards Mavroudi/Syrah
| 2006 | ISMAROS
★★ $ $ There's a lot of depth to the ripe, fresh blackberry, prune and dried fruit flavors here. Smooth tannins ensure a long, silky finish.

Vaeni Naoussa Grande Réserve | 2000 | NAOUSSA
★★★ $ $ Half of Naoussa's total production comes from this co-op winery. This Xynomavro is a great value: a mature, sophisticated red with mellowed tannins and cherry, leather and earth flavors.

united states

Americans first tried making wine with European grape varieties in Jamestown, Virginia, in the early 1600s. Franciscan missionaries brought viticulture to California in the 1770s, but it would be another 200 years before the world began to take American wine seriously. Today, every state makes wine, and the U.S. is the world's fourth-largest wine producer. Americans now drink more wine, too: The U.S. is the second-largest wine consumer in the world and should be the largest by 2012.

The United States: An Overview

California remains America's viticultural powerhouse, producing about 90 percent of the nation's wine, with Washington, New York and Oregon accounting for most of the remaining amount. The temperate West Coast makes fine wine from European *Vitis vinifera* varieties (grapes like Chardonnay, Cabernet Sauvignon, Pinot Noir). Other parts of the country with cold, harsh winters once grew only the heartier native American grapes, like *Vitis labrusca,* but have since switched over to European varieties and hybrids; winemakers in New York and Virginia are leading the charge. The classic American style, which often emphasizes bold flavors over subtlety, with ripe fruit and the generous use of oak, is also changing: Many of today's American wines are exhibiting more nuance and *terroir*.

california

California sunshine is a mixed blessing for viticulture. Producers must struggle to find areas that are cool enough to keep grapes from ripening too fast, and thus ensure proper flavor development. Some of the best wines are made in coastal regions tempered by Pacific breezes, as well as in vineyards at higher elevations. Luckily, California happens to have a bounty of such areas up and down the coast.

California: An Overview

The northernmost of California's important wine regions is the North Coast, including Napa, Sonoma, Mendocino and Lake counties. Mendocino's Anderson Valley provides the perfect climate for Chardonnay and Pinot Noir, as well as high-quality sparkling wines (see p. 255). In Sonoma, the legendary Alexander, Russian River and Dry Creek valleys are home to elegant Chardonnays, spicy Zinfandels and fruity Sauvignon Blancs. East of Sonoma is the smaller yet more renowned Napa Valley, where the country's greatest Cabernets and Bordeaux-style blends are made. Nearby, Carneros makes great Chardonnays, Pinot Noirs and sparkling wines. The vast Central Coast region extends southward from Santa Cruz to the top of Los Angeles County. Generally speaking, Pinot Noir and Chardonnay grow well throughout this area; Zinfandel and France's Rhône grape varieties—Syrah, Grenache, Mourvèdre and Viognier—also produce some superb wines here. Farther inland, east of San Francisco Bay, Lodi, in the Central Valley, and the Sierra Foothills region are famous for old-vine Zinfandels.

California Wine Labels

Most California labels list the winery name, AVA (American Viticultural Area), vintage and grape. U.S. law dictates that a wine labeled with an AVA must contain at least 85 percent grapes from that region. If an AVA wine lists a vintage date, 95 percent of the fruit must be from that year's harvest. Wines with the name of one grape, often called varietal wines, must contain 75 percent of that variety, though regulations in certain counties are stricter. Blending, however, is an important winemaking technique, and a combination of different grapes can produce wines of greater complexity. Some of California's finest wines are blends of various Bordeaux grapes (see p. 159), a style that carries the legally recognized moniker *Meritage* (pronounced like "heritage"), although most producers use a proprietary name instead—for instance, Beringer Vineyards' "Alluvium" blends. The term *Reserve* has no legal definition, but generally connotes wines of higher quality.

california whites

California's varied geography gives its winemakers the latitude to craft white wines in a range of styles, from light, floral and crisp to big, dense and high in alcohol. Many of the best whites, though, are produced in the state's cooler regions, such as Sonoma County's Russian River Valley.

CALIFORNIA WHITES

chardonnay

California's most planted variety, Chardonnay accounts for about as much of the state's wine production as Cabernet and Merlot combined. In fact, California's hallmark style of Chardonnay—with butterscotch, tropical fruit and oak flavors—was synonymous with "white wine" in the U.S. for years. While that rich, opulent style still exists, especially in large-production popular brands, the trend today is toward leaner, more elegant and food-friendly Chardonnays balanced with refreshing acidity and minerality.

chardonnay recommendations

Barra of Mendocino | 2008 | **MENDOCINO**
★★ $ $ Octogenarian Charlie Barra has been farming organically here since the 1950s. His silky Chardonnay has vibrant nut, vanilla and caramel aromas, apple and lemon flavors and a butterscotch finish.

Beaulieu Vineyard | 2008 | **CARNEROS**
★★ $ $ Famed wine consultant Michel Rolland works on Beaulieu's Private Reserve Cabernet, yet this more affordable offering from the winery seems also to be made in his signature rich style. Ripe and lush, it balances creamy pear and crisp apple flavors.

Bennett Family The Reserve | 2007 | **RUSSIAN RIVER VALLEY**
★★★ $ $ A welcome change from the many overblown, heavy Chardonnays, Bennett Family's delicious 2007 is austere and elegant, with clean apple flavors, good acidity and a mouthwatering finish.

Buena Vista | 2007 | **CARNEROS**
★★ $ $ Buena Vista's estate-harvested Chardonnay is classic California in style: butter, nut, toast and vanilla flavors with a rich texture.

Chalone Vineyard Estate Grown | 2008 | CHALONE

★★★ **$ $** Chardonnay reminiscent of Burgundy has been Chalone's trademark since its first commercial vintage in 1966. This gorgeous wine, with its refined flavors of crisp apple and subtle toast, continues that legacy.

Clos Pegase Mitsuko's Vineyard | 2008 | CARNEROS

★★★ **$ $** Visionary Jan Shrem purchased a 50-acre vineyard in Calistoga in 1983. Today, he owns 400 additional acres in the northern and southern ends of the Napa Valley, including this Carneros property, named for his wife. His 2008 is expertly balanced, offering layers of rich apricot and dried fruit flavors.

Cuvaison | 2008 | CARNEROS

★★ **$ $** Cuvaison has been crafting delicious, dependable wines for more than four decades. This beautiful Chardonnay is soft and fruity, with fine acidity and a finish that lingers.

star producers
california chardonnay

Aubert

Mark Aubert's résumé includes stints at Peter Michael Winery, Colgin Cellars and Bryant Family Vineyard. His blockbuster Sonoma Chardonnays are truly exceptional.

Hartford Court

Don Hartford and winemaker Jeff Mangahas craft single-vineyard Russian River Valley Chardonnays with a distinctly elegant character.

Kistler Vineyards

Steve Kistler eschews trendy Dijon clones for old California vines, and his wines stand out for their Old World style.

Kongsgaard

This Napa winery produces tiny amounts of terrific Burgundy-inspired wines. They are hard to find but worth the hunt.

Patz & Hall

For more than 20 years, Patz & Hall has been making evocative single-vineyard Chardonnays, sourced from some of California's most coveted vines.

Peter Michael Winery

Because of the succession of talented winemakers at Peter Michael estate—including Helen Turley, Mark Aubert and Luc and Nicolas Morlet—the wines are always world-class.

Edna Valley Vineyard Paragon | 2008 |
SAN LUIS OBISPO COUNTY
★ ★ $ $ Layers of clay and volcanic rock in Edna Valley's estate vineyard yield a surprisingly elegant wine marked by crisp overtones and a creamy texture. And it comes at a great price.

Fetzer Vineyards Valley Oaks | 2008 | **CALIFORNIA**
★ $ Forever dependable for affordable and delicious wines, Fetzer does not disappoint with this light-bodied, tasty Chardonnay that is a hard-to-beat value.

Foxglove | 2008 | **CENTRAL COAST**
★ ★ ★ $ $ Fermented and aged in stainless steel without malolactic fermentation (which imparts a creamy, soft quality), Foxglove Chardonnay displays a crisp underlying acidity supporting flavors of tropical fruit, honeysuckle and orange blossom. This is a delicious value from Varner Wine.

Grgich Hills Estate | 2007 | **NAPA VALLEY**
★ ★ ★ $ $ $ Mike Grgich has been king of the opulent, balanced California Chardonnay since the 1970s. His full-bodied 2007 is peach-scented and floral, with a pronounced minerality that keeps it elegant.

Kazmer & Blaise Boon Fly's Hill | 2007 | **CARNEROS**
★ ★ ★ $ $ $ K&B keeps production low and quality high, as is evidenced by this spectacular 2007 Chardonnay. It's brawny yet refined, full of honeydew and ripe peach flavors and mouthwatering acidity.

Lafond SRH | 2007 | **STA. RITA HILLS**
★ ★ ★ $ $ The Santa Rita Hills area has proven to be especially good terroir for Burgundy grapes, which often achieve greater ripeness here than in their home turf. This beautiful Chardonnay is intensely tropical on the nose, and has loads of dried fruit, pear and apricot flavors on the broad, complex palate.

Landmark Overlook | 2008 | **SONOMA COUNTY**
★ ★ ★ $ $ Landmark's proprietor, Damaris Deere Ford (John Deere's great-great-granddaughter), specializes in bright, focused Chardonnays. This standout bottling shows juicy flavors of apple, pear and papaya, and a solid beam of refreshing acidity that helps balance the opulent finish.

Lolonis | 2007 | **REDWOOD VALLEY**
★ ★ $ $ All Lolonis wines are made with organically grown grapes. Restrained without being lean, the Redwood Valley Chardonnay features notes of smoke, butter and toast.

Londer Vineyards Corby Vineyards | 2008 |
ANDERSON VALLEY

★ ★ **$ $ $** One of Londer's Pinot Noirs has been compared to Grand Cru Burgundy, but don't overlook the winery's Chardonnays. A pleasant touch of smoke on the nose of this lovely wine is followed by crisp, clean flavors of citrus and mineral that linger on the palate.

Luli | 2008 | SANTA LUCIA HIGHLANDS

★ ★ ★ **$ $** Master Sommelier Sara Floyd and the acclaimed Pisoni family crafted this Chardonnay with grapes from multiple Santa Lucia Highlands vineyards for added complexity. The result is a wine bursting with fresh pineapple and lemon curd aromas and citrus zest and tropical fruit flavors.

Morro Bay Split Oak Vineyard | 2008 | CALIFORNIA

★ **$** Always a dependable bargain, Morro Bay's Chardonnay features apple flavors with a touch of marzipan. Aged *sur lie* (on lees), the wine is creamy from start to finish.

Picket Fence | 2007 | RUSSIAN RIVER VALLEY

★ ★ ★ **$ $** Because half of this wine was aged in new French oak barrels and the whole underwent partial malolactic fermentation, it has layers of decadent, creamy flavors and a round mouthfeel. Ripe apple and apricot flavors are buoyed by refreshing acidity that keeps the long, superb finish crisp.

Sbragia Family Vineyards Home Ranch | 2007 |
DRY CREEK VALLEY

★ ★ **$ $** At first this wine seems to be dominated by its rich, creamy texture. But fragrant notes of apple, sweet pear and citrus soon reveal themselves, as it builds up to a powerful, mineral-laden finish.

Sonoma-Cutrer | 2008 | SONOMA COAST

★ ★ **$ $** Although Sonoma-Cutrer also produces limited amounts of Pinot Noir, Chardonnay has been its calling card for three decades. The 2008 is characterized by ripe apple, pear and quince flavors laced with minerals, spice and tangy acidity.

Souverain | 2008 | ALEXANDER VALLEY

★ ★ **$ $** Notes of creamy butterscotch take center stage in this opulent Chardonnay, thanks to malolactic fermentation and aging *sur lie*.

Talbott Logan | 2007 | MONTEREY COUNTY

★ ★ ★ **$ $** Created as a less expensive alternative to Talbott's signature Chardonnay, Logan has a fruit-forward style, with apple, pear and apricot notes. And like its sibling, it boasts a long, plush finish.

Testarossa Castello | 2008 | CENTRAL COAST
★★ $ $ Fresh tangerines and Meyer lemons mark the nose of this Central Coast white. It's crisp and delicious, displaying bright apple flavors layered with spicy vanilla notes.

Varner Spring Ridge Vineyard Bee Block | 2008 | SANTA CRUZ MOUNTAINS
★★★ $ $ $ Twin brothers Bob and Jim Varner craft this distinctive Chardonnay. A faint hint of smoke reveals the judicious use of oak, and citrus and mineral flavors round out the palate.

Wente Vineyards Riva Ranch | 2008 | ARROYO SECO
★★ $ $ Founded 125 years ago, Wente Vineyards is the oldest continuously operated family-owned winery in the U.S. Made from grapes grown in the family's Riva Ranch vineyard, this wine shows off a range of flavors—guava, pear and nectarine—with a pleasant spicy edge.

William Hill Estate Winery | 2007 | NAPA VALLEY
★★★ $ $ Winemaker Ralf Holdenried is as involved in the vineyard as he is in the winery. His luscious, complex Chardonnay is dripping with sweet pineapple and lemon curd aromas that lead to flavors of citrus zest and tropical fruit underscored by cleansing minerals.

CALIFORNIA WHITES

sauvignon blanc

The Sauvignon Blanc grape of France's Bordeaux and Loire Valley regions is second in popularity only to Chardonnay among California's white varieties. Its defining tropical fruit and citrus flavors distinguish California Sauvignon Blancs from the grassy character of most New Zealand versions.

sauvignon blanc recommendations

Brander | 2009 | SANTA YNEZ VALLEY
★★ $ Argentina native Fred Brander founded his winery in 1975. Three years later, his Sauvignon Blanc landed Santa Barbara County its first gold medal at the Los Angeles County Fair. The 2009 vintage is crisp and juicy, with notes of lemon, lime, herb, pear and minerals.

DeLoach Ritchie Vineyard | 2008 | RUSSIAN RIVER VALLEY
★★ $ $ Burgundy's Boisset family purchased this longtime Russian River Valley producer in 2003. This lively Sauvignon is full of acacia and honeysuckle aromas and ripe fig and melon flavors.

Ferrari-Carano Fumé Blanc | 2009 | SONOMA COUNTY
★ ★ $ With its blend of Dry Creek, Alexander and Russian River Valley grapes, this wine has a heady, complex nose of ripe pear, citrus and fresh herbs. Its not-too-tart acidity provides a beautiful frame for the long finish.

Flora Springs Soliloquy Vineyard | 2008 | OAKVILLE
★ ★ $ $ Fresh apple, persimmon and apricot define the core of this wine, while vibrant notes of lime, spice and minerals add nice accents.

Foursight Charles Vineyard | 2008 | ANDERSON VALLEY
★ ★ $ $ Made from grapes grown in Foursight's Anderson Valley vineyard, this wine boasts lemon, lime and orange aromas, followed by sweet flavors of marzipan and bright, fresh herbs.

Frog's Leap | 2009 | RUTHERFORD
★ ★ $ $ After tart Granny Smith apples jump out of the glass, the Frog's Leap 2009 Sauvignon Blanc reveals ample grapefruit and grass flavors and a relatively full body.

Geyser Peak Winery | 2008 | CALIFORNIA
★ ★ $ Geyser Peak's 2008 vintage, made primarily with grapes grown in Sonoma County, is rich and intense, with notes of guava, lime and fresh-cut grass. Mouthwatering acidity breaks through on the long, luscious finish.

Hanna | 2009 | RUSSIAN RIVER VALLEY
★ ★ ★ $ $ In contrast to the previous year, Hanna's 2009 growing season was graced with mild weather. The resulting wine is complex and dense, with flavors of pink grapefruit, lemon and passion fruit.

Honig | 2009 | NAPA VALLEY
★ ★ ★ ★ $ $ With its use of solar panels, biodiesel fuels and natural predators for insect control, Honig is an exceptionally "green" producer. In this outstanding wine, sumptuous flavors of green apples and pears are uplifted by fresh acidity and a touch of minerals.

Lail Vineyards Blueprint | 2008 | NAPA VALLEY
★ ★ ★ $ $ $ Lail's Blueprint Sauvignon Blanc joins its more established sibling, Blueprint Red. Only the second vintage made, the 2008 is intriguing, marked by dried fruit and ripe apricot flavors and a juicy, citrusy finish.

Main Street Winery | 2008 | MONTEREY COUNTY
★ ★ $ Sourced mostly from Main Street's marine-influenced estate vineyard in Santa Barbara County, this Sauvignon Blanc is a great value, delivering soft, easy-to-drink flavors of citrus and pear.

Markham Vineyards | 2008 | NAPA VALLEY
★★★ $ Markham has earned a reputation for terrific, fruit-forward Sauvignon Blancs, and this vintage clearly shows why. Citrus zest aromas precede flavors of honeysuckle and fig, with grassiness coming through at the end.

Mason | 2008 | NAPA VALLEY
★★★ $ $ Mason also produces red wines but truly excels with Sauvignon Blanc. The beautiful 2008 shows passion fruit and grapefruit flavors and a savory, herbal quality.

Paul Dolan Vineyards | 2007 | MENDOCINO COUNTY
★★ $ $ Paul Dolan's organic and biodynamically grown grapes highlight the region's unique terroir. Aromas of tropical fruit come together with bright citrus and pineapple flavors before the soft, grassy finish.

eat here now

BOTTEGA Celebrity-chef Michael Chiarello is back in a restaurant kitchen for the first time in close to a decade. He serves excellent house-cured *salumi*, homemade pickled vegetables and hand-rolled pastas at his 90-seat Napa restaurant. *Yountville, Napa Valley;* botteganapavalley.com

Santa Barbara Winery | 2008 | SANTA YNEZ VALLEY
★★ $ Up-front green apple and fig give way to juicy notes of ripe pear and fresh-cut grass and a subtle underlying tartness in this Santa Ynez gem.

Schug | 2008 | SONOMA COUNTY
★★ $ $ Walter Schug founded his winery in 1980 after his tenure as the founding winemaker at Joseph Phelps Vineyards. This 2008 Sauvignon Blanc bears the aromas and flavors of tangy lemon and lime, with smoky overtones, and shows a nice intensity on the finish.

SeaGlass | 2009 | SANTA BARBARA COUNTY
★ $ Delicate lemon zest aromas, a touch of minerals, and mouthwatering fruit on the finish make this light-bodied wine a perfect food companion for warm-weather fare.

Slingshot | 2008 | NAPA VALLEY
★★ $ $ Slingshot's Sauvignon Blanc is soft and chalky in the mouth; bright acidity and firm minerals add great balance.

Sterling Vineyards | 2008 | NAPA COUNTY
★ $ Made from grapes grown largely in northern Napa Valley, plus some from Mendocino, Lake and Sonoma counties, this light-bodied wine has notes of bright citrus and fresh grass and a spicy finish.

other california whites

The most widely planted white after Chardonnay is French Colombard, used mainly for bulk wines. Pinot Grigio, grown throughout the state, can yield delicious, citrusy wines, particularly from cooler regions. Rhône varieties include Viognier and, in small amounts, Marsanne and Roussanne.

other california white recommendations

Au Bon Climat Hildegard | 2006 | SANTA MARIA VALLEY
★★★ $ $ $ Named for a wife of Charlemagne, this elegant Pinot Gris–Pinot Blanc–Aligoté blend could be mistaken for a white Burgundy. Elegant toast flavors are woven with bright citrus and flowers.

Big House White | 2009 | CALIFORNIA
★ $ This nice white blend offers melon, apricot and mineral flavors. It's also available in a party-friendly, three-liter Octavin box.

Bray Vineyards Verdelho | 2008 | SHENANDOAH VALLEY
★★ $ $ Made from the Verdelho grape, popular in parts of Portugal and Australia, this white offers citrus aromas, zippy acidity, a waxy texture and loads of tropical flavors.

Chimney Rock Elevage Blanc | 2008 | NAPA VALLEY
★★★ $ $ $ A blend of Sauvignon Blanc and Sauvignon Gris, this grassy, citrus-laden white is luscious and surprisingly brawny.

Christine Andrew Viognier | 2007 | LODI
★★ $ Showing expressive aromas of mango, peach and orange blossom, this is a plush, big, yet delightfully crisp Viognier.

Cline Viognier | 2009 | NORTH COAST
★ $ Subtle floral and melon aromas give way to mouthwatering pineapple, passion fruit and lychee flavors.

Dancing Coyote Albariño | 2009 | CLARKSBURG
★ $ Though Albariño wines typically hail from Spain, this refreshing California version offers a great mix of melon, pear and minerals.

Dashe McFadden Farms Dry Riesling | 2008 | POTTER VALLEY
★★★ $ $ Husband-and-wife team Michael and Anne Dashe have released only three vintages of this terrific Riesling. Made from organic grapes, it oozes honeysuckle, peach, mineral and petrol flavors right up through the completely dry, medium-long finish.

Ironstone Obsession Symphony | 2008 | CALIFORNIA
★ ★ ★ $ The rarely seen Symphony grape, a cross between Muscat of Alexandria and Grenache Gris, was developed in 1948. It makes a captivating wine here, expressing a range of peach, rose and lychee notes, at a wonderfully low price.

Lazy Creek Vineyards Gewürztraminer | 2007 | ANDERSON VALLEY
★ ★ ★ ★ $ $ Lazy Creek is the second-oldest winery in the Anderson Valley. This outstanding, multifaceted white displays honey and baked pear on the nose. Its flavors are concentrated, and an uplifting acidity brings the wine to life.

Mandolin Riesling | 2008 | MONTEREY
★ $ Perfect for everyday drinking, this Monterey Riesling provides plenty of easy-to-enjoy peach, pear and wet stone flavors.

Navarro Vineyards Gewürztraminer | 2008 | ANDERSON VALLEY
★ ★ ★ $ $ With a floral, mineral nose and a full-bodied yet brightly acidic palate, this stellar white is reminiscent of its Alsace counterparts. Navarro also makes an unfermented Gewürztraminer grape juice that is great for kids.

Parducci Sustainable White | 2008 | MENDOCINO COUNTY
★ ★ $ Tart and medium-bodied, this unusual blend of Chenin Blanc and Sauvignon Blanc, with smaller percentages of Viognier, Muscat Canelli and Tocai Friulano, is a real value for its round, pleasing texture and abundance of ripe pear and citrus flavors.

Pine Ridge Chenin Blanc/Viognier | 2008 | CALIFORNIA
★ ★ $ The peach and mineral flavors one expects from Chenin Blanc are elevated by Viognier's tropical zing in this delicious blend.

Qupé Bien Nacido Hillside Estate Roussanne | 2007 | SANTA MARIA VALLEY
★ ★ ★ ★ $ $ $ Stylistically, this Roussanne is entirely Californian. Oaky and bold yet balanced, it's a creamy white full of satisfying apricot, peach and tropical fruit flavors that go on and on.

Tamás Pinot Grigio | 2008 | CENTRAL COAST
★ $ Aromas of bright citrus and apple lead to a juicy, ripe, medium-bodied palate that makes this Pinot Grigio good for casual sipping.

Thomas Fogarty Gewürztraminer | 2008 | MONTEREY COUNTY
★ ★ $ $ This is a well-built Gewürztraminer perfect for those who prefer a dry style. Boasting lychee and rose petal aromas, it unleashes all the warm citrus and spice flavors characteristic of the grape.

california rosés

California could be blamed for the poor reputation of rosés in America. The state's blush wines—sweet, simple pink wines made from the red Zinfandel grape—share only their color with traditional dry rosé, yet have long cast a negative light on these wines. But with the increase in dry, food-friendly rosés imported from Spain and France, California is responding with true rosé, typically made from Sangiovese, Grenache, Pinot Noir and even Cabernet Sauvignon.

california rosé recommendations

Bonterra Vineyards Rosé | 2008 | MENDOCINO COUNTY
★★ $ Made with organic grapes, this vivid pink rosé evokes summer flowers, berries and red cherries. With loads of refreshing acidity and a touch of herbs, it's balanced and delicious.

Eberle Steinbeck Vineyard Syrah Rosé | 2008 | PASO ROBLES
★★ $ $ Bold yet slightly rustic cherry aromas carry through on the palate along with dried red fruit flavors in this rich, dark rosé. It has plenty of acidity to offset the plush, mouth-coating, black fruit flavors.

Francis Coppola Sofia | 2009 | MONTEREY COUNTY
★★ $ $ Cranberry aromas up-front in this lean, dry rosé are rounded out by dried cherry, strawberry and vanilla nuances and a touch of tannin with a burst of acidity at the end.

Ménage à Trois Rosé | 2008 | CALIFORNIA
★★ $ An interesting blend of red and white grapes, this is a very tasty, if unconventional, pink wine made by Folie à Deux. The flavors of Gewürztraminer—lychee and rose petal—predominate, complement-ed by the ripe berry notes from Syrah and Merlot.

Navarro Vineyards Rosé | 2009 | MENDOCINO
★★ $ $ Flowers and bubble gum introduce this lively rosé, which delivers loads of juicy watermelon and berry flavors. It's tasty and refreshing, thanks to an electric acidity.

Quivira Vineyards and Winery Grenache Rosé | 2009 |
DRY CREEK VALLEY
★★★ $ With a lovely salmon color and delicate dried fruit and herb flavors, this has much in common with French rosés. A blend of 90 percent Grenache and 10 percent Mourvèdre grapes (biodynamically grown), it reveals hints of orange and melon amid ample wild berries.

Tablas Creek Vineyard Rosé | 2009 | **PASO ROBLES**
★ ★ $ $ Aromas of blackberries and smoke turn juicy on the palate of this Mourvèdre-Grenache-Counoise blend. It's generous, spicy and slightly rustic, with a bone-dry finish.

Valley of the Moon Rosato di Sangiovese | 2009 |
SONOMA COUNTY
★ ★ $ Sangiovese is intensely fruity here, with a brilliant magenta color, a nose of watermelon and berry and an off-dry palate with light tannins. The slightest touch of fizz adds to the wine's refreshment.

california reds

Cabernet Sauvignon put California on the international map back in the 1970s, most famously when Stag's Leap Wine Cellars' Cabernet beat the French competition at a blind tasting in Paris in 1976. Although Cabernet remains the state's iconic wine, California grows more Zinfandel, producing both anonymous sweet blush wines and impressively spicy, jammy, dry reds. Rhône reds, led by Syrah, often blended with Grenache and/or Mourvèdre, thrive in the California sun. Petite Sirah can also do well, although winemakers use it mostly to add color and tannin to blends.

CALIFORNIA REDS

cabernet sauvignon & bordeaux blends

Cabernet Sauvignon is the king of *all* grapes in California, thanks to its ability to create wines of extraordinary complexity, concentration and longevity. Some of the world's most expensive wines are the so-called cult Cabernets of Napa Valley. While Cabernet grown on California's valley floors can develop intense berry flavors, many high-end winemakers prefer to use fruit from hillside vineyards; these vines tend to yield smoky, earthy, blackberry-flavored wines. Cabernet blends beautifully with other grapes, particularly Bordeaux varieties such as Merlot, Cabernet Franc and Petit Verdot. Most of California's top Bordeaux blends use proprietary names, like Joseph Phelps Insignia.

cabernet sauvignon recommendations

Atlas Peak | 2005 | **NAPA VALLEY**

★★★ $ $ $ An above-the-fog-line vineyard location means that Atlas Peak's grapes benefit from both abundant sunshine and cool daytime temperatures. The beautifully crafted 2005 is firm yet generous, with equal parts black fruit, herbs and earth.

Brandlin | 2007 | **MOUNT VEEDER**

★★★ $ $ $ $ Vibrant black cherry, fresh currant and wild berry flavors are underscored by pleasing earth and mineral characteristics and notes of dusty herbs in this supple, refined Cabernet.

Cakebread Cellars | 2007 | **NAPA VALLEY**

★★★ $ $ $ $ Made with grapes sourced from throughout Napa Valley, Cakebread has earned a loyal following over the years. Its 2007 is somewhat tight and lean, with chewy tannins framing ample fruit.

Cliff Lede | 2007 | **STAGS LEAP DISTRICT**

★★★ $ $ $ Cliff Lede's wines are made in an impressive gravity-flow winery (i.e., no pumps are used to move grapes or wine). The 2007 Cabernet shows a spicy bouquet, a pronounced black pepper quality and a silky texture.

Corison Kronos Vineyard | 2005 | **NAPA VALLEY**

★★★ $ $ $ $ Be patient with Cathy Corison's hand-crafted, estate-grown Cabernet. Somewhat tightly wound, it needs a bit of time in the glass for the hefty tannins to soften and reveal a wonderful mix of black cherry, currant, anise, mineral, sage and leather flavors.

Dancing Bull Vintage Blend | 2006 | **CALIFORNIA**

★ $ A juicy, easy-drinking wine perfect with food or without, Dancing Bull's Cabernet is full of mouthwatering raspberry and black cherry flavors, and is a great pour for large gatherings.

Darms Lane | 2007 | **NAPA VALLEY**

★★★ $ $ $ Bold currant notes come on strong in this dense and concentrated Cabernet. It is herbal, rustic and savory, with firm, persistent tannins that impart real substance.

Diamond Creek Volcanic Hill | 2007 | **NAPA VALLEY**

★★★★ $ $ $ $ When the late Al Brounstein planted Bordeaux varieties on Diamond Mountain in 1968, not many people in the state showed much interest in these grapes. Today, the pioneering estate is known for dense, full-bodied reds like this Cabernet, packed with tar, tobacco and ripe black fruit encased in big tannins.

Faust | 2007 | NAPA VALLEY

★ ★ ★ $ $ $ Perhaps better known for Quintessa, another one of his California estates, and Veramonte, his Chilean label, Agustin Huneeus is also the proprietor at Faust, which turns out this expertly crafted Cabernet. Juicy berry and cocoa flavors are punctuated by notes of soft chalk and earth.

Ghost Pines | 2007 | NAPA COUNTY/SONOMA COUNTY

★ ★ ★ $ $ Named for the gray pines that are native to the Napa Valley, Ghost Pines' 2007 Cabernet is a solid-value wine. Its soft, chalky palate balances notes of sweet black fruit.

Gnarly Head | 2007 | CALIFORNIA

★ ★ $ Grapes from vineyards in Lodi and Monterey go into Gnarly Head's Cabernet, yielding a fruit-forward wine with a formidable body and soft tannins—this is an outstanding bottle for the low price.

Hall Kathryn Hall | 2006 | NAPA VALLEY

★ ★ ★ ★ $ $ $ $ The eco-friendly Hall has crafted yet another winning wine. The estate's flagship wine, this Cabernet is big and stunning, with an impressive array of flavors; medium-firm tannins balance black and red fruit flavors through the brawny finish.

visit here now

750 WINES Wine seller David Stevens and his wife, Monica, opened this sleek shop to offer the ultimate in customer service: private, one-on-one tastings by appointment, hard-to-find bottlings and a concierge service to arrange visits to topflight wineries. *St. Helena, Napa Valley; 750wines.com*

Harlan Estate | 2006 | NAPA VALLEY

★ ★ ★ ★ $ $ $ $ For more than two decades, Bill Harlan has been making extraordinarily delicious—and extraordinarily expensive—wines at his hillside vineyard in western Oakville, and he never misses. His meaty, alluring 2006 weaves slate, licorice and cassis aromas with opulent waves of black fruit flavors. The finish is dry and tight, a good indicator that the wine will age remarkably well.

Hawk Crest | 2006 | CALIFORNIA

★ $ Hawk Crest has been produced since 1974, and great value has always been the brand's trademark. This well-built Cabernet shows a backbone of dark cherry flavors that are tailor-made for food pairing.

Healdsburg Ranches | 2007 | SONOMA COUNTY

★ $ The soft red fruit in Healdsburg Ranches' light-bodied Cabernet plays well with its chalky palate and mild tannins.

Heitz Cellar Bella Oaks Vineyard | 2005 | **NAPA VALLEY**
★★★ **$ $ $** Heitz Cellar's Bella Oaks Cabernet is aged for more than three years in oak before it is bottled, resulting in a big, intense wine with firm tannins and rich, concentrated fruit.

Howell at the Moon | 2006 | **HOWELL MOUNTAIN**
★★★ **$ $ $ $** There's a savory quality to this terrific wine, with sage and earth notes infusing ultraripe prunes and mouth-coating black fruit flavors. Firm tannins provide a solid frame.

Hundred Acre Kayli Morgan Vineyard | 2007 | **NAPA VALLEY**
★★★★ **$ $ $ $** It's easy to see why this pricey wine—around $300 a bottle—is one of the most coveted Cabernets from California. Incredibly elegant, pure, powerful and distinct, it stands out among its Napa peers for its irresistible mix of cassis, coffee, cocoa and earth flavors. Though young, the 2007 is already remarkably approachable.

star producers
california cabernet sauvignon

Colgin Cellars
Ann Colgin was an art historian before she became a winemaker, which may explain why she crafts wines with a rare, artistic refinement.

Harlan Estate
This 240-acre premium Napa estate provides grapes for both Harlan and The Maiden, two of the region's most sought-after Bordeaux-style blends.

Hundred Acre
Although consulting winemaker Philippe Melka helps craft Hundred Acre's prized wines, owner Jayson Woodbridge is the bigger-than-life driving force behind the legend.

Robert Mondavi Winery
The late Robert Mondavi's brand was synonymous with quality and dynamism in California, and his legacy of crafting outstanding, benchmark wines continues.

Schrader Cellars
Fred Schrader's small-batch, single-vineyard Napa wines are often experimental yet always reliably excellent.

Shafer Vineyards
Producer of the elite cult Cabernet Hillside Select, among others, father-and-son duo John and Doug Shafer have been making great wines in Stags Leap for over 30 years.

Irony | 2007 | NAPA VALLEY
★★★ $ Multiple Napa vineyards contributed fruit for this great-value Cabernet, which offers a mélange of black currant, tobacco and cocoa. It's wonderfully complex for its price.

Jade Mountain | 2007 | NAPA/SONOMA/LAKE COUNTIES
★★ $ Jade Mountain's winemaker believes that blending grapes from different premium appellations yields great wines. The 2007 Cabernet is juicy and easy to drink.

Jarvis | 2003 | NAPA VALLEY
★★★★ $ $ $ $ The slight brown hue of this wine suggests its maturity. Full of beautiful fig and date flavors layered with earth and leather, this is a broad-shouldered Cabernet that still possesses formidable heft and power for a wine of its age.

Jekel Vineyards | 2007 | ARROYO SECO
★ $ Founded in 1972, Jekel was one of Monterey's pioneering wineries. Its light-bodied Cabernet delivers ample plum and cherry flavors.

Louis M. Martini Monte Rosso Vineyard | 2006 |
SONOMA VALLEY
★★★★ $ $ $ $ It's easy to understand why the Monte Rosso Vineyard is the subject of so much talk: This is a truly great wine—with earth and forest nuances built on top of berry and mocha flavors—that demonstrates real power in the lengthy finish.

Palmaz Vineyards | 2006 | NAPA VALLEY
★★★★ $ $ $ $ Abundant black fruit flavors—both fresh and dried—are the hallmark of this massive Cabernet. There's plenty of earthy rusticity and finesse to lend elegance without stifling the wine's powerful personality.

Peju Provence | 2006 | NAPA VALLEY
★★★ $ $ $ An image of Peju's impressive 50-foot tower graces the label of this outstanding red. Marked by fig, earth and berry flavors, it's full-bodied and has strong yet well-integrated tannins.

Rodney Strong | 2007 | SONOMA COUNTY
★★ $ $ Rodney Strong's Sonoma Cabernet is built around rich black currant, blackberry, cedar and earthy mineral flavors. The palate is intensely fruity but nicely structured, too.

Stewart | 2006 | NAPA VALLEY
★★★ $ $ $ $ Black cherry and currant flavors serve as the perfect counterpoint to this wine's bone-dry, tannic palate, which also possesses a distinct leathery edge.

163

Terlato Family Vineyards | 2006 | STAGS LEAP DISTRICT

★★★ $ $ $ Stags Leap District is probably Napa's most lauded AVA for Cabernet Sauvignon. Terlato's full-bodied wine—with its complex notes of currant, mocha, mineral and espresso—is a testament to the appellation's truly exceptional terroir.

Terra Valentine | 2006 | SPRING MOUNTAIN DISTRICT

★★★ $ $ $ Tightly wound, with firm tannins wrapped around a core of dried currant, plum and spicy blackberry flavors, this full-bodied wine offers equal parts grace and muscle.

337 | 2007 | LODI

★★ $ Named for the French vine clone from which it is made, 337 is a California Cabernet that distinctly recalls Bordeaux. In the glass, pleasant berry meets soft tannins before the juicy finish.

Two Angels | 2007 | SONOMA VALLEY

★★ $ $ From grapes grown on the Sonoma side of the Mayacamas Mountains, Two Angels Cabernet is somewhat closed at first, but opens up to reveal delicious cherry, chocolate and chalk flavors.

Yorkville Cellars | 2007 | YORKVILLE HIGHLANDS

★★ $ $ Among the first in the region to be certified organic (in 1986), Yorkville Cellars' vineyards yield a reliably tasty wine with easy-drinking flavors of raspberry and soft chalk.

bordeaux blend recommendations

Boëté Reserve Cheval Rouge | 2006 | CARMEL VALLEY

★★★ $ $ A blend of Cabernet Sauvignon, Cabernet Franc and Merlot, Boëté's Cheval Rouge was produced with the help of consulting winemaker Dave Coventry. It's a balanced yet intense wine with abundant ripe currant, spice and mineral flavors and well-integrated tannins to offset the plush texture.

Chappellet Mountain Cuvee | 2007 | NAPA VALLEY

★★ $ $ All five Bordeaux grapes—Cabernet Sauvignon, Merlot, Malbec, Cabernet Franc and Petit Verdot—made it into this blend. It's finely tuned and big, displaying dried currant, sage and mineral flavors with hints of nuts and earth.

Chateau St. Jean Cinq Cépages | 2006 | SONOMA COUNTY

★★★ $ $ $ $ Margo Van Staaveren has had a hand in making wine at Chateau St. Jean for nearly three decades. Her 2006 Cinq Cépages, a superb blend dominated by Cabernet Sauvignon, has notes of minerals, herbs and anise and big tannins that ensure a long finish.

Eponymous Macallister Vineyard | 2007 | SONOMA COUNTY
★★ $ $ $ This dense blend of Cabernet Sauvignon, Merlot and Cabernet Franc is quite opulent, characterized by dust, herbs, leather and currants. Firm tannins make it a perfect candidate for cellaring.

Ferrari-Carano Trésor | 2006 | SONOMA COUNTY
★★★ $ $ $ Ferrari-Carano's Trésor, French for "treasure," lives up to its name, with enough youthful flourishes and cherry flavors to be drinkable now, as well as the earth, chocolate and herb notes and full body to make it ageworthy.

Girard Artistry | 2007 |
NAPA VALLEY
★★★ $ $ $ Produced from a blend of all five Bordeaux varieties, Artistry displays the colors and aromas of deep dark fruit—black cherries, blackberries and prunes—with a charmingly spicy kick.

Jayson | 2007 | NAPA VALLEY
★★★★ $ $ $ Jayson Pahlmeyer's mission when he launched this winery in the 1980s was to craft "California Mouton," and his wines can indeed be counted on to deliver power and fruit tempered by elegance and finesse. Graphite and spice aromas are layered over plum and blackberry flavors in this well-structured red.

visit here now

BERNARDUS LODGE & WINERY At this luxurious Carmel Valley restaurant-winery-resort, chef Cal Stamenov's terrific California cooking pairs with an 1,800-bottle wine list. Among the highlights: winery-only bottlings of Bernardus's own acclaimed wines. *Carmel Valley; bernardus.com*

Joseph Phelps Insignia | 2006 | NAPA VALLEY
★★★★ $ $ $ $ Cabernet Sauvignon and just a touch of Petit Verdot make up Joseph Phelps's beautiful Insignia. Its muscular, tannic style enhances the rich flavors of wild berries, pencil lead and licorice.

Justin Vineyards & Winery Justification | 2007 | PASO ROBLES
★★★ $ $ $ With masculine aromatics—leather, tar and cedar—this sultry blend of 65 percent Cabernet Franc and 35 percent Merlot is all swagger up-front but then reveals a softer side, with juicy cherries, dusty tannins and good acidity.

Kathryn Kennedy Winery Lateral | 2007 | CALIFORNIA
★★★ $ $ $ This St-Émilion–style Merlot-centric blend is the Kathryn Kennedy Winery's most popular wine for good reason. Firm and concentrated, with a wealth of dried currant, earth and mineral flavors, it has fine-grained tannins on the plush finish.

Napanook | 2006 | **NAPA VALLEY**

★★★ **$ $ $** Modesty is a virtue in this smooth, medium-bodied blend of four of the five Bordeaux varieties. Powerful, rich notes of black and red currants harmonize beautifully with spice, anise and mocha nuances in this plush red.

Opus One | 2006 | **OAKVILLE**

★★★★ **$ $ $ $** Since Michael Silacci took the helm as winemaker in 2004, Opus One has had a run of excellent vintages. The 2006 wafts smoked meat and toasted herb aromas, followed by generous flavors of ripe cherry and currant upheld by a beam of vibrant acidity.

Quintessa | 2007 | **RUTHERFORD**

★★★★ **$ $ $ $** Since 1990, owners Agustin and Valeria Huneeus have managed the Quintessa vineyards with sustainable practices, and the wines are all the better for it. This elegant, well-textured blend offers notes of spicy currants, chalky minerals and dusty sage, while a judicious amount of oak marks the powerful finish.

Rivino Sedulous | 2006 | **MENDOCINO**

★★ **$ $** There's a splash of Viognier in this Merlot–Cabernet Franc blend, which displays a seductive lusciousness rounded out with sweet black cherry, violet and dusty spice flavors.

Roy Estate | 2007 | **NAPA VALLEY**

★★★★ **$ $ $ $** The late Charles Roy founded this estate with his wife Shirley, and his legacy lives on in this refined yet decadent red. The 2007 layers blackberries, chocolate and coffee flavors with silky tannins; this would benefit from some time in the cellar.

CALIFORNIA REDS

merlot

Americans drink nearly as much Merlot as Cabernet—and consumption is rising. The "other half" of the grape duo that creates the great Bordeaux and California Bordeaux-style blends, Merlot can add a velvety quality to Cabernet's power. In the 1990s, overproduction led to a sea of inferior California Merlot and to the grape's public thrashing in the movie *Sideways*. Fortunately, that reputation for mediocrity is increasingly unwarranted, and shrewd shoppers will look to Merlot for wines that are less expensive than Cabernet but no less sophisticated.

merlot recommendations

Bonterra Vineyards | 2007 | MENDOCINO COUNTY

★ ★ $ $ Bonterra is one of the most commercially successful wineries using organic grapes, which means their wines are not hard to find. Its Merlot is light-bodied and refreshing, with loads of red fruit, juicy acidity, vanilla and notes of cocoa.

Clos Du Val | 2007 | NAPA VALLEY

★ ★ $ $ From the pioneering Napa Valley winery comes this powerful Merlot, offering aromas of plums, berries, earth, flowers and a touch of chocolate cake. It is medium-bodied and soft, with lingering notes of toasted oak.

eat here now

GOTT'S ROADSIDE Brothers Joel and Duncan Gott use artisanal ingredients and modern flavors to update classics at their roadside stand. Their offerings include a Wisconsin sourdough cheeseburger and white pistachio milkshakes. *St. Helena, Napa Valley; gottsroadside.com*

Concannon Selected Vineyards | 2007 | CENTRAL COAST

★ $ A super value from the Central Coast, this Merlot shows a great combination of savory herbs, bell pepper and sarsaparilla alongside traditional juicy fruit and chocolate flavors.

Cycles Gladiator | 2007 | CALIFORNIA

★ $ Another terrific value, this well-structured wine is made with grapes from regions throughout the state and mixes wonderfully ripe cherry and spice cake flavors with tasty cocoa notes and plush tannins.

Delicato Family Vineyards | 2008 | CALIFORNIA

★ ★ $ It's hard to believe how inexpensive this is. Around $6 buys you a delicious combination of luscious blueberry, cherry and vanilla flavors framed by subtle tannins.

Duckhorn Vineyards | 2007 | NAPA VALLEY

★ ★ ★ $ $ $ The tightly wound dark fruit on display in this standout Merlot is permeated by nuances of fresh fennel, licorice, earth and spice. It has superb structure, thanks to the addition of 10 percent Cabernet Sauvignon and a touch of Petit Verdot, and a lively acidity that keeps it fresh.

Frei Brothers Reserve | 2007 | DRY CREEK VALLEY

★ ★ $ $ Frei Brothers may no longer be the most talked-about estate, but it's well worth rediscovering this Sonoma stalwart. Small additions of Petite Sirah and Zinfandel add intrigue to Merlot's classic cherry flavors, which are augmented by spice, cocoa and cedar.

Joseph Carr | 2007 | NAPA VALLEY
★★ $ $ Sommelier-turned-*négociant* Joseph Carr offers this pretty, medium-bodied Merlot, with a touch of eucalyptus and resin on the nose and hints of dill amid flavors of raspberries and blackberries.

Merriam Vineyards | 2005 | RUSSIAN RIVER VALLEY
★★ $ $ Hailing from the Windacre Vineyard, located in the warmest corner of the cool-climate Russian River Valley appellation, this wine demonstrates its origins with a vibrant acidity and tart cherry flavors. It's fresh and expertly balanced.

Napa Cellars | 2007 | NAPA VALLEY
★★ $ $ Wafting nice cedar pencil, dill and mint aromas alongside traditional plum, this is a dark, juicy yet firm Merlot, with fresh oak, chocolate and supple tannins coming to the forefront.

181 | 2008 | LODI
★★ $ This is the sister wine to the 337 Cabernet, and it too is named for its French vine clone. It's a jammy Merlot with great balance, a medium body and notes of ginger, allspice and clove.

Raymond Estates R Collection | 2006 | CALIFORNIA
★★ $ Combining fruit from Napa Valley, Sierra Foothills and San Joaquin Valley, this deliciously ripe Merlot offers saucy berry and red currant flavors enhanced by the right amount of vanilla-tinged oak.

Silverado Vineyards | 2006 | NAPA VALLEY
★★★ $ $ $ Silverado is named for a mining town, and fittingly, ample graphite, mineral and dust notes infuse this red's dried berry and cherry flavors. It is an earthy and rugged wine, with powerful tannins and cedar notes.

Trefethen Family Vineyards | 2006 |
OAK KNOLL DISTRICT OF NAPA VALLEY
★★★ $ $ $ This is super-ripe and effusive, with pungent cherry, lilac, vanilla, fennel and cocoa on the nose. Yet it also possesses a Bordeaux-like finesse, with complex touches of leather, bright red fruit flavors and a gorgeous, mouthwatering acidity.

Twenty Rows | 2008 | NAPA VALLEY
★★★ $ $ Merlot is rarely as massive as this brawny wine. Dark, smoky fruit, clove and licorice flavors are laced with gingery spice notes on the full-bodied, powerful, yet balanced palate.

Twisted | 2008 | CALIFORNIA
★ $ Simple, clean and fruity, this is an ideal summer picnic red full of juicy blueberry flavors and just enough light tannins and acidity.

CALIFORNIA REDS

pinot noir

Pinot Noir is one of the most persnickety of grapes, hard to grow even in its homeland of Burgundy. California vintners have wrestled with it for decades, trying to replicate the smoky, earthy qualities that mark French examples. The best California Pinot Noirs come from the Russian River Valley, Carneros, Anderson Valley and the Central Coast. The trend among most small producers is for rich, robust Pinots that bear only passing resemblance to the wines of Burgundy. These producers have staked their claims in the AVAs of Santa Barbara County, including Santa Maria Valley, Santa Ynez Valley and Sta. Rita Hills.

pinot noir recommendations

Au Bon Climat La Bauge Au-dessus | 2007 |
SANTA MARIA VALLEY

★★★ $ $ *La bauge au-dessus* means "the wallow up above," a reference, perhaps, to the wine's high-elevation origins. It's dominated by berry and cherry flavors with an alluring, green tea–like, savory edge.

Breggo Ferrington Vineyard | 2007 | ANDERSON VALLEY

★★★ $ $ $ A bit of time in the glass allows the cocoa, spice, tea and smoke flavors to emerge from underneath this Pinot's up-front blackberry pie aromas. Supple tannins give a soft texture to the fruit-forward, cola-accented palate.

Carpe Diem Firepeak Vineyard | 2007 | EDNA VALLEY

★★ $ $ Winemaker Christian Roguenant brings real French pedigree to this Pinot Noir. It's sensuous and full-bodied, with damp leaves, sassafras and earth interwoven with dried figs and licorice.

Castle Rock | 2008 | CENTRAL COAST

★★ $ This generous, juicy Pinot is anything but subtle. Jammy, bold, ripe fruit flavors have a sweet cola quality and a tasty peppery finish.

C. Donatiello Winery Maddie's Vineyard | 2008 |
RUSSIAN RIVER VALLEY

★★★ $ $ $ $ Made with organic grapes, this shows a Burgundy-like elegance in the pepper, flower and leather flavors that highlight a base of ripe raspberries and warm, sweet spice.

Cherry Pie Huckleberry Snodgrass | 2007 | SONOMA COAST
★★★★ $ $ $ Jayson Woodbridge of Layer Cake fame created this wine, and it's true to its name. Baked cherry pie flavors ooze over the palate, which is filled out with pretty sassafras, smoldering tobacco and spice; ample tannins add balance.

Cobb Coastlands Vineyard | 2007 | SONOMA COAST
★★★★ $ $ $ $ Cobb Wines specializes in single-vineyard Pinot Noir. Reminiscent of a blueberry pie, complete with spice and vanilla ice cream, this wine is especially delicious. It's medium-bodied and ripe, with a solid frame of fine tannins adding good structure.

Cuvaison | 2008 | CARNEROS
★★ $ $ $ Cuvaison's 400-acre Carneros estate vineyard yields the fruit for this bright, full-bodied wine, which is characterized by smoky blackberry and pencil lead notes and a lovely acidity.

star producers
california pinot noir

Kosta Browne Winery
A decade ago, as coworkers in a Santa Rosa restaurant, Dan Kosta and Michael Browne pooled their tip money to buy grapes. Today their Pinot Noirs are some of California's best.

Loring Wine Company
Brian Loring, a self-professed "Pinot freak," gave up his career as a software engineer to focus on crafting these stellar wines.

Paul Hobbs Winery
Hobbs's ultra-natural approach to winemaking—he uses indigenous yeasts and eschews filtration—results in spectacular Cabernet Sauvignons and Pinot Noirs.

Rochioli Vineyards & Winery
A champion of Russian River Pinot Noirs, banker-turned-winemaker Tom Rochioli has a knack for crafting world-class wines year after year.

Siduri
Texas natives Adam and Dianna Lee debuted Siduri's first vintage in 1994, and their wines—25 each year—now serve as benchmarks for California Pinot Noir.

Talley Vineyards
This southern Central Coast winery makes elegant, intense Pinot Noirs that easily outshine any others in the region.

Darcie Kent Vineyards West Pinnacles Vineyard | 2007 |
MONTEREY
★★★ $ $ This wine is produced at the Monthaven Winery. With pretty aromas of sweet cola, clove and earth, it's a medium-bodied Pinot Noir featuring tart cherry flavors, hints of wild mushroom and a true elegance.

Domaine Alfred Chamisal Vineyards | 2007 | EDNA VALLEY
★★ $ $ $ This is voluptuous, sexy and supple, with dark fruit and licorice at the forefront. Although it's made in a blockbuster style, the slightly bitter tannins prevent it from being overblown.

Educated Guess | 2007 | NAPA VALLEY
★★ $ $ Made with grapes from Carneros and Spring Mountain District, this delicious red oscillates between cherry-cola flavors and layers of fresh cherries and spiced vanilla.

Esser | 2008 | CALIFORNIA
★★ $ $ Esser blends wines from many different appellations for this Pinot Noir, but the largest contribution (46 percent) comes from the North Coast's Solano County. Red currant and black fruit come on strong, with simple touches of licorice, cola and spice peeking through toward the end.

Etude | 2007 | CARNEROS
★★★ $ $ $ Winegrower Tony Soter believes Pinot Noir is the best vehicle for studying wine—in musical terms, an *étude*. This rich wine, imparting black plum, raspberry jam, kirsch and sultry baking spice, is robust and perfectly harmonious.

Five Rivers | 2008 | CALIFORNIA
★ $ This is pure and simple Pinot enjoyment, with tart berry, pomegranate and cranberry flavors laced with a touch of dark chocolate.

Fogdog | 2007 | SONOMA COAST
★★ $ $ $ This is indeed as dense as a thick fog, with complex aromas from spice cake to fresh black currants. The wave of spice continues on the palate, which has complementary notes of black cherry and cola and ends on a mineral note.

Gary Farrell Russian River Selection | 2007 |
RUSSIAN RIVER VALLEY
★★★ $ $ $ This is the entry-level Pinot from Gary Farrell, a pioneer with the grape in the Russian River Valley. The wine's charming cherry-cola flavors are augmented by ripe raspberry and nutmeg flavors, and the finish has a savory edge.

Gloria Ferrer Rust Rock Terrace | 2005 | CARNEROS
★★★ $ $ $ Gloria Ferrer uses Dijon and Pommard clones for this wine, which gives it a detectable Burgundy character. Well-knit flavors of dark fruit and mocha have a generous touch of toasted oak and ample earthy nuances, too.

Husch | 2007 | ANDERSON VALLEY
★★★ $ $ This Pinot evokes part spicy cedar closet and part fresh-baked strawberry-rhubarb pie, a marriage of flavors that works brilliantly. The medium-bodied palate is exquisitely balanced with loads of invigorating acidity and vanilla.

Jargon | 2008 | CALIFORNIA
★ $ Few $10 Pinot Noirs are as drinkable as this. Light and lovely, it presents a mix of tannins, berry flavors and sweet blueberry notes.

Kali Hart | 2007 | MONTEREY COUNTY
★★ $ $ Kali Hart is proprietor Robb Talbott's youngest daughter, and her namesake wine is solid, fresh and vibrant, with herbal, Bing cherry and exotic spice notes.

Kenwood Vineyards | 2008 | RUSSIAN RIVER VALLEY
★★ $ $ This under-$20 wine entices with aromas of raspberry pie filling and zesty acidity driving blackberry and vanilla flavors. Hints of licorice and supple tannins make it a great partner for food.

MacPhail Toulouse Vineyard | 2007 | ANDERSON VALLEY
★★★ $ $ $ MacPhail produced only 20 barrels of this powerful Pinot. It's worth tracking down for its decadent combination of blueberry, blackberry, root beer, spice and cedar flavors woven with licorice and fine tannins.

Philo Ridge Vineyards | 2006 | ANDERSON VALLEY
★★ $ $ This juicy Pinot offers up candied apple, maraschino cherry and dried flower aromas. In the mouth it's fresh and light-bodied, with just enough earth and tannins to keep it interesting.

Prophet Teac Mor Vineyard | 2007 | RUSSIAN RIVER VALLEY
★★★ $ $ $ Unlike many of the fruit-forward Pinots from California, this is profoundly earthy, with mushroom and soil flavors enveloping smoky oak and dark fruit. It has mouthwatering acidity and a long-lasting, lovely finish.

Rodney Strong | 2008 | RUSSIAN RIVER VALLEY
★★ $ $ This drinkable crowd-pleaser features ripe red fruit flavors enhanced by toasted oak, espresso and spice notes, along with soft tannins and acidity.

Sanford La Rinconada Vineyard | 2008 | STA. RITA HILLS
★★★ $ $ $ Made from a blend of three Dijon clones, this is classic Sta. Rita Pinot Noir from the region's pioneering producer. Even with its impressive weight, it manages to stay bright and balanced, with luscious flavors of cherry, berry, peppery licorice and spice cake.

Sea Smoke Southing | 2007 | STA. RITA HILLS
★★★ $ $ $ This outstanding red's seductive nose of spicy root beer, earth and cherry gives way to a rich palate heaped with dark fruit and firm tannins. Complete with nuances of spices, herbs and damp leaves, it walks the line between boldness and elegance.

Sequana Sarmento Vineyard | 2008 | SANTA LUCIA HIGHLANDS
★★ $ $ $ Crafted by Pinot specialist James MacPhail, this is unapologetically oak-laden and New World in style, but it's not over-the-top. Its cherry, raspberry and vanilla flavors show hints of cloves.

news from california

Value News

Thanks to a few large harvests and a weak economy, California has recently seen a boom in *négociant* wines. Négociants purchase excess grapes or even finished wine from established wineries, then release wines at bargain prices under different labels. Often these brands are forbidden to reveal their sources, but people still try to find out. Names to look for include Cameron Hughes, Joseph Carr, Castle Rock and Bon Anno.

Vintage Notes

The 2007 harvest was spectacularly good in northern California. While not as exceptional as 2007, the 2008 vintage was still quite good; 2009 was top-quality in Napa and Sonoma only for growers who harvested before the massive October rains. Statewide, however, 2009 was the second-largest harvest in California history.

Winemaker to Watch

One of Bordeaux's superstar winemaking consultants, Stéphane Derenoncourt released his first Napa wine in 2009. His eponymous 2006 Napa Valley Cabernet is an impressive debut—though selling $220-a-bottle Cabernet, even with a famous name, isn't as easy as it once was.

Siduri Rosella's Vineyard | 2008 | SANTA LUCIA HIGHLANDS
★★★ $ $ $ Siduri crafts a wide range of consistently great single-vineyard Pinots from California and Oregon. This one shows perfect balance, with spice, smoke and oak infusing black cherry flavors.

Terlato Family Vineyards | 2008 | RUSSIAN RIVER VALLEY
★★★ $ $ $ Pinot reveals its sleek side here, with flamboyant strawberries laced with spice, vanilla and cinnamon. The fruit is incredibly pure, and silky tannins round out the ultrapolished package.

Testarossa Palazzio | 2008 | CENTRAL COAST
★★★ $ $ $ *Testarossa,* Italian for "redhead," is winery cofounder Rob Jensen's nickname, but could also refer to the red cherry and red berries on display in this stellar wine. Baking spice, earth and cedar round out the seductive palate.

Villa Mt. Eden Grand Reserve Bien Nacido Vineyard | 2006 |
SANTA MARIA VALLEY
★★ $ $ This wine, from a cool harvest season in one of California's cooler-climate AVAs, shows lovely tart cherry and pomegranate fruit flavors and an underlying earthiness on a medium-bodied palate.

CALIFORNIA REDS

syrah

California's love affair with France's Rhône grape varieties began with Syrah. In cooler climates it yields lean and elegant wines, with spicy berry flavors and smoky aromas—occasionally comparable to northern Rhône wines. Syrah from warmer parts of the state tends to more closely resemble Australian Shiraz (the same grape), displaying spicy, dark berry flavors and often a high alcohol content.

syrah recommendations

Beckmen Vineyards Estate | 2008 | SANTA YNEZ VALLEY
★★★ $ $ Tom and Steve Beckmen specialize in Rhône grapes, and their affordable Syrah is a winner. Delicious blueberry and blackberry flavors are layered with dried herbs, figs and milk chocolate.

Bota Box Shiraz | 2008 | CALIFORNIA
★ $ $ (3 L) This compact box holds four bottles of wine. With light tannins and flavors of jam, candied fruit and grape bubble gum, it's juicy, affordable and refreshing (especially with a slight chill).

Bradford Mountain Grist Vineyard | 2006 | DRY CREEK VALLEY
★★★ $ $ $ Made from organic grapes, this Syrah is rich yet bright and balanced. Dark berries, cedar and spice dominate the nose, while the palate shows violets, plums and figs.

Chance Creek | 2005 | MENDOCINO
★★ $ $ There's an up-front smokiness in this tasty red, which is infused with flavors of roasted plums, sweet red peppers and blackberries. Mellow tannins make it easy to drink.

Daniel Gehrs | 2006 | SANTA BARBARA COUNTY
★★ $ $ Daniel Gehrs crafts this wine in a lighter style than many California Syrahs. With ample acidity and heaps of tart cherry and pomegranate flavors, it's fruity and satisfying.

star producers
california syrah

Alban Vineyards
John Alban pioneered Rhône grapes in the U.S., and his passion for Syrah is evident in his voluptuous wines.

Beckmen Vineyards
"Rhone Rangers" Tom and Steve Beckmen are responsible for an impressive line of Santa Barbara estate-grown Syrahs, including Block Six and Clone #1 from their Purisima Mountain Vineyard.

Carlisle Winery & Vineyards
A young *négociant* firm with a small vineyard of its own, Carlisle produces old-vine Zinfandel as well as exceptional and affordable Syrahs.

Saxum Vineyards
Saxum's James Berry Vineyard, the source of its superior Syrah, has been lauded as one of the best for Rhône varieties in all of California.

Sine Qua Non
Winemaker Manfred Krankl is one of California's hardest-working viticulturists, always striving for Syrahs of rare purity and richness.

Tensley Wines
Colson Canyon is the best-known wine that Joey Tensley makes, and the only one aged in new French oak, but all of his Santa Barbara Syrahs are terrific.

Dogwood Cellars | 2007 | DRY CREEK VALLEY

★★ $ $ This lovely Syrah has an alluring combination of dark chocolate, violets and blueberry on the nose. The palate is awash with supple ripe fruit and very fine tannins, with cocoa on the finish.

Jaxon Keys Wilson Vineyard | 2007 | MENDOCINO COUNTY

★★ $ $ Bold mocha and blackberry aromas lead to sumptuous flavors of blueberry and raspberry underscored by leather and wet leaves. Berries take over once again on the lingering, smooth finish.

Jorian Hill | 2007 | SANTA YNEZ VALLEY

★★ $ $ On the homestead of Gary and Jeanne Newman, seven and a half acres are dedicated to their hand-tended vineyards, which yield this excellent Syrah. It offers dark cassis, cocoa and earth flavors laced with tar and firm tannins, and ends on a spicy note.

Mariah | 2006 | MENDOCINO RIDGE

★★ $ $ Sultry, smoky and peppery, with intriguing notes of clove and sweet tobacco, Mariah is a complex wine. Dense cherry and black plum flavors are silky on the firm yet polished palate.

Novy Family Winery | 2007 | SANTA LUCIA HIGHLANDS

★★★ $ $ Adam and Dianna Lee of Siduri, who own Novy with members of Dianna's family, crafted this incredibly rich wine. Exuberant, spicy red fruit flavors layered with smoldering tobacco and herbs lead up to a plush finish—at around $25, this is a lot of wine for the price.

Obsidian Ridge | 2007 | RED HILLS LAKE COUNTY

★★ $ $ This standout blend of five Syrah clones was aged in barrels from Kádár, Hungary, for 18 months, which imparted an underlying smoked meat quality to bold mocha and blackberry flavors.

Scribe | 2004 | NAPA VALLEY

★★★ $ $ $ Bountiful sweet vanilla and floral aromas are offset by pepper and meat notes in this berry-flavored wine. It's brawny yet balanced, and its substantial alcohol (14.8 percent) is well integrated.

6th Sense | 2007 | LODI

★★ $ $ This wine is typical of Michael-David Winery and Lodi grapes, showing powerful berry, chocolate and cola flavors, as well as nice nuances of cedar, smoky oak, white pepper and hints of sausage.

Stama | 2007 | CALAVERAS COUNTY

★★ $ With a whopping 15.89 percent alcohol, this ripe and fruity Syrah has aromatic hints of witch hazel and mint and a palate that packs a fruity explosion of cherry cough drops. The wine lacks much structure or tannin but is undeniably delicious.

Ventana | 2007 | **ARROYO SECO**
★★ $ $ With its slightly rustic style and dried cherry, leaves, cola and charred herb flavors, this wine represents an interesting change of pace for Monterey County. Less slick than many other wines from the region, it's immensely drinkable and pleasingly earthy.

Wrath Doctor's Vineyard | 2007 | **SANTA LUCIA HIGHLANDS**
★★★ $ $ $ This is textbook Syrah, with the power and ripeness typical of California and the savory, meaty quality of the northern Rhône. Chewy black fruit wrapped in bacon and smoke—with a kick of pepper and sage—is held together with firm tannins and acidity.

Zaca Mesa | 2006 | **SANTA YNEZ VALLEY**
★★★ $ $ A great value in a very ripe New World style, Zaca Mesa's Syrah is a terrific mix of cascading berry, chocolate and cinnamon. The abundant fruit is balanced by vibrant acidity and light tannins.

CALIFORNIA REDS

zinfandel

In the early 1990s, DNA testing shattered the myth that Zinfandel was a native American grape variety, as many had long believed. Alas, Zinfandel turns out to be identical to an obscure Croatian grape called Crljenak Kastelanski, though how exactly it became Zinfandel, an important variety in California capable of producing world-class wines, remains a mystery. Regardless, Zinfandel's long-established relationship with California (dating as far back as the 1850s) gives it a uniquely American identity. The most prized versions come from vineyards planted with gnarled old vines— some a century old—whose low yield results in grapes of extraordinary richness and concentration.

zinfandel recommendations

Artezin | 2007 | **DRY CREEK VALLEY**
★★ $ $ This Zinfandel is blended with 9 percent Petite Sirah, which adds notes of fresh herbs and pepper to the classic flavors of ripe blackberries and cassis, all nicely supported by velvety tannins.

Barefoot | NV | **CALIFORNIA**
★ $ This medium-bodied quaffer presents juicy cherry and raspberry flavors, a pleasant hint of sweet spice and gentle tannins.

Bella Big River Ranch | 2007 | ALEXANDER VALLEY
★★★ $ $ $ Made from vines planted in 1905, this Zinfandel is bursting with dark plum, raspberry, vanilla and wildflower aromas that take a spicy turn on the somewhat oaky, silky palate.

Brazin Fall Creek Vineyard | 2007 | DRY CREEK VALLEY
★★ $ $ After spending 17 months in American and French oak casks, this Zinfandel is full-bodied and over-the-top. Its intensely juicy raspberry flavors are jammy, candied and spicy, with a hint of smoke.

Candor Lot 2 | NV | CALIFORNIA
★★ $ $ Made by Hope Family Wines, producers of the popular Liberty School brand, this red progresses from raspberry on the nose to dark fruit in the mouth, where spice and tannins add complexity.

Chiarello Family Vineyards Giana | 2008 | NAPA VALLEY
★★★ $ $ $ Winery owner Michael Chiarello is perhaps better known as a chef in the Napa Valley. Jammy, oaky and delightfully tasty, his 2008 Zinfandel is a cut above the competition.

Claudia Springs John Ricetti Vineyard | 2007 | REDWOOD VALLEY
★★★ $ $ This delicious Zinfandel is a spicy, superbly balanced powerhouse of a wine sourced from a tiny one-acre vineyard parcel that has existed since Prohibition.

Dancing Bull Winemaker's Reserve | 2007 | CALIFORNIA
★ $ Fun, tasty and thoroughly likable, Dancing Bull's Zinfandel is always a great buy. The 2007 delivers black cherry and raspberry jam flavors, a medium body and tannins that linger without overpowering.

Elyse Korte Ranch | 2007 | NAPA VALLEY
★★★ $ $ $ The Korte Ranch vineyard, located just north of St. Helena, is planted with old-vine Zinfandel. This splendid wine is polished, ripe and inky, with mouth-filling charred oak and plum flavors supported by earthy tannins.

Kunde Family Estate | 2006 | SONOMA VALLEY
★★ $ $ Kunde adds 7 percent Petite Sirah and 3 percent Syrah to this Zinfandel and ages it in oak for 16 months. The result is an enticing combination of intense raspberry, pomegranate and spice flavors, with firm tannins holding it all together.

Lake Sonoma Winery | 2007 | DRY CREEK VALLEY
★★ $ $ Barrel-aged for 18 months, this full-bodied red is ripe with dark berries and black pepper. Persistent tannins carry through on the subtly smoky finish.

Limerick Lane Collins Vineyard | 2007 | **RUSSIAN RIVER VALLEY**
★ ★ ★ ★ $ $ Zinfandel accounts for 90 percent of Limerick Lane's production, and the winery's expertise with the grape is evident here. Nearly purple in color, this wine has robust and silky flavors of raspberry, baking spice, vanilla and pomegranate.

Ottimino Rancho Bello Vineyard | 2006 | **RUSSIAN RIVER VALLEY**
★ ★ $ $ Rancho Bello Vineyard is farmed with no irrigation, which results in grapes with concentrated flavors. In this brash wine, scrumptious raspberry and juicy strawberry take center stage, while a kick of spice and nice tannins play a supporting role.

Peju | 2006 | **NAPA VALLEY**
★ ★ $ $ Perhaps it's the addition of 5 percent Cabernet, or the fact that 25 percent of the wine was aged for 16 months in new oak barrels, but the result is a monster of a wine packed with big, bold cooked fruit flavors.

taste here now

SEGHESIO FAMILY VINEYARDS The winery produces some of the best Zinfandel in Sonoma, from their basic Sonoma Zin to their luscious Home Ranch. The best place to sample them is upstairs at their weekly "Family Table" tastings, where chef Jon Helquist prepares small plates of the family's traditional Italian dishes to pair with a flight of five or more wines. *Healdsburg, Sonoma; seghesio.com*

Philo Ridge Vineyards | 2006 | **MENDOCINO**
★ ★ $ $ Philo Ridge's winery is powered by solar and wind energy. This lovely wine is equal parts earth and fruit, with ample baked fruit, baking spice and leaves bound together by gentle tannins.

Porter-Bass | 2005 | **RUSSIAN RIVER VALLEY**
★ ★ ★ $ $ Made with grapes from Porter-Bass's certified biodynamic vineyard, this wine entices with aromatic mocha and blackberry and a hint of cedar. The flavors are deliciously plummy, with lots of earth, and fine-grained tannins accompany a long finish.

Robert Biale Vineyards Stagecoach Vineyards Biale Block | 2007 | **NAPA VALLEY**
★ ★ ★ $ $ $ The Biale Block at Stagecoach Vineyards is a four-acre plot of Zinfandel planted in 1999. This rich, smooth wine has flavors of dark, wild berries and a long and smoky finish.

Rosenblum Cellars Rockpile Road Vineyard | 2007 | **ROCKPILE**
★ ★ ★ $ $ $ Zinfandel is Rosenblum's specialty—the winery produces more than a dozen different bottlings each vintage. The Rockpile Road Vineyard release is bold and rich, with bright raspberry and baked fruit flavors and gratifyingly chewy tannins.

Sanctuary Mariah Vineyard | 2006 | MENDOCINO RIDGE

★★ $ $ This North Coast red is concentrated and deep. The ripe nose offers a bushel of dark berries, while the succulent palate delivers plum, strawberry jam and softened tannins.

Sin Zin | 2008 | ALEXANDER VALLEY

★★ $ $ A friendly and very drinkable crowd-pleaser, Sin Zin is surprisingly restrained, with earthy flavors of raspberry and spice, a medium body and velvety tannins.

Sobon Estate Rocky Top | 2007 | AMADOR COUNTY

★★★★ $ $ This is a positively stunning wine with an incredibly complex nose of clove, blackberry and cedar. On the palate, it is pleasingly full and firm, and at well under $20 a bottle, it's a steal.

star producers
california zinfandel

Dashe Cellars

Husband-and-wife winemaking team Michael and Anne Dashe craft a range of superlative single-vineyard wines, most famously their Zinfandels.

Hendry

Since 1939 the Hendry family has grown a variety of grapes on their 117-acre Napa property, but it's the prized Block 7 that produces their acclaimed Zinfandels.

Martinelli Winery

Russian River veteran Martinelli produces its concentrated Jackass Hill Zinfandel with the help of famed consulting winemaker Helen Turley.

Ravenswood

Ravenswood's early focus on Zinfandel—and its mantra of "no wimpy wines"—results in ripe, intense wines that many try to emulate.

Robert Biale Vineyards

Biale began selling its grapes to other producers in the 1930s, but it was only 20 years ago that Aldo and Robert Biale began bottling their own great old-vine Zinfandels.

Seghesio Family Vineyards

This Sonoma stalwart has been producing wine for more than 100 years but didn't focus on old-vine Zinfandels until the mid-1990s.

Villa Mt. Eden Grand Reserve Antique Vines | 2005 |
AMADOR COUNTY/NAPA VALLEY
★ ★ $ Produced from vines planted between 1908 and 1968, this
rich and lively red has a polished texture and well-focused blackberry,
black cherry, oak and spice flavors.

XYZin Vine Age Series 10 Year Old Vines | 2007 | CALIFORNIA
★ ★ $ $ This wine is crafted using an oak regimen of new and old
French, American and Hungarian barrels. The combination yields a
leathery, plum-infused wine with a medium body, subtle tannins and
loads of ripe dark fruit.

other california reds

European immigrants brought many different Mediterranean grape cuttings with them long before U.S. Customs
prohibited such souvenirs, though most were used to produce simple jug wines. In the 1980s, a group of winemakers
calling themselves the "Rhone Rangers" looked beyond
the popular Cabernet Sauvignon and began experimenting
with varieties such as Grenache, Mourvèdre, Carignane,
Syrah and Petite Sirah, which they claimed were ideally
suited to California's Mediterranean-type climate. The gam-
ble has paid off, as these grapes are now producing some of
California's most interesting and delicious wines. A similar
movement to establish Italian grapes in the state is represented mostly by Barbera and some Sangiovese (the wines
are dubbed "Cal-Ital"). The sun-loving Spanish Tempranillo
grape also produces some good wines here.

other california red recommendations

Altamura Sangiovese | 2006 | NAPA VALLEY
★ ★ ★ $ $ $ This is a really lovely, elegant wine with plenty of ripe
fruit, spice and peppery-strawberry aromas that carry through on the
palate, where silky fruit meets lively acidity.

Bokisch Vineyards Liberty Oaks Vineyard Tempranillo
| 2007 | JAHANT
★ ★ $ $ The growers-turned-winemakers at Bokisch know how to
coax all the right flavors from the Tempranillo grape. This bright wine
delivers cherry, cassis and vanilla alongside tobacco and spice.

Brutocao Hopland Ranches Quadriga | 2006 | MENDOCINO

★★ $ $ This blend of Italian grapes—Sangiovese, Primitivo, Barbera and Dolcetto—is smoky and dark, with licorice, tar and herb notes infusing a base of fleshy red fruit flavors.

Clendenen Family Vineyards Nebbiolo | 2003 | SANTA MARIA VALLEY

★★★ $ $ $ From a small, less-than-two-acre plot, Jim Clendenen makes a Nebbiolo that is surprisingly Barolo-like in its combination of delicate violet, fresh fruit and earth aromas. Beautifully supple, it has a good, driving acidity and a nice leathery quality on the finish.

Di Arie Barbera | 2007 | SIERRA FOOTHILLS

★★ $ $ This terrific California interpretation of Barbera oozes earth and cherries. A medium body, notes of licorice and zippy acidity make this a very fresh, food-friendly wine.

Domaine de la Terre Rouge Tête-à-Tête | 2006 | SIERRA FOOTHILLS

★★ $ $ Delicate tart cherry, raspberry and cranberry flavors have a medium weight on the palate in this appealing blend, which has a dry, mineral-laden, yet juicy finish.

Earthquake Petite Sirah | 2007 | LODI

★★★ $ $ Petite Sirah is famous for its inky, almost jet-black color. In this example, the flavors are also ultradark—black licorice, black-berries, burnt sugar, cigar ash—and linger impressively, thanks to powerful tannins.

Girasole Vineyards Sangiovese | 2008 | MENDOCINO

★ $ Organic Sangiovese grapes yield this berry- and sage-scented wine that's juicy and rustic, with ample tart cherry and tar flavors.

Greg Norman Petite Sirah | 2007 | PASO ROBLES

★★ $ Another ultraripe, dark Petite Sirah, this is a very powerful example, oaky and firm, yet deftly balanced by nuances of rose, plum and vanilla.

Il Podere dell'Olivos Teroldego | 2005 | CENTRAL COAST

★★ $ $ Au Bon Climat Winery makes this plush, full-bodied red, weaving licorice, cedar, graphite and smoke with ripe black fruit, light tannins and invigorating acidity.

Karly Wines El Alacrán Mourvèdre | 2008 | AMADOR COUNTY

★★ $ $ $ Taking its name from the Spanish word for "scorpion," this is a wonderfully fruity, exotic red that reveals lovely notes of san-dalwood throughout the very dry finish.

LangeTwins Petite Sirah/Petit Verdot | 2008 | CALIFORNIA

★★ $ $ This unusual blend from a fifth-generation farm family is marked by berry, baking spice and dark chocolate aromas. Well-integrated tannins provide a nice frame for juicy, enjoyable flavors of cloves and blueberries.

Liberty School Cuvée | 2007 | SONOMA COAST

★★ $ Profoundly dark and concentrated, with an opaque violet color, this Syrah-dominated Rhône blend offers succulent fruit, spice and toasted oak aromas. The flavors are intense and tightly wound, showing impressive power, especially for such an affordably priced wine.

Murrieta's Well Zarzuela | 2007 | LIVERMORE VALLEY

★★ $ $ Flowers, leather and spice jump out of the glass in this blend of Spanish and Portuguese grapes. It's a delicate, medium-bodied wine, with rose, plum pudding and elegant herb details and soft tannins.

Noceto Sangiovese | 2007 | AMADOR COUNTY

★★ $ $ A respected Italian grape specialist in California, Vino Noceto crafts wines with Barbera and Moscato Bianco as well as Sangiovese. Displaying wonderful varietal character—dried cherry, wild strawberry, leather and tar—this wine is plush and ripe.

taste here now

BONNY DOON VINEYARD
Winemaker Randall Grahm is best known for Rhône varieties such as Syrah. His new tasting room and Cellar Door Café are located in downtown Santa Cruz. At the Cellar Door, chef Charlie Parker's menu echoes the winery's focus on organic and biodynamic farming. *Santa Cruz; bonnydoonvineyard.com*

Quivira Vineyards and Winery Grenache | 2008 | DRY CREEK VALLEY

★★ $ $ The Grenache grape shows its distinctive earthy side here, with subtle leather and damp leaves complementing rustic cherry, plum and mulberry flavors.

Renwood Barbera | 2007 | AMADOR COUNTY

★★ $ $ Far riper than Italian Barbera, this is balanced by fine tannins supporting concentrated chocolate-covered raisin and black plum flavors. Smoky oak and notes of licorice add intrigue.

Ridge Lytton Springs | 2007 | DRY CREEK VALLEY

★★★ $ $ $ In this masterful blend, Zinfandel provides the jammy and supple blueberry and strawberry fruit; Petite Sirah contributes intensity, structure and tannins; and Carignane, along for the ride, adds hints of rustic spice on the finish.

Seghesio Family Vineyards Sangiovese | 2007 |
ALEXANDER VALLEY

★ ★ ★ **$ $** Seghesio has the oldest plantings of Sangiovese in North America. This delicious, powerful rendition features cherry and blueberry flavors, with herbs, spice, anise and leather in the mix.

Seven Daughters | NV | CALIFORNIA

★ ★ **$** There's an addictive candied cherry quality to this bright, tasty red, a hodgepodge of Merlot, Cabernet Franc, Cabernet Sauvignon, Syrah, Zinfandel, Carignane and Alicante Bouschet.

Shenandoah Vineyards ReZerve Barbera | 2007 |
AMADOR COUNTY

★ ★ **$ $** Shenandoah's organic grapes produce a highly aromatic Barbera brimming with violet, tar and dill notes. The palate leans toward richer cherry and strawberry flavors flecked with fresh herbs.

star producers
other california reds

Bonny Doon Vineyard
Bonny Doon is renowned for its eccentric celebrity winemaker Randall Grahm, its eye-catching bottle labels and, of course, an excellent Rhône-inspired range of red and white wines.

Edmunds St. John
Steve Edmunds is a founding member of the California Rhone Rangers, and his reds are consistently elegant, vibrant and pure.

The Ojai Vineyard
Regardless of challenging conditions, winemaker Adam Tolmach proves year after year that he is an expert at coaxing both power and structure out of his grapes.

Palmina
Husband-and-wife team Steve and Chrystal Clifton make some of the best New World iterations of Italian varieties.

Ridge
Whether blending Bordeaux grapes for its iconic Monte Bello or combining Rhône grapes with Zinfandel to make its Lytton Springs, Ridge is a master at creating balanced wines that are full of character.

Tablas Creek Vineyard
Founded as a joint venture between American importer Robert Haas and Château de Beaucastel, Tablas Creek produces terrific Rhône-variety red and white blends.

Treana | 2007 | PASO ROBLES

★★★ $ $ $ Ripe berries meet pine, tar, menthol, sage and leather in this dense, savory Cabernet-Syrah blend. The body shows great balance and elegance, and with bright acidity and medium-weight tannins, it achieves more than just sheer power.

Verdad Tempranillo | 2007 | SANTA YNEZ VALLEY

★★ $ $ With small additions of Grenache and Syrah, this Tempranillo actually tastes more Spanish than many modern Spanish reds, with its balanced Old World style and modest alcohol level. It boasts aromas of dried cherry, flowers and toast, with berries, cocoa and leather coming together nicely on the palate.

oregon

Although Oregon is sandwiched between Washington to the north and California to the south, its wines are very different from those of its neighbors. Western Oregon's cool climate is especially suited to growing Pinot Noir, as well as Pinot Gris and Chardonnay. The state's wineries are mostly small, and their total production is far less than that of Washington, New York or California. While the absence of mega-producers means that there are few inexpensive options, Oregon has earned a well-deserved reputation for its high-quality boutique wines.

Oregon: An Overview

The hub of Oregon wine production is the Willamette Valley. Located in the state's northwestern corner and protected against strong winds from the Pacific by the Coast Ranges, the wine region experiences relatively cool temperatures and abundant moisture. Fortunately for vintners, Pinot Noir has taken to the area particularly well. To the south, in the warmer wine regions of the Umpqua, Rogue and Applegate valleys, Bordeaux and Rhône varieties tend to outperform Pinot. Northeast of the Willamette Valley, the Columbia Gorge and Valley regions run along the Washington State border, meeting the Walla Walla Valley, where Cabernet Sauvignon reigns, and Merlot and Syrah are also produced, but in lesser volumes.

Oregon Wine Labels

Oregon's labeling rules are somewhat stricter than the federal standard followed in other wine-producing states. Certain wines labeled by grape variety must consist of 75 percent of that grape in accordance with federal mandate, but others, such as wines made with Pinot Noir, Pinot Gris, Riesling and Chardonnay, are held to an even higher state standard of 90 percent. In addition, wines that bear specific region names must contain 95 percent grapes from that region, a slightly higher proportion than the 85 percent federal standard.

oregon whites

While Pinot Noir is Oregon's pride, the state's whites can be impressive. The most important white is Pinot Gris, which finds a middle ground between the generous Alsace style and refreshing Italian Pinot Grigio. Chardonnay shows great promise in Oregon, while light-bodied, dry Rieslings have achieved some success in certain areas, particularly in the Willamette Valley.

oregon white recommendations

Adelsheim Chardonnay | 2008 | WILLAMETTE VALLEY
★★ $ $ Just the right amount of oak aging adds delightful notes of hazelnut to this sophisticated Willamette Valley Chardonnay. Its pronounced red apple and pear flavors are nicely restrained and linger on the peach-accented, crisp finish.

Anne Amie Vineyards Cuvée A Amrita | 2008 | WILLAMETTE VALLEY
★★ $ $ The distinctive floral quality of Viognier meets bright tangerine and zesty grapefruit flavors in this fresh and zippy blend, which also includes Pinot Gris, Müller-Thurgau, Pinot Blanc, Chardonnay and Gewürztraminer. It's entirely dry and medium-bodied, with an intriguing stony quality woven throughout.

Arcane Cellars Pinot Gris | 2009 | WILLAMETTE VALLEY
★ $ $ Spicy melon flavors dominate this light-bodied, vibrant Pinot Gris. There's a slight fizz and a bit of sweetness, as well as refreshing notes of zesty citrus.

A to Z Riesling | 2007 | OREGON

★★★ $ This fast-growing *négociant* stays true to its founding mission: producing affordable wines that overdeliver on quality. Medium-bodied and crisp, this terrific white shows great Riesling character in the form of waxy apple flavors laced with floral and petrol aromas.

The Eyrie Vineyards Pinot Gris | 2008 | DUNDEE HILLS

★★★ $ $ Eyrie is credited with planting America's first Pinot Gris vines. Its 2008 is made in a full-bodied, plush style, with generous flavors of intense tropical fruit, pear and spice highlighted by whiffs of flint and smoke.

Montinore Estate Almost Dry Riesling | 2008 | WILLAMETTE VALLEY

★★ $ Lithe and fresh, this biodynamically farmed and crafted Riesling has a touch of sweetness to its bright citrus and key lime flavors.

Phelps Creek Vineyards Estate Reserve Chardonnay | 2008 | COLUMBIA GORGE

★★★ $ $ This superbly balanced Chardonnay features a combination of apple, pear, buttered toast and hazelnut flavors punctuated by notes of spice. Complex and elegant, it's made from Burgundy's famous Dijon clones, grown in volcanic soils.

Valley View Anna Maria Viognier | 2008 | APPLEGATE VALLEY

★★ $ $ With a modest alcohol level of 12.9 percent, this is a fine example of a balanced Viognier, showing a lean texture and crisp acidity, which is so often lacking in many wines from this grape. Fragrant orange peel and floral aromas follow through on the palate, along with tropical flavors of papaya and guava.

WillaKenzie Estate Pinot Gris | 2008 | WILLAMETTE VALLEY

★★★ $ $ Lush fruit meets mineral-laden acidity in this beautiful wine. In spite of rich, bready aromas, it's light and fresh on the palate, with notes of vanilla, golden apple and melon and a lively acidity.

Willamette Valley Vineyards Dry Riesling | 2008 | WILLAMETTE VALLEY

★★ $ Relatively low in alcohol (12.5 percent) and bone-dry, this Riesling is austere and minerally. Flavors of peach and other stone fruit as well as a kick of zesty citrus and loads of acidity fill it out.

Wine by Joe Pinot Blanc | 2009 | OREGON

★★ $ Pinot Blanc is often an uninspiring grape, but not here: With pretty vanilla cream, pear and mineral flavors, this expressive white shows hints of banana and a snappy, flinty finish.

oregon reds

Oregon has benefited from the surging demand for Pinot Noir. Although the climate in the Willamette Valley is challenging, in the best vintages Oregon Pinots achieve an admirable balance between the earthy, more astringent style of Burgundy and the robust and ripe styles of California. In recent years, a few *négociant* labels (which produce wines from grapes grown by others) have made these Pinots more accessible, but most Oregon reds command premium prices, especially the Pinots of the Willamette Valley and its six subappellations.

oregon red recommendations

Argyle Reserve Series Nuthouse Pinot Noir | 2006 | **WILLAMETTE VALLEY**
★★★ $ $ $ Argyle wines are reliable across the price spectrum, and this upper tier offering does not disappoint. It's an elegant, supple Pinot Noir that is velvety and lush, with just the right touch of cinnamon and tannins to offset ripe cherry and spicy-sweet cola flavors.

Aubichon Pinot Noir | 2008 | **WILLAMETTE VALLEY**
★★ $ $ $ Now in its second year of release, Aubichon's Pinot has grown a bit bolder and more powerful, but is still nicely balanced. Abundant dark cherry and plum flavors infused with hints of spice and green peppercorn are framed by generous tannins.

Chehalem 3 Vineyard Pinot Noir | 2008 | **WILLAMETTE VALLEY**
★★ $ $ This stellar Willamette Valley producer (pronounced *shuh-HAY-lum*) blends grapes from three different vineyards to remarkable effect here: Packed with ripe and tart cherry, cedar and spicy oak flavors, this is a delicate, balanced, food-friendly Pinot Noir.

Cliff Creek Cabernet Sauvignon | 2006 | **SOUTHERN OREGON**
★★★ $ $ Cliff Creek winemaker Joe Dobbes illustrates the potential of Cabernet in Oregon. This gorgeous, medium-bodied red offers cassis and chocolate infused with nuances of sage, licorice and oak.

Cooper Mountain Vineyards Reserve Pinot Noir | 2007 | **WILLAMETTE VALLEY**
★★ $ $ Intriguing pine resin and dusty cherry flavors are on display in this unusual Pinot. Made with organic grapes, it has a charming rustic quality, rounded out by wild raspberry and earth flavors.

De Ponte Cellars Pinot Noir | 2007 | DUNDEE HILLS

★★ $ $ $ Strawberry and raspberry flavors are nicely woven with hints of forest and vanilla in this juicy, earthy, beautifully bright wine.

Dobbes Family Estate Grande Assemblage Cuvée Syrah
| 2006 | ROGUE VALLEY

★★ $ $ Black as ink, with heady aromas of caramel and maple, this decadent Syrah pours across the palate with blackberries and vanilla. There are hints of dill, herbs and a bold smoky quality throughout.

Domaine Serene Grace Vineyard Pinot Noir | 2007 |
WILLAMETTE VALLEY

★★★★ $ $ $ $ Few wines can justify a price tag this steep, but this Domaine Serene does exactly that. Preceded by dried flower, herb and berry aromas, the palate is rich and soft, with wave after wave of grilled peach and wild berry flavors that have incredible length.

where to go next
willamette valley, oregon

The Allison Inn & Spa
The Willamette Valley's first luxury resort, located in Newberg, is truly first class. *2525 Allison Ln., Newberg; theallison.com*

Domaine Drouhin
The wildly successful, internationally acclaimed Oregon outpost of the famous Burgundy wine family. *6750 Breyman Orchards Rd., Dayton; domainedrouhin.com*

The Eyrie Vineyards
Oregon winemaking pioneers continue to make some of the state's finest wines. *935 NE 10th Ave., McMinnville; eyrievineyards.com*

Inn at Red Hills
This 20-room Dundee hotel from the owners of Bergström Wines features a wine bar and an excellent restaurant, Farm to Fork. *1410 N. Hwy. 99W, Dundee; innatredhills.com*

Nick's Italian Cafe
An Oregon wine-country classic offering tasty old-school Italian dishes and a stellar local wine list. *521 NE 3rd St., McMinnville; nicksitaliancafe.com*

Thistle
Eric Bechard's affordable restaurant only uses produce from six local farms. *228 N. Evans St., McMinnville; thistlerestaurant.com*

Erath Prince Hill Pinot Noir | 2006 | DUNDEE HILLS

★ ★ ★ $ $ $ Erath makes this with grapes from a prized single vineyard, and the result is a delicious, jammy wine marked by wild raspberry and strawberry flavors that taste as though they were dipped in caramel. Notes of coffee also appear on the plush, finely tuned palate.

Le Cadeau Vineyard Diversité Pinot Noir | 2008 |
WILLAMETTE VALLEY

★ ★ ★ $ $ $ *Diversité* refers to the many different Pinot Noir clones grown throughout Le Cadeau vineyard. This diversity yields a smoke- and blackberry-laden wine that is dense yet bright. A spine of acidity and notes of spice and pepper keep it balanced.

star producers
oregon pinot noir

Argyle Winery

Since its founding in 1987, Argyle has ranked among Oregon's best wineries for its powerful, beautifully textured Nuthouse and Willamette Valley Pinot Noirs.

Bergström Wines

One of the youngest winemakers in Oregon, Josh Bergström has already established his eponymous Pinot Noirs as among the finest in the region.

Domaine Serene

Ken and Grace Evenstad's love of Pinot Noir led them to the Dundee Hills region in 1989, where they continue to produce Domaine Serene's outstanding reds.

Penner-Ash Wine Cellars

Lynn Penner-Ash is a winemaking veteran, having worked at Stag's Leap Wine Cellars in Napa and Oregon's Rex Hill before launching her own much-acclaimed Pinot Noir–focused brand.

St. Innocent Winery

Oenologist Mark Vlossak founded this Willamette Valley winery in 1988. Today, his six vineyard-designated and two blended Pinot Noir bottlings sell out almost immediately.

Stoller

Bill and Cathy Stoller craft stellar wines at their state-of-the-art, partially solar-powered, gravity-flow winery.

Meditrina {6} | NV | UNITED STATES
★★ $ $ Blending Pinot Noir with other grapes is normally taboo, but this combination of Pinot, Syrah and Zinfandel made by Oregon's famed Sokol Blosser estate works quite well. Plump, round strawberry, plum and pomegranate flavors are bolstered by light tannins.

Night & Day Southern Crossing | 2007 | ROGUE VALLEY
★★ $ This kitchen-sink blend of Cabernet, Merlot, Syrah, Sangiovese, Grenache and Cabernet Franc, made by A to Z Wineworks, results in a dense, fruit-driven wine with loads of ripe, dark berries. Zippy acidity and firm tannins keep it balanced.

Panther Creek Freedom Hill Vineyard Pinot Noir | 2007 | WILLAMETTE VALLEY
★★ $ $ $ A highly distinctive mix of smoked plum, root beer and meat aromas introduce this wine, while the flavor profile is decidedly fruitier: Plush and supple blackberries and raspberries finish with cola, dried cherry and ample tannins.

Ponzi Vineyards Pinot Noir | 2008 | WILLAMETTE VALLEY
★★★ $ $ $ Second-generation winemaker Luisa Ponzi is at the helm today and she continues the winery's tradition of producing balanced, well-crafted wines. The 2008 boasts ample crushed berries, with equal parts violets and cedar, and a pleasing tartness at the end.

Siduri Pinot Noir | 2008 | CHEHALEM MOUNTAINS
★★★ $ $ Pinot specialist Siduri always delivers. This fabulously earthy, complex red has true Burgundy flair, offering dried cranberry, cherry and herb flavors, with chocolate and spice on the finish.

Sineann Abondante | 2007 | COLUMBIA VALLEY
★★ $ $ The crushed berry and floral aromas in this red blend lead to bright flavors of boysenberries and plums, with a fair amount of minerals, smoke and cedar in the mix. The finish features enticing notes of tart cherry and chocolate.

Stoller JV Estate Pinot Noir | 2007 | DUNDEE HILLS
★★ $ $ JV stands for *jeunes vignes*, or "young vines," which are clearly expressed in the pure, juicy cherry and candied apple flavors on display in this enjoyable Pinot Noir. Touches of earth and mineral add a delightful refinement.

Torii Mor Pinot Noir | 2008 | WILLAMETTE VALLEY
★★ $ $ There's a lovely kick of honey graham cracker on the palate of this food-friendly, medium-bodied Pinot Noir. Thanks to loads of acidity and spice, its tart cherry-vanilla flavors are tasty and balanced.

washington state

Washington is the second-largest wine-producing state in the U.S., with more than four times the number of wineries it had a decade ago. And the industry continues to accelerate, with record-breaking harvests each vintage, divided almost equally between whites and reds. While Washington produces more and more high-end wine, it is the state's vast output of excellent, affordable wines that has made wine drinkers take note.

Washington State: An Overview

Most winemaking in Washington takes place inland, where vineyards are sheltered from the coastal weather by the Cascade Range and enjoy sunny, relatively dry summers. The state's largest wine region is the Columbia Valley, which encompasses many prominent subregions, including the Yakima Valley, Red Mountain and the Walla Walla Valley (the last of which, in southeastern Washington, straddles the border with Oregon).

Washington State Wine Labels

Washington wine labels include basic information such as grape, winery, vintage and region where the grapes were grown. Some Washington wines are blends of Bordeaux varieties and are labeled *Meritage* (see p. 148); other wineries give proprietary names to their signature blends.

washington state whites

Washington was a white wine–centric state before its reds gained success. Cool nights allow vintners to make crisp, citrusy Chardonnays that are typically lighter and more refreshing than full-bodied California versions. Riesling production has increased dramatically, thanks to a resurgent interest in the grape among American wine drinkers. Washington Rieslings range in style from dry to sweet. Washington State Gewürztraminer is ripe, tropical and floral, usually in an off-dry style.

washington state white recommendations

Cadaretta SBS Sauvignon Blanc/Semillon | 2008 |
COLUMBIA VALLEY

★ ★ $ $ The addition of 21 percent Semillon adds weight and texture to the Sauvignon Blanc in this blend. A crisp acidity enlivens flavors of grass and lime, and the citrusy finish lingers nicely on the palate.

Chateau Ste. Michelle & Dr. Loosen Eroica Riesling | 2008 |
COLUMBIA VALLEY

★ ★ ★ $ $ This white displays an impressive balance between razor-sharp acidity and a slight sweetness. It's a particularly floral Riesling, offering a wealth of peach, honey and mineral flavors.

Columbia Crest Grand Estates Chardonnay | 2008 |
COLUMBIA VALLEY

★ ★ $ Fans of an oaky Chardonnay will appreciate this well-made—and well-priced—example. It's medium-bodied and bright, with buttery oak flavors complemented by apple and tart pear.

Columbia Winery Cellarmaster's Riesling | 2008 |
COLUMBIA VALLEY

★ $ Off-dry but not cloying, this food-friendly wine has layers of honeyed peach, lime and wet slate offset by zesty acidity.

Covey Run Riesling | 2008 | COLUMBIA VALLEY
★ ★ $ A dependable value for everyday drinking, Covey Run's Riesling is straightforward and delicious, packed with peach, citrus and honey flavors and just a hint of pineapple.

Cupcake Vineyards Riesling | 2009 | COLUMBIA VALLEY
★ ★ $ Its name may suggest sweetness, but this Riesling is entirely dry and crisp, marked by quaffable flavors of lime and honeydew.

DeLille Cellars Chaleur Estate | 2008 | COLUMBIA VALLEY
★ ★ ★ ★ $ $ $ This oaked, full-bodied blend of 62 percent Sauvignon Blanc and 38 percent Semillon is reminiscent of a fine white Bordeaux. Layered and creamy, with a fine yet rich texture, it offers a captivating mix of toast, citrus, honey and grass flavors.

Milbrandt Vineyards Evergreen Vineyard Chardonnay
| 2008 | COLUMBIA VALLEY

★ ★ $ $ Barrel fermentation and aging *sur lie* contribute a round, voluptuous quality to this single-vineyard Chardonnay. Peach, apple and banana aromas are followed by tropical fruit and oak flavors.

Poet's Leap Riesling | 2008 | **COLUMBIA VALLEY**
★★ $ $ Demonstrating a rare elegance, this dry Riesling made by Long Shadows Vintners offers mouthwatering flavors of petrol, peach and honeysuckle that are beautifully integrated.

Snoqualmie Naked Chardonnay | 2008 | **COLUMBIA VALLEY**
★ $ "Naked" (organically grown) Chardonnay grapes are used for this wine, which is unoaked and full of ripe pear and apricot flavors.

washington state reds

Cabernet Sauvignon production is increasing in Washington and surpassed Merlot some years ago. Washington's best Cabernets, Merlots and Bordeaux-style blends have smooth textures and bold fruit flavors, though they tend to be more restrained than California's riper-style reds. Syrah is Washington's brightest up-and-comer, responsible for many of the state's finest wines. Washington Syrahs often possess a subtlety missing in warm-region versions. The state also grows modest quantities of Cabernet Franc, Malbec and Pinot Noir, as well as a small but important amount of Lemberger (also called Blaufränkisch).

washington state red recommendations

Amavi Cellars Syrah | 2007 | **WALLA WALLA VALLEY**
★★ $ $ Aged in barrels for 15 months, this Syrah provides rich, succulent flavors of oak, plum, and spice, all framed by tannins.

Arbor Crest Wine Cellars Stillwater Creek Vineyard Cabernet Sauvignon | 2007 | **COLUMBIA VALLEY**
★★ $ $ $ One of Washington's earlier wine properties, this estate was built in 1924 and purchased by Arbor Crest in 1985. Its 2007 Cabernet is medium-bodied and full of generous black currant and cedar flavors that are highlighted by a pronounced herbal character.

Betz Family Winery Père de Famille Cabernet Sauvignon | 2007 | **COLUMBIA VALLEY**
★★★ $ $ $ An enticing nose of smoke and flowers introduces this formidable beauty. Powerful and impressive flavors of raspberry, earth, charred oak and spice are held together by velvety tannins that guarantee a lengthy finish.

Buty Rediviva of the Stones | 2007 | **WALLA WALLA VALLEY**
★ ★ ★ $ $ $ Buty combines 77 percent Syrah with 23 percent Cabernet Sauvignon to craft this tantalizing wine. The classic trademarks of Syrah—dark fruit, rich mocha and spice—are expertly woven with Cabernet's cassis flavors and fine-grained tannins to create a beautifully vivacious wine.

Chateau Ste. Michelle Canoe Ridge Estate Merlot | 2006 | **HORSE HEAVEN HILLS**
★ ★ $ $ The Horse Heaven Hills appellation was established in 2005, and quickly earned a reputation for quality. This red is big and robust, with firm tannins and flavors of blackberry, dark cherry and oak.

star producers
washington state reds

Andrew Will Winery
Founded in 1989 by former restaurant wine buyer Chris Camarda, this winery specializes in Bordeaux-style blends of rare elegance.

Buty Winery
Caleb Foster and his wife, Nina Buty (pronounced "beauty") Foster, first came to Walla Walla for college and now make seductive red blends worthy of their name.

Cayuse Vineyards
The scion of a Champagne-producing family in France, Christophe Baron brings years of experience to his stony-soiled Walla Walla vineyards, where he makes complex, earthy reds.

Gorman Winery
Chris Gorman's range of splendid red wines, with names like The Evil Twin, The Bully and The Pixie among them, are made from some of the state's best Cabernet Sauvignon, Merlot and Syrah grapes.

Leonetti Cellar
Father-and-son winemaking team Gary and Chris Figgins are famous for their lush Walla Walla Valley Merlots, but their Cabernet Sauvignons and Sangioveses are also great.

Quilceda Creek
This boutique winery produces the state's most iconic Cabernet Sauvignon, complex and cellar-worthy enough to rival the best in Napa.

Cougar Crest Estate Winery Reserve Syrah | 2006 |
WALLA WALLA VALLEY
★★★ $ $ $ Plum and toasted, charred oak aromas are powerful yet elegant here, rounded out with flavors of jammy dark fruit, smoke and silky tannins on the refined palate.

DiStefano Meritage | 2005 | **COLUMBIA VALLEY**
★ $ $ Cabernet Franc imparts a distinct herbal quality to this blend, which also includes about a third each of Merlot and Cabernet Sauvignon. Full-bodied and tannic, this displays cassis and spice flavors infused with pleasant notes of cedar.

Kiona Lemberger | 2006 | **RED MOUNTAIN**
★★★ $ Vinified from the Lemberger grape—also known as Blaufränkisch—this medium-bodied red offers generous dark berry flavors and a long and juicy finish supported by soft, smooth tannins.

Kontos Cellars LVLL Stone Tree Vineyard Malbec | 2007 |
WAHLUKE SLOPE
★★★ $ $ $ This inky Malbec is deliciously hedonistic: Aromas of plum and cranberry precede the ultraripe, full-bodied palate, which is dominated by oak-infused blackberries and firm tannins.

L'Ecole Nº 41 Seven Hills Vineyard Estate Syrah | 2007 |
WALLA WALLA VALLEY
★★★★ $ $ $ Don't be fooled by the playful label (which features an eight-year-old's watercolor)—this is a very serious wine. A classic New World–style Syrah, it delivers a cascade of luscious dark fruit, spice and oak flavors encased in ripe, chewy tannins.

Nicholas Cole Cellars Michele | 2006 | **WALLA WALLA VALLEY**
★★ $ $ $ This is a big, full-bodied and polished Bordeaux-style blend with loads of blackberry jam and vanilla flavors and integrated tannins on the finish.

Otis Kenyon Syrah | 2007 | **WALLA WALLA VALLEY**
★★ $ $ Made in a very modern style, this weighty, meaty Syrah shows off layer after layer of spicy vanilla and raspberry flavors. Polished tannins add a welcome dimension to the fruit.

Owen Roe Red Willow Vineyard Cabernet Sauvignon
| 2007 | **YAKIMA VALLEY**
★★★★ $ $ $ $ Owen Roe's standout Cabernet is powerfully built, yet still shows grace. It's hard not to love this youthful and ebullient wine for its gorgeous red currant and spice flavors, rich, soft tannins and lengthy, compelling finish.

Red Diamond Merlot | 2007 | WASHINGTON STATE

★ $ This instantly likable Merlot has soft tannins and a whiff of chocolaty oak amid pleasant flavors of blackberry and plum.

Seven Hills Syrah | 2007 | WALLA WALLA VALLEY

★ ★ ★ $ $ Seven Hills fermented this Syrah with the skins of Viognier grapes. The result is a deep-colored, highly aromatic Syrah with a floral nose and black cherry and subtle oak flavors.

Sparkman Ruby Leigh | 2007 | RED MOUNTAIN

★ ★ ★ $ $ $ The desertlike Red Mountain appellation gets only five inches of rain a year, yet grapevines thrive here. This Bordeaux blend is dominated by Merlot and is somewhat big in structure, marked by red fruit flavors, spice, oak notes and silky tannins.

where to go next
walla walla, washington

Dunham Cellars

Eric Dunham, who makes some of the best Cabernet Sauvignons and Syrahs in Washington State, also produces actor Kyle Mac-Lachlan's small-production Cabernet, Pursued by Bear, which is well worth looking for. *150 E. Boeing Ave., Walla Walla; dunhamcellars.com*

Jimgermanbar

This open, airy bar has terrific cocktails and seasonal "Etruscan" snacks, including homemade chorizo poached in red wine. *119 Main St., Waitsburg; jimgermanbar.com*

Monteillet Fromagerie

The Monteillets craft ten wonderful farmstead goat's- and sheep's-milk cheeses. *109 Ward Rd., Dayton; monteilletcheese.com*

Saffron Mediterranean Kitchen

Go for the excellent paella and Mediterranean-inspired seasonal dishes. *125 W. Alder St., Walla Walla; saffron mediterraneankitchen.com*

Walla Walla Roastery

The house-roasted coffee is great, as is the baklava made by local nuns. *290 A St., Walla Walla; wallawallaroastery.com*

Su Lei Beet Red | 2007 | WALLA WALLA VALLEY
★★ $ $ Made with two-thirds Cabernet and one-third Syrah, this vibrant blend shows a great balance between power and structure. Its effusive, juicy red and black cherry flavors are complemented by fine-grained tannins.

Woodward Canyon Merlot | 2007 | COLUMBIA VALLEY
★★★ $ $ $ From one of Washington State's most esteemed and collected producers comes this earthy, intensely herbal Merlot. Sweet and savory flavors of spice, plum and oak abound on the full-bodied, broad yet firm palate.

other united states wines

A handful of non–West Coast producers in the U.S. have been able to overcome the challenges of harsh climates, poor soils, a highly competitive wine market and distribution difficulties to achieve great success. Today, every state can claim at least one winery, and some of America's fastest growing wine regions are in the least likely of locations.

Other United States Wines: An Overview

Climate is the biggest challenge facing vintners in most states. Since cold winters or hot, humid summers spell trouble for traditional European *Vitis vinifera* grape varieties (like Chardonnay, Cabernet Sauvignon, Sauvignon Blanc), winemakers in many states often choose to work with the heartier native American or French-American hybrid grapes that can endure such conditions. Two areas of New York are exceptions: While the Finger Lakes region in the western part of the state continues to grow some hybrid grapes, the trend here is toward *Vitis vinifera* varieties, which grow well along the deep glacial lakes. Long Island, New York's fastest-growing region, has a maritime climate suited to white and red European grapes.

Outside of New York, mid-Atlantic and Midwestern states are taking advantage of hybrid grapes that more closely resemble *vinifera* in flavor, while new wineries focused on *vinifera* grapes are proliferating in Virginia and Maryland. In the Southwest, Arizona winemakers are currently working with Rhône Valley varieties, and Texas is producing considerable quantities of quality *vinifera*-based white and red wines. The high-elevation vineyards of New Mexico are the source of some especially fine sparkling wines (see p. 255), as well as appealing reds.

Other United States Wines Grapes & Styles

Parts of the Northeast—especially New York's Finger Lakes region—enjoy ideal conditions for growing certain white grape varieties, particularly Riesling and Gewürztraminer. Chardonnay and Sauvignon Blanc benefit from the slightly longer growing season on Long Island, which produces a few good-quality sparkling wines and dry, crisp rosés. Hybrid grapes such as Vidal Blanc are used to make delicious dessert wines in New York, Virginia and Texas. Despite a relatively warm, humid growing season, Virginia winemakers produce a number of high-quality, dry white wines from Chardonnay and Viognier grapes. With a growing season marked by relatively cool nights and warm, dry days—much like that of southeastern Washington State to the west—Idaho is also becoming a source of well-crafted *vinifera*-based white wines.

Red wine producers are doing well in many pockets throughout the country. Long Island vintners work with Cabernet Sauvignon, Merlot and Cabernet Franc, while winemakers in the cool-climate Finger Lakes region farther north focus on Cabernet Franc and Pinot Noir, which can excel in good vintages, such as 2007. In Virginia, local grape varieties like Norton grow alongside increasing amounts of *vinifera* varieties, such as Cabernet Sauvignon, Merlot and (surprisingly) Tannat, a powerful red grape native to the Madiran region of southwestern France. In wine regions in Texas and Arizona, Merlot and Cabernet Sauvignon vines do well, and producers are also creating some interesting red wines with Grenache, Mourvèdre, Tempranillo and Sangiovese. Pinot Noir does unexpectedly well in New Mexico's high-elevation vineyards.

other u.s. wines recommendations

WHITES

Barboursville Vineyards Reserve Viognier | 2008 | VIRGINIA

★★ $ $ Italy's Zonin family owns this Virginia estate, where Viognier thrives. The 2008 features lovely apricot, orange blossom and peach flavors, with hints of butter and spice and a tangy citrus finish.

Bouké White Table Wine | 2008 |
NORTH FORK OF LONG ISLAND, NEW YORK

★★ $ $ An uncommon blend of Chardonnay, Pinot Gris, Sauvignon Blanc and Gewürztraminer results in a delicious white with generous floral and citrus flavors perked up by vibrant acidity.

Cinder Viognier | 2009 | SNAKE RIVER VALLEY, IDAHO

★★ $ $ Lively peach, guava and pineapple flavors have a slight sweetness in this Idaho white, which makes it a perfect choice for spicy cuisine. Look also for Cinder's crisp rosé, full of wild strawberry and dried cherry flavors.

Hermann J. Wiemer Dry Gewürztraminer | 2008 |
FINGER LAKES, NEW YORK

★★ $ $ Wiemer crafts its wines in the German style, so although this is labeled dry, it has a touch of sugar beautifully balanced by zippy acidity. Flowers, cloves and lychee dominate the juicy palate.

Peconic Bay Winery La Barrique Chardonnay | 2007 |
NORTH FORK OF LONG ISLAND, NEW YORK

★★ $ $ Peconic Bay's medium-bodied Chardonnay nicely integrates ample toasted oak with ripe flavors of apples and peaches. The long finish is crisp and marked by notes of butterscotch and nutmeg.

Ste. Chapelle Dry Riesling | 2008 | SNAKE RIVER VALLEY, IDAHO

★★ $ Wine production began in Idaho as early as the 1860s; Ste. Chapelle is one of the finest modern-day producers in the state. The excellent Riesling is an amazing value for its mix of bold fruit flavors—green apple, white peach and citrus—underscored by racy acidity and interesting whiffs of petrol.

REDS

Dos Cabezas WineWorks El Norte | 2008 | ARIZONA

★★ $ $ Rhône grapes tend to perform well in Arizona, as this blend of Grenache, Mourvèdre and Syrah illustrates. Pungent aromas of berries, flowers and smoky oak up-front are followed by super-ripe flavors of dark fruit and caramel brought out by the desert sunshine.

Linden Hardscrabble | 2006 | VIRGINIA

★★★ $ $ $ This blend of Cabernet Sauvignon, Merlot, Petit Verdot and Cabernet Franc has a supple palate of red berry flavors laced with dusty cocoa, tobacco, spice and graphite. Hints of fennel at the end add a nice touch of complexity.

Llano Estacado Signature Mélange | 2008 | TEXAS

★ $ This is a simple, fruity red that calls to mind Hawaiian Punch. Made with Carignane, Grenache, Syrah, Mourvèdre and Viognier, with a touch of tannic structure and minerality to keep it food-friendly and balanced, it's a perfect summer picnic red.

Macari Dos Aguas | 2007 |
NORTH FORK OF LONG ISLAND, NEW YORK

★★ $ $ The mixed berry flavors on display in this Bordeaux blend—a combination of Cabernet Sauvignon, Merlot, Cabernet Franc and Malbec—are expertly offset by soft tannins, hints of savory herbs and a rich vanilla quality.

Pellegrini Vineyards Merlot | 2005 |
NORTH FORK OF LONG ISLAND, NEW YORK

★★ $ $ The combination of red berry and pronounced barnyard aromas makes this excellent Merlot reminiscent of a Bordeaux. The supple, earthy palate also features rustic tannins.

Shinn Estate Vineyards Cabernet Franc | 2007 |
NORTH FORK OF LONG ISLAND, NEW YORK

★★★ $ $ $ Shinn's ripe take on Cabernet Franc could win over many drinkers who don't normally love this grape. Flavors of dark berry, black tea and roasted tomatoes are balanced by firm tannins, and a leafy, herbal quality adds a nice touch of elegance.

Stone Hill Winery Cross J Vineyard Norton | 2007 |
HERMANN, MISSOURI

★★ $ $ Few outside the region are familiar with Missouri's state grape, Norton, and this gorgeous wine serves as a perfect introduction. It has cinnamon and clove-infused berry aromas, a soft texture and loads of mouthfilling boysenberry and licorice flavors that are round and plush.

australia

Australia is known, a bit unfairly, for full-bodied, affordable wines that are delicious but not very sophisticated. The downside of that reputation is that it has made the path more challenging for the nation's premium and boutique producers—many of whom are now concentrating on more graceful, aromatic styles. The truth is that Australia has a robust and wildly diverse wine world, with far more to offer than many wine drinkers suspect.

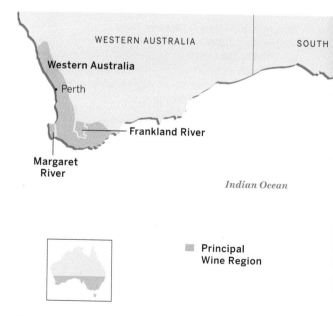

WESTERN AUSTRALIA

SOUTH

Western Australia

• Perth

Frankland River

Margaret River

Indian Ocean

▨ Principal Wine Region

Australia: An Overview

Australia has more than 2,000 wineries spread across 64 designated growing regions in six states. This island continent's sheer size and diversity allow winemakers to produce a vast array of wines. South Australia is the hub of the industry and the home to the majority of the country's most acclaimed regions, among them the Shiraz-centric Barossa Valley and McLaren Vale, and the Clare and Eden valleys, home to Australia's top Rieslings. In Victoria, Pinot Noir thrives in the Yarra Valley, near Melbourne, while Cabernet Sauvignon does well in Coonawarra. The Hunter Valley region in New South Wales, north of Sydney, is known for its Shiraz, Semillon, Cabernet and Chardonnay. Western Australia excels with Bordeaux blends, both red and white, and makes some of the country's finest Chardonnays.

Australian Wine Labels

Most Australian labels specify producer, region, vintage and grape. Blends tend to be named with the dominant grape listed first; sometimes only the initials of the blend are given, as in "GSM" (Grenache, Shiraz, Mourvèdre).

australian whites

White wines account for less than half of Australia's production. The most popular is Chardonnay. Riesling, Semillon and Sauvignon Blanc are also grown, along with such varieties as Verdelho, Muscat and Colombard.

AUSTRALIAN WHITES

chardonnay

Chardonnay was widely planted throughout Australia in the 1970s, and today is the country's primary white grape. Most of Australia's Chardonnay exports to the U.S. are mass-produced, multiregion blends made in a full-bodied, often lightly sweet style, bearing the designation South Australia, or the even larger South Eastern Australia (a zone about five times the size of California encompassing all of New South Wales, Victoria and Tasmania, and parts of Queensland and South Australia). Leaner versions come from cooler regions, such as South Australia's Adelaide Hills, Mornington Peninsula in Victoria, and Tasmania. The Margaret River region in Western Australia makes Chardonnay of exquisite elegance.

chardonnay recommendations

Giant Steps Sexton Vineyard | 2006 |
YARRA VALLEY
★★★ **$ $ $** This wine's rich and creamy texture is just the icing on the cake: Full-bodied, lush flavors of citrus and minerals are underscored by a touch of smoke, thanks to a judicious use of oak.

Jacob's Creek Reserve | 2007 | **SOUTH AUSTRALIA**
★ **$** Here's another terrific wine for every day. A backbone of acidity offsets citrus and sweet pear flavors through the zesty finish.

Leeuwin Estate Prelude Vineyards | 2007 | MARGARET RIVER
★★★ $$$ Wine legend Robert Mondavi helped select Leeuwin's vineyard site and acted as a consultant to the winery during its infancy. This 2007 Chardonnay is intensely tropical, bursting with pineapple, passion fruit and thick quince paste flavors that culminate in a long, plush finish.

Marquee Classic | 2008 | VICTORIA
★★ $ An outstanding value, this Victoria Chardonnay boasts a range of Bosc pear, peach and nectarine flavors perfectly balanced with a spicy, white peppery edge.

Philip Shaw № 11 | 2007 | ORANGE
★★★ $$ This Chardonnay hails from one of the highest-altitude wine regions in Australia. Its nose of sweet pineapple and lemon curd precedes generous, complex layers of flavor, including stony minerals, citrus zest and ripe tropical fruit.

Stonier | 2007 | MORNINGTON PENINSULA
★★ $$ Inviting aromas of quince and sweet apple jump out of the glass of this medium-bodied wine, followed by spicy fruit flavors, tangy acidity and a pleasing minerality.

taste here now

PORT PHILLIP ESTATE The spectacular rammed-earth and limestone cellar door (Australiaspeak for tasting room) has six luxury guest rooms with sweeping views of Westernport Bay. While Port Phillip's wines aren't sold in the U.S., the estate's winemaker, Sandro Mosele, also makes the stellar wines from Kooyong, which are. *Red Hill South, Mornington Peninsula, Victoria; portphillipestate.com.au*

Thorn-Clarke Terra Barossa | 2008 | EDEN VALLEY
★★★ $ Though trained as a chemical engineer, winemaker Derek Fitzgerald put his talent to use in the winery instead, where he crafts stunning wines like this one. A powerful nose of nectarine, vanilla and melon is complemented by the addition of pear and spice on the broad, complex palate.

The Wishing Tree Unoaked | 2008 | WESTERN AUSTRALIA
★ $ Always a dependable bargain, The Wishing Tree is crammed with all the bright, juicy citrus, pear and apple flavors that define well-made unoaked Chardonnay.

Yalumba The Y Series Unwooded | 2009 | SOUTH AUSTRALIA
★★ $ Bright pineapple and pear aromas are augmented by full-bodied flavors of juicy apple in this standout value wine. A mouthwatering acidity keeps it beautifully balanced.

other australian whites

Riesling is Australia's second most important grape in terms of quality white wine production. The Clare Valley produces mainly austere, dry, long-aging versions with pronounced mineral qualities. Good Sauvignon Blanc can also be found in Australia, though the Semillon grape tends to perform much better here, yielding mostly dry white wines with intriguing honey-lemon flavors. Producers in Western Australia in particular blend Sauvignon Blanc and Semillon into herb-scented white wines abbreviated as either SBS or SSB, depending on which grape dominates. The widely grown Portuguese grape Verdelho produces a few noteworthy wines that can display a lovely mix of citrus, herb and nut flavors.

other australian white recommendations

Big Woop! White Wine | 2008 | SOUTH EASTERN AUSTRALIA
★★★ $ (1 L) Winemaker Ben Riggs adds a bit of Pinot Gris to this outstanding Chardonnay-Viognier blend, achieving a rich, aromatic wine upheld by refreshing acidity. At around $15 for a full liter, it's an exceptional bargain.

Brokenwood Semillon | 2008 | HUNTER VALLEY
★★ $ $ Vibrant acidity, abundant ripe pear, zesty citrus and golden apple flavors and an ethereal delicacy mark this charming Hunter Valley Semillon.

Cullen Ephraim Clarke Sauvignon Blanc/Semillon | 2008 |
MARGARET RIVER
★★★ $ $ $ This lightly oaked blend of 81 percent Sauvignon Blanc and 19 percent Semillon is alive with gorgeous aromas of sweet lime zest and vanilla. Grapefruit and peach flavors dominate the long, citrus-laden finish.

d'Arenberg The Hermit Crab Viognier/Marsanne | 2008 |
ADELAIDE
★★★ $ $ Tropical fruit, honeysuckle and baking spice flavors abound in d'Arenberg's Rhône-style blend. Made with mostly Viognier and some Marsanne, it has a cleansing acidity—perfect for offsetting the waxy texture—which reverberates through the plush finish.

Kaesler Old Vine Semillon | 2008 | BAROSSA VALLEY
★ ★ $ $ Crisp, tangy grapefruit flavors characterize this Aussie white from start to finish. It's bright and broad on the palate, ending with an elegant dose of minerals.

Kilikanoon Mort's Block Watervale Riesling | 2009 |
CLARE VALLEY
★ ★ ★ $ $ Founded in 1997, Kilikanoon has come a long way in a relatively short time. This wine is a textbook example of crisp, dry and mineral-rich Clare Valley Riesling, and it's utterly delicious. Tart green apple, sweet pineapple and honeysuckle flavors are perfectly integrated and refined.

Penfolds Thomas Hyland Riesling | 2008 | ADELAIDE
★ ★ ★ $ Best known for its flagship wine Grange, Penfolds is capable of excellent wines across the price spectrum. This delightful white shows off bold flavors of ripe pear, apple and lime that are at once succulent and bright.

Petaluma Hanlin Hill Riesling | 2008 | CLARE VALLEY
★ ★ ★ $ $ There's an impressive purity to the fruit flavors and steely acidity in this terrific, multilayered Riesling. Lemon-lime zest, petrol and delicate white flower aromas pave the way for enticing pineapple and quince flavors.

Pewsey Vale Riesling | 2009 | EDEN VALLEY
★ ★ ★ $ $ Pewsey Vale was the first vineyard in Eden Valley, and it remains one of the finest, with a long tradition of excellent Riesling. Zippy and elegant, this combines pineapple and mineral flavors with a tangy, citrusy acidity.

Plantagenet Riesling | 2008 | GREAT SOUTHERN
★ ★ $ $ Great Southern—confusingly located in Western Australia—is not terribly well known, but wines like this illustrate the region's potential. Juicy melon, lime and nectarine flavors anchor this crisp, polished Riesling.

St. Hallett Riesling | 2008 | EDEN VALLEY
★ ★ ★ $ $ A razor-edged acidity gives this focused Riesling an incredibly lengthy finish after a burst of flinty lime and citrus flavors.

Woop Woop Verdelho | 2009 | SOUTH EASTERN AUSTRALIA
★ ★ $ Light-bodied and immensely gulpable, Woop Woop's Verdelho shows just how enjoyable this often underappreciated grape can be: Tart apple, citrus and tropical flavors are nicely woven together with mineral acidity throughout.

australian reds

Shiraz is Australia's claim to wine fame, though Cabernet Sauvignon is widely produced and performs well in many regions. Merlot plantings have increased significantly, but the grape has yet to yield results on a par with the country's Shiraz and Cabernet. There is a niche following for some high-quality Pinot Noirs from a handful of the country's cooler wine regions, while the more obscure varieties Grenache and Mourvèdre are gaining ground, especially in South Australia's McLaren Vale and Barossa Valley.

AUSTRALIAN REDS

cabernet sauvignon

Cabernet Sauvignon may be second to Shiraz in popularity among Australians, but it's responsible for many of the country's best reds. Australian Cabernets run the gamut from simple and light to complex and full-bodied; the finest are capable of extensive aging. Warmer regions tend to bring out berry and chocolate flavors, while cooler-climate areas like Western Australia's Margaret River produce more refined Cabernets. Tiny Coonawarra, with its distinctive "terra rossa" soil, is responsible for some of the country's greatest Cabernets. Australian winemakers blend Shiraz with Cabernet for everyday wines as well as iconic ones such as Penfolds Grange.

cabernet sauvignon recommendations

Angove Family Winemakers Vineyard Select | 2007 |
COONAWARRA
★★★ **$ $** Smooth and velvety tannins frame the spicy black currant flavors in this outstanding Cabernet. Notes of red peppers and juicy raspberries come through on the earthy finish.

Faldo | 2006 | **COONAWARRA**
★★ **$ $** Following the lead of fellow golfers-turned-winery-owners Greg Norman and Ernie Els, Nick Faldo established this estate in 2000. His 2006 Cabernet kicks off with cherries, raspberries and a hint of cocoa; a spice character comes through on the palate.

Heartland | 2008 | SOUTH AUSTRALIA

★ ★ $ $ An avalanche of mouthwatering blackberry, sage and dark chocolate flavors mark this red; the silky mouthfeel is bolstered by moderate tannins.

Henry's Drive Vignerons The Trial of John Montford | 2007 | PADTHAWAY

★ ★ ★ $ $ $ Named after the trial of an obscure 19th-century bandit, this Cabernet is thoroughly modern in style. Rich, ripe, and powerful, it still manages to exhibit a rare finesse amid flavors of wild blackberry, cherry and mint.

Jacob's Creek Reserve | 2006 | SOUTH AUSTRALIA

★ ★ $ There is a Chianti-like quality to this South Australian Cabernet in the form of dark cherry, bitter tea and earth flavors held together by dry, dusty tannins. The medium-long, full and juicy finish is unmistakably Australian.

Kangarilla Road | 2007 | MCLAREN VALE

★ ★ $ $ This wine is all about fruit: An explosion of cherries, mulberries and raspberries coats the palate, while nuances of herbs and a soft finish keep it balanced and enjoyable.

Penley Estate Phoenix | 2008 | COONAWARRA

★ ★ $ $ Sixteen months spent maturing in both new and old French oak barrels has endowed this full-bodied Cabernet with charming earth and tobacco notes, which are rounded out with blackberry and cherry flavors. Although its tannins are firm, it's approachable now.

AUSTRALIAN REDS

shiraz

Shiraz, Australia's most planted and beloved grape, is remarkably different from its counterpart in France, Syrah. With a more explosive array of concentrated berry flavors as well as pronounced spice notes, Shiraz is without a doubt Australia's defining wine. Grown in a variety of regions throughout the country, Shiraz is at its best in the Barossa Valley and McLaren Vale in South Australia, Hunter Valley in New South Wales and several Victoria regions. Shiraz is often aged in American oak (rather than French barrels), which seems to complement its jammy, ripe fruit flavors— and adds to its affordability.

shiraz recommendations

Blackbilly | 2007 | MCLAREN VALE
★ ★ ★ $ $ This beautiful, mouthwatering Shiraz displays a vibrant mix of blueberry and currant flavors wrapped in ample tannins. On the wonderfully complex, lingering finish, there are notes of black pepper and coffee.

Block 50 | 2007 | CENTRAL RANGES
★ $ A perfect everyday pour, this delivers bright raspberry, ripe plum and spicy-vanilla flavors bolstered by ripe tannins.

Château Tanunda Grand Barossa | 2007 | BAROSSA VALLEY
★ ★ $ $ Up-front berry and spice flavors define this well-crafted red; sweet vanilla tannins and a lovely earthiness complete the package.

The Chook Shiraz/Viognier | 2008 | SOUTH AUSTRALIA
★ ★ $ $ Winemaker Ben Riggs and Tony Parkinson, proprietor of Penny's Hill, collaborate to make this wine. It's rich and round, with luscious dark berry flavors, and the addition of 6 percent Viognier comes through in notes of apricots and the smooth mouthfeel.

Cimicky Trumps | 2008 | BAROSSA VALLEY
★ ★ $ $ This amped-up red has a terrific concentration of cherry, raspberry and plum. A hint of peppery spice adds complexity to the solid core of fruit, while plush tannins hold it all together.

Cluster M45 | 2006 | HEATHCOTE
★ ★ ★ $ $ $ $ This splendid Shiraz has an impressive pedigree: It's the result of an intercontinental partnership between Jasper Hill and Michel Chapoutier, the famous Rhône producer. Notes of earth, barnyard and game underscore dark cherry flavors, while plush tannins add depth and structure.

Domaine Terlato & Chapoutier Shiraz/Viognier | 2007 | VICTORIA
★ ★ ★ ★ $ $ Globe-trotting Michel Chapoutier has a hand in this excellent wine, too. Working with American importer Anthony Terlato, he has produced a sleek wine full of fruit—blueberry, raspberry and raisins—as well as nuances of dark chocolate and spice.

Expatriate | 2007 | MCLAREN VALE
★ ★ ★ ★ $ $ $ This red, produced by Corrina Rayment, shows both power and refinement, the result of fruit from 65-year-old vines. Brimming with blueberry, plum, vanilla, leather and spice flavors, it's unbelievably smooth and lingers on the palate.

Henry's Drive | 2007 | PADTHAWAY
★ ★ ★ $ $ $ Fans of hedonistic wines will appreciate this full-bodied Shiraz. It displays floral aromatics alongside a core of raspberry and red currant flavors and cushy tannins for balance.

Jasper Hill Georgia's Paddock | 2006 | HEATHCOTE
★ ★ ★ $ $ $ $ Jasper Hill makes its wines from grapes grown biodynamically, without vine grafting or irrigation. The result is a youthful red that is bright yet concentrated and full of cherry and raspberry flavors that are fused with brawny tannins.

Jenke Vineyards | 2006 | BAROSSA
★ ★ $ $ Red currant, sweet oak and anise aromas are woven with licorice, mocha and blackberry flavors in this well-knit Shiraz.

The Lackey | 2007 |
SOUTH AUSTRALIA
★ ★ $ An appealing earthiness and leathery tannins augment the classic sweet blackberry, blueberry and raspberry flavors in this full-bodied Shiraz made by Kilikanoon.

Layer Cake | 2009 |
SOUTH AUSTRALIA
★ ★ ★ $ A truly phenomenal value, Layer Cake's Shiraz boasts rich, complex flavors of fresh plum and sage and a satiny finish—a lot of sophistication for the low price.

Massena The Eleventh Hour
| 2006 | BAROSSA VALLEY
★ ★ ★ $ $ $ The 60-year-old vines used to make this wine were almost bulldozed, until—at "the eleventh hour"—the grower listened to Massena's pleas to leave them. This is huge, full of berry flavors tightly wound with minerals and tannins.

Morse Code | 2008 | PADTHAWAY
★ $ This crowd-pleasing Shiraz made by Henry's Drive is marked by soft tannins, dark berry flavors and notes of tobacco.

Mr. Riggs The Gaffer | 2008 | MCLAREN VALE
★ ★ ★ $ $ Heady, floral aromas meld with huckleberry and plum flavors in this massive wine. Though it's big, the well-grained tannins and focused finish ensure that it's anything but clumsy.

taste here now

GIANT STEPS WINERY
Founder Phil Sexton set up an industrial-chic complex where the winery occupies one side of the building while the other side houses a bistro, coffee roaster, bread baker, pizza maker and cheese room. Visitors can taste the Giant Steps wines as well as bottles from Sexton's less expensive label, Innocent Bystander. *Healesville, Yarra Valley, Victoria; giant-steps.com.au*

Occam's Razor | 2006 | **HEATHCOTE**

★★★ $ $ $ Strong tannins hold this wine together and frame the flavors of blackberries and black cherries that ooze onto the palate. Notes of bay leaf come through on the powerful finish.

Penley Estate Special Select | 2005 | **COONAWARRA**

★★★ $ $ $ This brazenly decadent Shiraz is all about bright, juicy blackberry and blueberry flavors. Hints of earth, coffee and leather emerge with time, followed by firm tannins.

Piping Shrike | 2008 | **BAROSSA VALLEY**

★★ $ $ The pronounced oak notes in this red add nice undertones of earth and spice to flavors of cherry, plum and currant.

Rocky Gully Shiraz/Viognier | 2007 | **FRANKLAND RIVER**

★★★ $ $ Plush and spicy, this shows blackberry, white pepper and violet flavors, dusty tannins and a juicy, savory finish.

star producers
australian shiraz

Barossa Valley Estate

Among the valley's most esteemed wineries, BVE is a cooperative of 80 longtime Shiraz growers who have joined forces to make top-notch wine.

Clarendon Hills

Francophile winemaker Roman Bratasiuk labels his wines "Syrah" rather than "Shiraz." Made from old vines, his superb Astralis is the most sought-after of his wines.

Elderton

Elderton's flagship wine, Command, is one of Australia's most coveted reds. The estate's Cameron and Allister Ashmead are more gently priced.

Henschke

If the price tag for Henschke's acclaimed and hard-to-find Hill of Grace Shiraz is too steep, its sibling wine Mount Edelstone is a delicious stand-in.

Jasper Hill

Originating in Victoria, not far from some of the better-known Shiraz regions in South Australia, Jasper Hill wines are as distinctive as their *terroir*.

Penfolds

Penfolds Grange is one of the world's most famous wines, and it's priced accordingly. But this Australian pioneer makes many other delicious wines for every budget and taste.

Shirvington | 2007 | MCLAREN VALE

★ ★ ★ ★ $ $ $ $ This wine is dense and incredibly dark: An opulent, rich palate showcases blueberry, plum and baking spice flavors. Notes of fragrant vanilla and the polished mouthfeel are evidence of its 14-month oak maturation.

The Standish Single Vineyard | 2006 | BAROSSA VALLEY

★ ★ ★ ★ $ $ $ $ This inky Barossa Shiraz exudes black cherry and blackberry aromas and nicely concentrated flavors of spice, coffee and tobacco. The supple finish is held up by firm tannins.

Taltarni T Series | 2006 | VICTORIA

★ $ Made with grapes from the cooler climates of Victoria, this medium-bodied red is full of blackberry, currant and sweet spice.

Thorn-Clarke Shotfire | 2008 | BAROSSA VALLEY

★ ★ ★ $ $ Somewhere between ripe plum aromas and spicy currant flavors lies the brilliance of this Barossa Shiraz. It's perfectly balanced, with a sweet vanilla essence shining throughout.

Two Hands Gnarly Dudes | 2008 | BAROSSA VALLEY

★ ★ ★ $ $ Black currant and persimmon flavors are accented by cinnamon and allspice in this alluring wine, which is fleshed out with integrated tannins.

2 Up | 2008 | SOUTH AUSTRALIA

★ ★ ★ $ 2 Up takes its name from a traditional Australian gambling game. In spite of its whimsical moniker, this is a complex wine, composed of ebullient raspberry and strawberry jam flavors, a plush, spicy mouthfeel and an invigorating acidity.

Wyndham Estate George Wyndham Founder's Reserve
| 2005 | SOUTH AUSTRALIA

★ ★ ★ $ $ This wickedly delicious Shiraz has aromas of cassis, pomegranate and mocha. Plums and spice dominate the palate throughout the moderately tannic, spicy finish.

Yalumba The Y Series Shiraz/Viognier | 2008 |
SOUTH AUSTRALIA

★ ★ $ Yalumba's low-priced Shiraz delivers spice, apricot and berry flavors and a soft finish (thanks to the addition of Viognier).

Zonte's Footstep Single Site Shiraz/Viognier | 2007 |
LANGHORNE CREEK

★ ★ $ There is nothing shy about this powerhouse wine. Bold flavors of tar, licorice and blackberry are woven with notes of raspberry jam and fine-grained tannins.

other australian reds

Australia's unheralded red grapes are Grenache and Mourvèdre, both originally from France's Rhône Valley. Grenache displays many of the same fruit-forward characteristics as Shiraz but with a lighter body, while Mourvèdre shows a smokier, spicier composition. Many vintners combine the two with Shiraz in blends labeled "GSM." Pinot Noir has been planted in several wine regions throughout Australia, though success is restricted mainly to the island of Tasmania and Victoria's Yarra Valley. Merlot production has increased in South Australia over the last decade.

other australian red recommendations

d'Arenberg The Stump Jump Grenache/Shiraz/Mourvèdre | 2008 | SOUTH AUSTRALIA

★★★ $ D'Arenberg named this range of great everyday wines in honor of the stump-jumping plow that made planting vineyards in Australia possible. In the GSM blend, there's a lovely minerality woven with ripe cherry, blackberry and raspberry flavors that are intense and delicious.

Deakin Estate Merlot | 2007 | VICTORIA

★ $ Although Deakin released its first wine in 1994, some of its vines are much older. The 2007 is a great value, packed with approachable, silky-textured flavors of berries and cherries.

Elderton Tantalus Shiraz/Cabernet | 2006 | SOUTH AUSTRALIA

★★ $ $ Elderton fashions a standout Shiraz-Cabernet blend here, marked by peppery blackberry and licorice flavors. Moderate tannins support the plush, smooth palate.

Epicurean Bistro Grenache | 2007 | MCLAREN VALE

★★ $ Aussie winemaker Stephen Pannell sourced the grapes for this alluring Grenache from some of the finest McLaren Vale vineyards. Notes of blackberry and spice meet sweet raspberry flavors in the soft finish.

Heartland Stickleback Red | 2008 | SOUTH AUSTRALIA

★ $ Surprisingly complex for its price, this unique blend of Shiraz, Cabernet, Dolcetto and Lagrein has a bright, peppery nose. Dried cherry, cranberry and spice emerge on the palate.

Hewitson Miss Harry | 2008 | BAROSSA VALLEY

★★ $ $ Dean Hewitson has made wine in France and Oregon, and his experience is clearly evident in this tasty blend: Shiraz, Grenache, Mourvèdre and Cinsault come together to offer earthy, forest floor nuances amidst juicy blackberry and cherry flavors.

Hope Estate Merlot | 2008 | HUNTER VALLEY

★★ $ Pharmacist-turned-winemaker Michael Hope and winemaker James Campkin craft a great Merlot, dominated by cherry and strawberry and notes of dusty sage on the soft, pleasurable finish.

Inkberry Mountain Estate Shiraz/Cabernet | 2008 | CENTRAL RANGES

★★ $ Ripe blackberry flavors have a kick of spice in Inkberry's Shiraz-Cabernet blend. There's a concentration on the lingering finish, and a bright, mouthwatering character that can be attributed to the intense sunlight on this high-altitude vineyard.

Innocent Bystander Pinot Noir | 2008 | VICTORIA

★★ $ $ Phil Sexton's Pinot Noir is bright and juicy, with surprisingly dense cherry and berry flavors.

John Duval Wines Plexus | 2007 | BAROSSA VALLEY

★★ $ $ $ John Duval spent 29 years as a winemaker at Penfolds before striking out on his own. This is Plexus's fifth vintage, and it shows beautiful cherry, cranberry and pepper flavors.

Kaesler Stonehorse Shiraz/Grenache/Mourvèdre | 2007 | BAROSSA VALLEY

★★★ $ $ The Kaeslers first planted vines in the Barossa Valley in 1893. Today, winemaker Reid Bosward is at the helm, and his medium-bodied 2007 is a focused, juicy wine with equal parts earth, tobacco, blackberry and spice.

Kilikanoon Killerman's Run Shiraz/Grenache | 2007 | SOUTH AUSTRALIA

★★ $ $ Kilikanoon playfully named this Shiraz-Grenache blend after Mr. Killerman, a famous local hermit. Fresh and dried cherry flavors are underscored by mocha nuances.

Penfolds Bin 138 Grenache/Mourvèdre/Shiraz | 2007 | BAROSSA VALLEY

★★★ $ $ Penfolds made their bin number wines exclusively for company directors until 1959, when they began releasing them to the public. This Bin 138 is full of classic blackberry, plum and dusty spice notes held together with fine-grained tannins.

Peter Lehmann of the Barossa Clancy's Shiraz/Cabernet Sauvignon/Merlot | 2007 | BAROSSA

★★ $ $ Peter Lehmann offers a twist on the region's standard blend of Shiraz and Cabernet with the addition of Merlot, which creates a balanced wine that has hints of sun-dried tomato and herbs infusing flavors of dark berries and spice.

Pillar Box Red | 2008 | PADTHAWAY

★ $ Named for Australia's elaborately designed postboxes, Henry's Drive Vignerons' terrific Pillar Box wines are nicely affordable. The 2008 shows meaty, savory flavors alongside ripe blackberries.

Rutherglen Estates Red | 2007 | RUTHERGLEN

★ $ Rutherglen's estate-grown blend of Shiraz and Durif grapes is firm in texture, with pretty berry and dusty spice flavors.

Shoofly Aussie Salute | 2007 | ADELAIDE

★★ $ Veteran winemaker Ben Riggs has crafted a luscious, mouth-filling blend of Grenache, Shiraz and Viognier. Rich with plum and cherry flavors, it has a note of fire-roasted beef on the smooth finish.

Taltarni Three Monks Cabernet/Merlot | 2006 | VICTORIA

★★ $ $ Owned by descendants of French wine merchants, Taltarni brings together Old World traditions with New World innovation. Their 2006 Three Monks blend reveals spicy aromas, soft berry and herb flavors and well-defined tannins.

Tapanappa Whalebone Vineyard Cabernet/Shiraz | 2005 | WRATTONBULLY

★★★★ $ $ $ $ Tapanappa's Whalebone blend features mostly Cabernet Sauvignon, along with Shiraz and Cabernet Franc. A mouth-ful of cocoa, spice, currants and blackberries, it displays fine tannins and a black pepper–infused finish.

Tir Na N'og Old Vines Grenache | 2008 | MCLAREN VALE

★★★★ $ $ A tremendous value, this old-vine Grenache offers a perfect mélange of refined blackberry, cherry and black pepper fla-vors. Its impressive depth and complexity, along with a lengthy finish and solid tannins, guarantee it has a long life in the cellar.

Torbreck Cuvée Juveniles | 2008 | BAROSSA VALLEY

★★★★ $ $ Winemaker David Powell named this Torbreck cuvée in honor of his Rhône-variety-loving friend Tim Johnston, who owns the Juveniles wine bar in Paris. A gorgeous blend of Grenache, Mataro and Shiraz, it's a lot of wine for the price, brimming with raspberry, pep-per, dried cherry and bittersweet chocolate flavors.

Two Hands Yesterday's Hero Grenache | 2008 |
BAROSSA VALLEY

★ ★ ★ **$ $ $** Michael Twelftree and Richard Mintz—the "two hands" responsible for the wines—founded their *négociant* business in 1999. Their mouthwatering 2008 Grenache offers silky and alluring dried cherry, blackberry and mocha flavors that show impressive length.

Wakefield Promised Land Shiraz/Cabernet | 2006 |
SOUTH AUSTRALIA

★ ★ **$** Wakefield's vineyards were once part of an ancient seabed, hence the seahorse on the label. From that fertile soil comes a well-made wine with black pepper and juicy blueberry flavors.

Wallace by Ben Glaetzer Shiraz/Grenache | 2008 |
BAROSSA VALLEY

★ ★ ★ **$ $** The grapes for this traditional Aussie blend are grown in the loamy soils of Barossa's Ebenezer subregion. The result is an elegant wine dominated by red cherry, raspberry and sage notes.

news from australia

Region to Watch

Mornington Peninsula, a gorgeous little strip of land lined with soft, sandy beaches in Victoria, just south of Melbourne, is home to around 50 wineries, many of them specializing in Pinot Noir and Chardonnay. One of the peninsula's many attractions is the Montalto winery, where the picnic staff will deliver meals to private spots set throughout the property. At Moorooduc Estate, owner Richard McIntyre bakes delectable sourdough bread in an outdoor wood-fired oven to sell in the winery's tasting room.

Winemakers to Watch

The Mac Forbes winery focuses on Pinot Noirs in the Yarra Valley and Rieslings in the Strathbogie Ranges, the latter a little-known area about two hours northeast of Melbourne.

Michael Dhillon is the winemaker of his family's Bindi estate in the hilly Macedon Ranges region, Australia's coolest area, just north of Melbourne. His stellar wines are wonderfully complex.

William Downie, former winemaker at Domaine Hubert Lignier in Burgundy, brings that experience to bear on his eponymous Pinot Noirs.

new zealand

Few countries are as closely identified with one grape as New Zealand is with Sauvignon Blanc. Though this variety represents more than half of the nation's wine output, wine production here is extremely varied, in fact. New Zealand's more than 600 wineries also make excellent Pinot Noir, Cabernet Sauvignon, Riesling and Chardonnay.

Principal Wine Region

Kumeu
Waiheke Island
Auckland

Tasman Sea

Gisborne

Hawkes Bay

Wairarapa
Martinborough
Nelson
Blenheim
Wellington
Marlborough

Waipara

Canterbury · Christchurch

Central Otago
Queenstown

South Pacific Ocean

New Zealand: An Overview

Despite the challenges of a highly unpredictable maritime climate, both of New Zealand's main islands, the North Island and the South Island, produce great wine. Sauvignon Blanc dominates the Marlborough region, on the north-eastern tip of the South Island. Pinot Noir also excels in Marlborough, as well as in cool Central Otago (also on the South Island) and in Martinborough, near the southern tip of the North Island. Many North Island producers focus on Bordeaux grapes; some make Syrah as well.

New Zealand Wine Labels

Labels generally list region, grape and vintage, and in some cases vineyard name. The term *Reserve* may be used to designate higher-quality wines but has no legal meaning.

new zealand whites

New Zealand has long been known as a white wine country. Its vivacious Sauvignon Blanc created a worldwide sensation in the 1980s, became firmly established in the 1990s and remains New Zealand's leading wine. Chardonnay is the second most planted white, and thrives in the warmer Gisborne region. Pinot Gris and Riesling are grown in much smaller quantities, yet make some standout whites.

NEW ZEALAND WHITES

sauvignon blanc

Most Americans are familiar with New Zealand Sauvignon Blancs: lively wines with invigorating flavors of grass, lime and tropical fruit. Over two-thirds of the country's Sauvignon Blanc is planted in Marlborough, on the South Island, and its wines have come to typify this style. North Island versions tend to be riper and more fruit-focused, but they are still generally unoaked, fresh and crisp.

sauvignon blanc recommendations

Brancott B (Letter Series) | 2009 | MARLBOROUGH
★ ★ $ $ Big, juicy and bright, with tropical fruit and tart berry aromas, this Brancott displays a lovely mix of bell pepper and green apple flavors, firm minerals and lively acidity on the palate.

Cloudy Bay | 2009 | MARLBOROUGH
★ ★ $ $ This producer kick-started the New Zealand Sauvignon Blanc craze in America. With a generous body and supple yet crisp flavors of pink grapefruit, guava and mango, the winery's 2009 Sauvignon Blanc is wonderfully balanced and delicious.

Cupcake Vineyards | 2009 | MARLBOROUGH
★ $ California-based Cupcake Vineyards makes wines in regions throughout the world. As tasty as lemonade, their refreshing Sauvignon Blanc is uplifted by hints of grapefruit and grass.

star producers
new zealand sauvignon blanc

Brancott
Brancott helped establish Marlborough Sauvignon Blanc as New Zealand's signature white wine by planting the region's first modern vineyards.

Cloudy Bay
One of the first world-famous New Zealand producers, Cloudy Bay crafts wines that recall white Burgundies in their elegance and complexity.

Craggy Range Winery
For its excellent Sauvignon Blancs and Bordeaux-style reds, Craggy Range has emerged as one of the country's most dynamic wineries.

Jackson Estate
Winemaker Mike Paterson endows each of Jackson Estate's four Sauvignon Blancs with a unique personality.

Kim Crawford Wines
This is one of the country's largest and best producers. Made from grapes grown in regions on both islands, its wines are always expressive, balanced and delicious.

Spy Valley Wines
Bryan and Jan Johnson launched their acclaimed label to showcase the great fruit from their Waihopai Valley (a.k.a. "Spy Valley") vineyards.

Dashwood | 2009 | MARLBOROUGH
★ ★ $ Peaches, layered with flavors of tangerine, dominate in this gorgeous wine. It has a bright acidity and a juicy, crisp finish.

Glazebrook Regional Reserve | 2009 | MARLBOROUGH
★ ★ $ Fuller-bodied than most Sauvignon Blancs, this beauty starts out with flinty mineral aromas followed by a flavor-packed palate of bright citrus and cantaloupe and a zesty lime finish.

Jackson Estate Stich | 2009 | MARLBOROUGH
★ ★ $ $ Named for founder John "Stich" Stichbury, this Sauvignon will appeal to fans of a slightly plush, ripe style. White peach and pineapple alternate with herbs, pepper and minerals on the round palate.

Kato | 2008 | MARLBOROUGH
★ ★ $ Loosely translated, *kato* means "to harvest" in the Maori language. This wine, with its ample ripe passion fruit flavors and notes of green pepper and chive, is a superb value.

Kim Crawford | 2009 | MARLBOROUGH
★ ★ ★ $ $ Kim Crawford harvests its Sauvignon Blanc grapes at night so they are naturally chilled before fermentation. The wine's upfront tropical fruit and grassy, nettle aromas are nicely balanced by lemon curd flavors that follow through on the silky-textured finish.

Martinborough | 2008 | MARTINBOROUGH
★ ★ ★ $ $ This cool-climate North Island producer may be famous for Pinot Noir, but winemaker Claire Mulholland's whites are also spectacular. This pineapple-scented Sauvignon Blanc bursts with lime and grapefruit flavors that are supported by a focused acidity.

Matua Valley | 2009 | MARLBOROUGH
★ $ Like a field of newly cut grass, this easy-drinking, lime-flavored wine is incredibly fresh. Matua is one of the region's oldest wineries and always provides great value.

Mount Nelson | 2009 | MARLBOROUGH
★ ★ ★ $ $ Marchese Lodovico Antinori made Sauvignon Blanc at Tuscany's Ornellaia before launching this New Zealand project with his brother Piero. The vivid, limeade quality on display here is filled out with zesty grapefruit and green herb notes.

Nobilo Icon | 2009 | MARLBOROUGH
★ ★ ★ $ $ From one of the area's larger producers comes this highly aromatic Sauvignon brimming with gooseberry, tropical fruit and bell pepper. Flavors of pineapple, fresh grass and citrus are mouthwatering and juicy through the crisp, flinty finish.

Saint Clair Family Estate Pioneer Block 1 Foundation
| 2009 | MARLBOROUGH

★★★★ $ $ Power and elegance are wonderfully balanced in this well-made wine. Concentrated and intense, it reveals layers and layers of flavors—nettle, dried pineapple, citrus zest, blackberry and gravel—all upheld by a bright acidity.

Wairau River | 2009 | MARLBOROUGH

★★ $ With highlights of tropical fruit and a touch of sweetness, this medium-bodied Sauvignon bursts with berry, tangerine and grapefruit flavors.

other new zealand whites

Chardonnay is grown in many regions on both islands. Although skilled winemakers have worked hard to produce high-quality Rieslings in New Zealand, the grape still ranks fourth in total acreage. Third-ranked Pinot Gris is responsible for a growing number of excellent whites.

other new zealand white recommendations

The Crossings Unoaked Chardonnay | 2008 | MARLBOROUGH
★★ $ $ Pleasantly fresh, lean and simple, this medium-bodied Chardonnay offers a mix of zippy green apple and peach flavors and a crisp, bone-dry finish.

Jules Taylor Wines Pinot Gris | 2008 | MARLBOROUGH
★ $ A decidedly New World take on the Pinot Gris grape, this lean, brash wine has a medium body, lots of grapefruit and citrus zest flavors and a lively spicy character.

Mohua Pinot Gris | 2009 | CENTRAL OTAGO
★★ $ $ Fresh, fruit-filled and downright delicious, this value label from Peregrine shows apple, pear and ripe melon flavors enlivened by a bracing, lime-infused acidity.

Spy Valley Wines Envoy Pinot Gris | 2008 | MARLBOROUGH
★★★ $ $ $ Pinot Gris takes on a rich, plush quality here, thanks to partial fermentation in oak and malolactic fermentation. It is packed with wonderfully ripe flavors of poached pear and figs, while notes of cinnamon, cloves and nutmeg add complexity to the creamy, full-bodied palate.

new zealand reds

New Zealand's efforts in red wine have been focused mainly on Pinot Noir, a grape that yields exceptional results here. New Zealand winemakers also produce many refined Cabernets and Merlots as well as some noteworthy Syrahs.

NEW ZEALAND REDS

pinot noir

In plantings, Pinot Noir is second only to Sauvignon Blanc in New Zealand. This notoriously finicky red variety thrives on both islands, thanks to cool temperatures moderated by the ocean's influence. On the North Island, Pinot Noir performs well in Martinborough. On the South Island, it does well in Marlborough and excels in Central Otago, in the southern part of the island, where the country's finest Pinot Noirs are made from low-yielding vines that produce intensely concentrated yet elegant wines.

pinot noir recommendations

Coopers Creek | 2008 | **MARLBOROUGH**
★★★ **$ $** Noted winemaker Kim Crawford helped put Coopers Creek on the map 20 years ago before starting his own label. Since 1998 Simon Nunns has been crafting outstanding wines here, like this steely, crisp, lean Pinot, with its rich berry flavors, chalky mouthfeel and minerally finish.

Crown Range | 2008 | **CENTRAL OTAGO**
★ **$ $** Aromas of autumn leaves, herbs and berries lead to lively flavors of tart cherry, plum and baking spices in this fresh, delicious red.

Felton Road | 2008 | **CENTRAL OTAGO**
★★★ **$ $ $** Felton Road's Bannockburn vineyards in Central Otago are among the southernmost vineyards on the globe. Mouthwatering acidity runs through the beautiful cherry fruit, black pepper and dusty spice flavors of this delicious wine.

Grove Mill | 2008 | **MARLBOROUGH**
★★ **$ $** Grove Mill is a "carboNZero" winery, boasting a minimal carbon footprint. Its Pinot is impressive, full of smoky black plum, cherry and toasted oak flavors; notes of mocha show on the bright finish.

Jules Taylor Wines | 2008 | MARLBOROUGH

★★★ $ $ Taylor worked at Kim Crawford, Saint Clair and Cape Campbell before starting her own label. Her experience shows here: Wonderfully spicy aromas of cinnamon, star anise, clove and candied ginger are followed by flavors of bright berry, orange zest and cola.

Mana NZ | 2008 | MARLBOROUGH

★★ $ $ This wine is made just for the U.S. market. Cherries and blackberries explode on the palate, accompanied by aromatic hints of chocolate, earth and leather. It has great structure, with fine tannins framing the citrus-tinged finish.

Mud House | 2008 | CENTRAL OTAGO

★★ $ $ A single estate vineyard grew the grapes for this sophisticated, light-bodied wine. Intriguing clove, spice, berry, tobacco and herb aromas are followed by fresh, exuberant fruit flavors and a hint of gingerbread.

news from new zealand

Vintage Notes

The 2009 vintage was terrific for New Zealand's top-value Sauvignon Blanc, yielding many excellent bottles for $15 or less. The stellar 2007 Pinot Noirs are great now but will also age well. Thanks to the small size of the crop, the 2007 Pinot Noirs are unusually concentrated.

Grape on the Rise

Syrah is growing in popularity among New Zealand winemakers. It has become increasingly important in the Hawkes Bay region, where many producers are pulling out Cabernet vines to make room for the Rhône variety. The region's Syrahs tend to be terrifically peppery— more reminiscent of Rhône versions than the jammy style of Australian Shiraz.

Winemakers to Watch

In 2009 Kevin Judd left his post at Cloudy Bay vineyards, where he had worked for 25 years. He has now released his own 2009 Marlborough Sauvignon Blanc under the label Greywacke (a reference to a local soil type) and is also working with Pinot Gris, Pinot Noir and Chardonnay. Judd is borrowing winery space from two other Cloudy Bay alums, James Healy and Ivan Sutherland, at their new property, Dog Point Vineyard.

Peregrine | 2007 | CENTRAL OTAGO

★ ★ ★ $ $ $ One of the most well-respected names in New Zealand crafts this solidly built, velvety red with aromas of dense blackberries and plums. Hints of tar, flowers and spice show on the medium-bodied palate, which is supported by supple tannins and minerals.

Rippon | 2007 | LAKE WANAKA, CENTRAL OTAGO

★ ★ ★ $ $ $ Rippon's tightly wound Pinot takes a bit of time in the glass to unfurl tart cherry, black fruit, cedar and spice aromas. Made from nonirrigated vines and fermented with indigenous yeasts, it's incredibly fresh, with flavors of plums, cassis and graphite.

Stoneleigh | 2008 | MARLBOROUGH

★ ★ $ $ Pretty cherry flavors are rounded out with oak, spice and cola; a tangy acidity gives the juicy, medium-bodied palate a nice jolt.

other new zealand reds

Cabernet Sauvignon and Merlot are the most widely planted red grapes on most of the North Island; more than half the vines are in Hawkes Bay. Alone or blended, these grapes can create elegant, Bordeaux-like reds. New Zealand produces small amounts of other Bordeaux varieties—chiefly Cabernet Franc and Malbec—and increasingly Syrah.

other new zealand red recommendations

Craggy Range Te Kahu Gimblett Gravels Vineyard | 2007 | HAWKES BAY

★ ★ ★ $ $ Super-ripe and luscious, with exotic aromas of sandal-wood, baking spice, dried cherries and cassis, Craggy Range's stellar blend of Merlot, Cabernet Franc, Cabernet Sauvignon, Malbec and Petit Verdot oozes dark fruit bolstered by ultrafine tannins.

Kennedy Point Syrah | 2008 | WAIHEKE ISLAND

★ ★ $ $ This distinctive, juicy Waiheke Island Syrah is not a power-house but delivers ample red fruit and violet flavors underlined by savory spice and well-integrated tannins.

Man o' War Syrah | 2008 | WAIHEKE ISLAND

★ ★ $ $ Funky, smoky and meaty, with peppercorn and exotic spice notes, this Syrah shows excellent character, complete with peppery red fruit flavors.

argentina

Argentina's status as a major wine producer is due largely to the appeal of its signature grape, Malbec. In the U.S., Malbec sales are among the fastest-growing of all red wines. But as the world's fifth-largest wine producer, Argentina also offers a range of other excellent wines, both red and white.

Principal Wine Region

CHILE

South Pacific Ocean

Salta
• Cafayate

ARGENTINA

La Rioja

Aconcagua
Casablanca
• Valparaíso
San Juan
☆ Santiago

Maipo
Rapel
• Colchagua
Mendoza   Buenos Aires ☆

Curicó
•Maipú
Maule
•Luján

Concepción
•Tupungato

Mendoza

South Atlantic Ocean

Río Negro
•
Neuquén

Argentina: An Overview

Argentina's wine regions enjoy both an abundance of sun and a reliable source of irrigation from the Andes mountains. The most internationally recognized of Argentina's wine regions is the central region of Mendoza, responsible for more than 80 percent of the country's wine production. Large and remarkably diverse, Mendoza produces both the intense Malbecs of Maipú and Luján de Cuyo (Argentina's oldest established wine region) and the more elegant reds of the Uco Valley. To the north, Salta province encompasses some of the highest-altitude vineyards in the world; Salta's Cafayate Valley yields some terrific white wines. La Rioja and San Juan are traditional wine regions moving quickly from bulk production to quality winemaking. The Río Negro and Neuquén areas in Patagonia are seeing major investments in new, modern wineries.

Argentine Wine Labels

Most Argentine wine labels identify grape variety, the region where the grapes were grown, the producer's name and the vintage. Producers often use the terms *Reserva* or *Reserve* on higher-quality wines, though these terms have no regulated or legal meaning.

argentine whites

Argentina's most distinctive white grape is Torrontés, which makes floral, light-bodied wines; Cafayate and parts of Mendoza both produce great examples. Though Torrontés sales have been rising steadily, Chardonnay is still the country's leading white wine export. Produced in most of Argentina's wine regions, these Chardonnays range in style from lightly oaked, light-bodied and refreshing to full-bodied, decadent and creamy. Sauvignon Blanc is the other white wine of real significance in Argentina. Pinot Gris (Pinot Grigio), Riesling, Semillon and Viognier play minor roles.

argentine white recommendations

Acordeón Torrontés | 2009 | CAFAYATE VALLEY
★ ★ $ A bold acidity gives this aromatic wine a Sauvignon Blanc–like character. Honeysuckle, peach and passion fruit flavors round out the palate, and notes of lime zest and minerals come in on the finish.

Alamos Torrontés | 2009 | SALTA
★ $ A value label from the Catena family, this light-bodied Torrontés is fresh and clean on the palate, with a fluffy lemon-cupcake quality. Its touch of sweetness is nicely balanced with lemon-lime acidity.

Altivo Reserva Chardonnay/Viognier | 2008 | UCO VALLEY
★ ★ $ $ Launched by Eugenio Bustos, an estate with a century-long heritage, this modern-style blend evinces Argentina's current climate of experimentation. Beautiful aromas of fruit, flowers and spice lead to a lively yet plush palate of citrus, melon and exotic spice.

Argento Reserva Torrontés | 2008 | SALTA
★ ★ $ $ This is a generous Torrontés, bursting with citrus and stone-fruit flavors laced with fresh herbal notes on the palate. Though full-bodied and rich, it shows a bright, zesty finish.

Catena Chardonnay | 2008 | MENDOZA
★ ★ $ $ Catena combines grapes from three high-altitude vineyards to craft this wine, which achieves a nice complexity for the price. Flavors of crisp apple, fig, pineapple, honey and butter are woven with vanilla and spice and finish fresh on the generous, balanced palate.

Colomé Torrontés | 2009 | CALCHAQUÍ VALLEY
★ ★ $ Made from grapes grown on 30- to 60-year-old vines and aged in stainless steel for three months, this lively yet delicate white displays effusive floral, passion fruit and pineapple aromas. Fruity, fresh citrus flavors are underlined by a razor-sharp acidity.

Crios de Susana Balbo Torrontés | 2009 | SALTA
★ ★ ★ $ Always a standout, the Crios Torrontés is highly aromatic, with rose petal, white peach and orange aromas joined by flavors of honeyed peaches, pears and tropical fruits. The full-bodied palate is well structured, its fruitiness offset by a lovely acidity.

Familia Zuccardi Santa Julia Torrontés | 2009 | MENDOZA
★ ★ $ While not quite as aromatic as many, this Torrontés offers a nice core of peach and nectarine flavors. Made from organic grapes, it is medium-bodied and has a vibrant, citrusy acidity and a pleasing mix of mint, thyme and bay leaf on the finish.

Grazioso Torrontés | 2008 | MENDOZA

★ $ This organic wine is a great value: Alpine herb and thyme notes add aromatic complexity to flavors of plums and peaches. On the palate, it offers a slick, rounded mouthfeel with a dry finish.

Inacayal Vineyards Torrontés | 2009 | MENDOZA

★ ★ $ Light-bodied and lovely, this Mendoza Torrontés offers hints of honey and very ripe fruit flavors in the form of pink grapefruit and zesty orange. Notes of fresh-picked herbs and a touch of tannin complete the finish.

Salentein Reserve Chardonnay | 2008 | UCO VALLEY

★ ★ ★ ★ $ $ Hailing from Mendoza's cool Uco Valley, this Chardonnay offers dense aromas of apricot, golden raisin and dates underscored by a whiff of nutmeg. The gorgeous palate, with its seductive spice, is reminiscent of poached pear and honey-coated baked apple; a lively acidity keeps the full body nicely balanced and fresh.

Tilia Chardonnay | 2008 | MENDOZA

★ ★ $ The highly regarded Bodegas Esmeralda makes this delicious value offering. About 30 percent of the wine is aged in oak for five months, which imparts touches of smoky oak and butter throughout, while the palate abounds with stone fruits, figs and citrus.

Trivento Reserve Torrontés | 2009 | MENDOZA

★ $ Light and fresh, with papaya, passion fruit and melon aromas, a featherweight body and super-crisp acidity, this white makes a great aperitif wine.

argentine reds

In the 1980s and 1990s, Argentina, like most New World winegrowing countries, focused on Cabernet Sauvignon. Today, while Cabernet remains an important grape here, many of Argentina's vintners have wisely chosen to promote their iconic red wine, Malbec. A Bordeaux native, the Malbec grape is a minor player in France these days, but thrives throughout Argentina, where it yields robust wines full of intense fruit flavors that are concentrated by oak aging. Bonarda, another popular Argentine red grape, makes pleasant, cherry-flavored, medium-bodied reds. In the San Juan and La Rioja regions, Syrah succeeds alongside Malbec, while in Patagonia, Pinot Noir shows great promise.

argentine red recommendations

Barda Pinot Noir | 2008 | PATAGONIA–RÍO NEGRO
★ ★ ★ $ $ Critics are buzzing about the potential of Pinot Noir in Argentina's Patagonia region, and this is a perfect example of why. Expertly balanced and wonderfully complex, it displays waves of delicious fruit, earth and herbs.

BenMarco Malbec | 2008 | MENDOZA
★ ★ $ $ Viticulturist Pedro Marchevsky makes these wines with his wife, the talented Susana Balbo. Their Malbec, containing 10 percent Bonarda, is a rich display of ripe, chewy huckleberry and cassis flavors layered with notes of toasted oak, sandalwood and spice.

Bianchi Particular Malbec | 2007 | SAN RAFAEL
★ ★ ★ $ $ Napa Valley's Robert Pepi is the consultant winemaker at this high-quality estate. The 2007 Malbec shows great intensity on the nose, with fruitcake, gingerbread, tobacco and spicy oak aromas. The palate is lively and fresh, packed with raspberry, cherry and pomegranate flavors held together with drying, spicy tannins.

Bodega Norton Malbec | 2009 | MENDOZA
★ $ This fresh, juicy wine was designed for pure drinking pleasure, and it delivers. Bright berry, tart cherry and pomegranate appear on the nose and follow through on the medium-bodied palate, which is supported by ample tannins on the finish.

Bodega Septima Gran Reserva | 2007 | MENDOZA
★ ★ $ $ This blend of Malbec, Cabernet Sauvignon and Tannat is tightly wound, yet slowly reveals hints of tar and flowers and waves of abundant oak. On the palate, generous red berry flavors are wrapped in very firm tannins and tinged with licorice and espresso.

Callia Alta Malbec | 2009 | TULUM VALLEY
★ $ A fantastic value from a subregion of San Juan, this red nicely balances blackberry fruit with spice and juniper aromas. It is medium-bodied and lively on the palate, with some underlying earthiness and a spicy finish.

Clos de los Siete | 2008 | MENDOZA
★ ★ ★ $ $ This gorgeous blend of Malbec, Merlot, Cabernet Sauvignon, Syrah and Petit Verdot was crafted by legendary winemaker Michel Rolland from his collective in the Uco Valley. Loaded with aromas of mocha, cassis, black pepper and violets, it offers a palate that is full yet not overly weighty, with a supple texture, lively acidity and exquisite balance.

Cruz Andina Malbec | 2007 | LUJÁN DE CUYO

★★ $ $ Two South American wine icons—Agustin Huneeus of Chile and Carlos Pulenta of Argentina—joined forces to make this well-priced Malbec. Its enticing black cherry and blackberry aromas are punctuated by spice and savory notes; the lingering finish is rounded out with vanilla, oak and super-fine tannins.

Doña Paula Estate Malbec | 2009 | MENDOZA

★★★★ $ $ Truly one of the best values out of Argentina, Doña Paula's estate Malbec wins countless accolades for its rich, rounded palate brimming with exotic spice, fragrant violets, black cherries and dried herbs—a lot of wine for the price.

Don Miguel Gascón Malbec | 2008 | MENDOZA

★ $ The winery where this Malbec is crafted was built in 1884 and provides a stark contrast to the wine's sleek, modern taste profile. This is a great-value wine offering beautiful smoky plum flavors, a supple palate and velvety tannins.

where to go next
buenos aires, argentina

Almacén Secreto

This private-house restaurant focuses on the foods and wines of the Salta region. *Aguirre 1242; almacensecretoclub. blogspot.com*

Gran Bar Danzon

At the city's first serious wine bar, all glasses feature a tag listing information about that particular wine. *Libertad 1161; granbardanzon.com.ar*

La Brigada

Meat-centric La Brigada in the boho San Telmo neighborhood is as famous for its beef as for its deep cellar. *Estados Unidos 465; labrigada.com*

La Vinería de Gualterio Bolívar

The entire wine list at this small place is available by the glass. Affordable tasting menus are prepared by a chef who trained at Spain's El Bulli. *Bolivar 865; lavineriadegualteriobolivar.com*

Parrilla Don Julio

At this insider's steak house, the list of 300-plus Argentine labels has lots of bottles for under $20. *Guatemala 4699*

Vinoteca de Palacio Duhau

Star sommelier Marcelo Rebolé pours 200 Malbecs at the Park Hyatt wine bar. *Alvear Ave. 1661; buenosaires.park.hyatt.com*

Durigutti Familia Malbec | 2005 | MENDOZA
★★★ $ $ $ This rich, dense red marries black plum aromas with chocolate, licorice, tar and cedary oak on the nose. Silky black fruit is laced with leather, mint and herbs on the palate, which is remarkably elegant despite the wine's sturdy structure and firm tannins.

Finca 8 Malbec | 2008 | UCO VALLEY
★★ $ $ Finca 8's owner, Hernán Fragueiro Frías, began his career in the business of fine cured *jamón* before turning to wine. Here, black cherry aromas, with hints of violets, fresh herbs and eucalyptus, lead to a palate filled with cocoa flavors and fine, dusty tannins.

Finca El Portillo Cabernet Sauvignon | 2008 | UCO VALLEY
★ $ This easy-to-drink Cabernet is made by the sister winery to the better-known Bodegas Salentein. It is a great deal for its generous berry and baking spice aromas and juicy plum and tart berry flavors with just a touch of leather and earth on the medium-bodied palate.

Finca [ñ] Malbec | 2007 | MENDOZA
★★ $ $ Those who love fruit-forward, silky-textured New World wines will be seduced by this Mendoza Malbec. Made with 5 percent Syrah, it is sweet and ripe, bursting with cassis and light oak notes, underscored by subtle whiffs of dill, sage and thyme.

Ichanka Bonarda | 2007 | FAMATINA VALLEYS
★★ $ This red hails from the hot, arid province of La Rioja (not to be confused with the famous Spanish wine region). Powerful and full-bodied—with 14.5 percent alcohol—it's a harmonious wine offering heaps of juicy blackberry flavors with hints of tar and spice.

Kaiken Malbec | 2008 | MENDOZA
★★ $ The Andes are little more than a speed bump for Chilean wine-maker Aurelio Montes, who crosses the mountain range to make this fruit-filled Argentine Malbec. The nose is tinged with spice, hints of coffee and dense berry that follow through on the palate.

La Posta Angel Paulucci Vineyard Malbec | 2008 | UGARTECHE
★★ $ $ From a Mendoza subregion on the southern edge of Luján de Cuyo comes this single-vineyard Malbec. Raspberry and black-berry flavors are laced with espresso and spice, while a pleasant earthiness and molten dark chocolate dominate in the long finish.

Layer Cake Malbec | 2008 | MENDOZA
★★ $ Ultraripe, chewy and juicy, this jammy red is filled with crushed berry and chocolate flavors accented by herbs, sweet spice and star anise. Firm tannins frame the rich, broad palate.

Lonko Single Vineyard Merlot | 2005 | PATAGONIA

★★ $ $ Like most producers in Patagonia, Lonko is relatively new, founded in 2001. This wine's mocha and cherry aromas lead to a wonderfully supple texture, fresh cherry-vanilla flavors and dusty tannins.

Luca Malbec | 2008 | UCO VALLEY

★★★ $ $ $ In this powerful wine, opulent dark fruit flavors meet sweet hoisin sauce and spice and are beautifully balanced by great acidity. Inky and rich, it is both silky and chewy, with a finish punctuated by notes of cedar, sandalwood and chocolate-covered raisins.

Luigi Bosca D.O.C. Malbec | 2007 | LUJÁN DE CUYO

★★ $ $ Compared to most other Luján de Cuyo Malbecs, this shows particular elegance and restraint, flaunting smoky plum, red fruit and dried flower aromas. The medium-bodied palate offers generous berry flavors alongside mocha, vanilla and tart cherries.

Maipe Bonarda | 2009 | MENDOZA

★★ $ A great example of how the Bonarda grape can overdeliver for the price, this inky, concentrated wine is made from 30-year-old vines and combines floral, crushed berry and caramel aromas. The plush, seductive palate is juicy and perfectly framed by fine tannins.

Mendel Malbec | 2007 | MENDOZA

★★★★ $ $ This outstanding wine is packed with smoky plum, cassis, and boysenberry aromas highlighted by savory meat and spice. It brandishes real power, with a gorgeous, silky texture, super-fine tannins and loads of bitter chocolate and espresso flavors.

The Show Malbec | 2009 | MENDOZA

★★ $ California's Three Thieves headed to South America to craft this plum-flavored, sultry Malbec for a great price. The spicy palate displays wonderful details of cinnamon and cloves, filled out with juicy black fruit flavors and hints of licorice, tar and mocha.

Siesta en el Tahuantinsuyu Cabernet Sauvignon | 2003 | MENDOZA

★★ $ $ Made by Ernesto Catena, son of the famous Nicolás Catena Zapata, this Cabernet is showing some age, revealing earthy, savory notes alongside dark berry flavors and hints of cocoa and coffee on the well-balanced finish.

Trapiche Malbec | 2009 | MENDOZA

★ $ Though perfect for everyday drinking, this light-bodied, entry-level wine also shows a bit of complexity, with exuberant acidity, fine tannins and earthy nuances joining red and black fruit flavors.

chile

Chile is known around the world as a major wine producer, but many wine drinkers are surprised to learn that it is also one of the oldest continually producing wine regions in the Americas. Over half of Chile's wine exports go to Europe, more than twice what it sends to the U.S. While Americans regard most Chilean wines as easy-drinking and affordable, Chile is also a great source for premium reds, and increasingly whites, that are well worth discovering.

Chile: An Overview

Chile is a long, narrow country, isolated and protected by its geography: To the north is the Atacama Desert, to the south icy Patagonia, to the west the Pacific coastal range and to the east the Andes mountains. Thanks to its location, Chile has famously escaped the devastating vine pest phylloxera that has plagued most wine regions. With its warm days, cool nights and long growing season, Chile's Central Valley is ideal for wine grapes. The famous regions of Maipo, the Curicó Valley and the Rapel Valley (which includes the Colchagua Valley) are all in the Central Valley. Slightly northward are the cooler Leyda and Casablanca valleys, where white grapes and Pinot Noir thrive. (See map, p. 226.)

Chilean Wine Labels

Chilean labels list grape and often a proprietary name for blends. More producers are using single-vineyard designations and adding the term *Reserva* to top-quality wines.

chilean whites

Chardonnay and Sauvignon Blanc are Chile's two most important white grapes. The Casablanca and Leyda valleys produce the finest Loire-like Sauvignon Blancs, while southern regions are having success with Chardonnay.

chilean white recommendations

Arboleda Sauvignon Blanc | 2008 | LEYDA VALLEY

★★ $ $ *Arboleda* means "grove," and Chilean native trees still grow among the winery's vines. Crisp and zesty, this citrusy white turns savory on the finish, with notes of thyme and chive.

Casa Marin Laurel Vineyard Sauvignon Blanc | 2008 | SAN ANTONIO

★★★ $ $ Laurel Vineyard is close to the Pacific, and there's a backbone of briny minerals in this outstanding white. Flavors of lime zest, white pepper and stones carry through on the bright, chalky finish.

Concha y Toro Marques de Casa Concha Chardonnay | 2007 | PIRQUE

★★★ $ $ Don Melchor Concha y Toro founded his winery in 1883, and his pioneering spirit lives on in the wines that bear his name. Bright and balanced, this apple-scented 2007 Chardonnay has lime zest, acacia flower and toasted oak notes on the creamy palate.

Cono Sur "Bicycle" Chardonnay | 2009 | CENTRAL VALLEY

★ $ Cono Sur's modern approach to winemaking results in straightforward, well-priced wines like this. A nose of honeysuckle and orange blossom is followed by juicy white peach flavors and lively minerals.

De Martino Legado Reserva Chardonnay | 2008 | LIMARÍ VALLEY

★★ $ De Martino's Legado line highlights the *terroir* of various regions. The lovely Limarí Valley Chardonnay displays star fruit, apple and pear flavors underlined by chalky minerals and vibrant acidity.

Emiliana Natura Sauvignon Blanc | 2009 | CASABLANCA VALLEY

★ $ Herbs, lime zest and minerals meet ripe fruit with a touch of creaminess in this great-value white.

Montes Classic Series Sauvignon Blanc | 2009 |
CASABLANCA VALLEY

★ $ This has the aromas and flavors of fresh-squeezed lemons and limes. It's clean, light and refreshing and has a nice low price.

Santa Ema Selected Terroir Chardonnay | 2009 |
CASABLANCA VALLEY

★★★ $ Santa Ema was founded by Pedro Pavone-Voglino, the son of Italian winemakers from Piedmont, in 1956. In this 2009 Chardonnay, ripe pear and lime zest aromas grow richer on the palate; they are accompanied by fig and grapefruit flavors, and minerals on the finish.

Terra Andina Reserva Chardonnay | 2008 | LIMARÍ VALLEY

★★ $ Fermented and aged in French oak for eight months, Terra Andina's Reserva Chardonnay is marked by kiwi and quince paste flavors; a bright, chalky minerality adds terrific balance.

Veramonte Reserva Sauvignon Blanc | 2009 |
CASABLANCA VALLEY

★ $ Vintner Agustin Huneeus helped grow Concha y Toro into Chile's largest winery before starting Veramonte, his own estate. The 2009 Sauvignon has grass, herb and grapefruit aromas that lead into flavors of kiwi and citrus, held up by zippy acidity.

Viña Litoral Ventolera Sauvignon Blanc | 2009 |
LEYDA VALLEY

★ $ *Ventolera* refers to the strong wind that blows from the Pacific Ocean through the Leyda Valley. Indeed, there's a distinct briny quality to the lime juice flavors of this delicious everyday white.

Viu Manent Secreto Sauvignon Blanc | 2009 |
CASABLANCA VALLEY

★★ $ Viu Manent's Secreto gets its name from the "secret" grapes that have been blended with the listed variety. In this case, Sauvignon Blanc and 15 percent other undisclosed grapes yield a plush wine with balancing acidity and seductive flavors of pear, kiwi and minerals.

chilean reds

About three-quarters of Chilean wines are red. Although the country is known as the Bordeaux of South America for its success with Cabernet Sauvignon and Merlot, Chile's most distinctive grape is Carmenère, a forgotten Bordeaux variety that was long mistaken for Merlot. Small amounts of Pinot Noir and some superb Syrah are also produced here.

chilean red recommendations

Agustinos Maitén Reserva Cabernet Sauvignon | 2007 |
ACONCAGUA VALLEY

★ $ Aromas of mint and sage dominate this old-fashioned Cabernet. Velvety tannins and mulled spice, currant and tobacco add charm.

Antiyal | 2007 | MAIPO VALLEY

★★★★ $ $ $ Antiyal's blend of Carmenère, Syrah and Cabernet Sauvignon is dark and brawny. Flavors of stewed plums and currants are laced with tobacco, olive and charred mesquite notes; it will benefit from a few years in the cellar.

Antu Ninquén Syrah | 2007 | COLCHAGUA VALLEY

★★★ $ $ Made with grapes grown on a mountaintop, this medium-bodied wine exhibits ripe flavors of blackberry and sweet spice. There are lovely notes of black tea and fresh berries on the lingering finish.

Casillero del Diablo Reserva Privada Cabernet Sauvignon/Syrah | 2007 | MAIPO VALLEY

★★ $ Named for a century-old legend about the devil stealing from founder Don Melchor's cellar, Casillero del Diablo's red blend is dark, fleshy and delicious. Black currant, spicy licorice and roasted coffee flavors are underscored by notes of loam and minerals.

Chono Reserva Syrah | 2008 | ELQUI VALLEY

★★ $ Chono is a small-batch winery named for a tribe that once lived in southern Chile. This intriguing Syrah reveals charcoal, tobacco and sage aromas and juicy flavors of macerated cherries and figs.

Hereu | 2006 | CENTRAL VALLEY

★★★ $ $ Like the winery's founder/winemaker, Arnaud Hereu, this Malbec-Syrah-Carignane blend has a big personality. Deep violet in color, it's dominated by currant, juniper and dried herb aromas that give way to a tightly woven palate of cassis, earth and savory spice.

Kingston Family Vineyards Lucero Syrah | 2008 |
CASABLANCA VALLEY

★★ $ $ Carl John Kingston's hope of finding gold and copper in Chile in the early 1900s led his family to the wine business instead. This standout red, which is rich yet light, has racy violet, blackberry, raspberry and sweet spice flavors around a core of minerals.

Koyle Cabernet Sauvignon | 2007 | COLCHAGUA–MAIPO VALLEY

★★ $ $ From the first Chilean winery to export to the U.S., this oozes plum, blackberry and fruitcake flavors with spicy oak notes.

Lapostolle Casa Carmenère | 2008 | RAPEL VALLEY

★ ★ $ In this lovely Carmenère from the Lapostolle family, supple currant and cocoa notes slowly build, augmented by toast, mineral and black cherry flavors that are taut and structured.

Los Vascos Domaines Barons de Rothschild (Lafite) Cabernet Sauvignon | 2008 | COLCHAGUA VALLEY

★ ★ $ French grape vines were first planted in these vineyards in the mid-1800s. Now produced under the leadership of the Rothschilds, the wines display true French flair, as evidenced in this solid Cabernet with blackberry and cherry flavors and vanilla and mineral nuances.

Matetic Vineyards EQ Syrah | 2007 | SAN ANTONIO

★ ★ ★ ★ $ $ $ Situated in the granite soils of the Rosario Valley, Matetic's winery is a popular tourist destination for its beauty as well as its stellar wines. This terrific, dark Syrah has currant, fig and blackberry flavors layered with notes of roasted vanilla and coffee; the finish shows a hint of graphite and lingers impressively on the palate.

news from chile

Earthquake Recovery

When an 8.8-magnitude earthquake hit Chile in February 2010, it caused widespread damage to the Chilean wine industry, specifically in the Maule, Cachapoal and Colchagua valleys, collapsing tanks and cracking barrels and bottles. It's estimated that Colchagua lost one-fifth of Chile's total stored wine, and the country is reporting an overall loss of approximately 12.5 percent, primarily from the 2009 vintage. Viu Manent and Los Vascos in Colchagua reported heavy wine losses, but many wineries were not hit as hard, since the quake came just as producers were preparing for harvest, when many tanks and storage areas were empty. The good news is that the harvest continued despite the upheaval. As for the pre-quake vintages, 2008 was small, thanks to a very dry growing season, which produced quite ripe, concentrated reds; and 2009 was also quite dry and warm, but with larger yields. The whites from 2009 are full-bodied, with more ripe, tropical characteristics and less acidity than those from cooler vintages.

Miguel Torres Manso de Velasco Old Vines Cabernet Sauvignon | 2006 | CURICÓ VALLEY

★ ★ ★ ★ $ $ $ Spanish winemaking icon Miguel Torres crafts this powerful wine, which offers concentrated plum, prune and fig flavors laced with sage, cocoa and aged tobacco. The long finish is polished and has incredible purity, despite its obvious heft.

Montes Alpha Carmenère | 2007 | COLCHAGUA VALLEY

★ ★ $ $ Montes' Alpha line is more expensive than some of its other popular offerings but worth every penny. This well-structured Carmenère shows juicy currant, roasted vanilla and cherry flavors.

MontGras Reserva Carmenère | 2009 | COLCHAGUA VALLEY

★ ★ ★ $ A superb Carmenère for a great price, this fleshy-textured wine offers classic flavors of plum, cherry, tobacco and toast.

Pangea Apalta Vineyards Syrah | 2006 | COLCHAGUA VALLEY

★ ★ ★ ★ $ $ $ Viña Ventisquero's pairing of superstar Australian winemaker John Duval and Chilean master Felipe Tosso has resulted in this exceptional Syrah. Berry, fig, chocolate and licorice flavors are earthy and solid; it's drinkable now but will improve with age.

Santa Carolina Reserva Pinot Noir | 2008 | MAULE VALLEY

★ ★ $ Inexpensive Pinot Noir is rarely this good: Aromas of raspberries and roses are echoed on the silky palate alongside earth notes.

Santa Rita Medalla Real Carmenère | 2008 | COLCHAGUA VALLEY

★ ★ ★ $ $ Cool breezes from the Pacific Ocean blow over Santa Rita's vineyards, enabling the grapes to ripen while maintaining a mineral-laden acidity. This delicious Carmenère shows weighty plum and violet flavors accented with tobacco, herbs and vanilla.

Seña | 2006 | ACONCAGUA VALLEY

★ ★ ★ ★ $ $ $ $ South America's Eduardo Chadwick and California wine legend Robert Mondavi cofounded this winery (today the Chadwick family runs the show). Sleek and refined, Seña's blend of Cabernet Sauvignon, Merlot, Carmenère and Cabernet Franc yields layers of ripe raspberry flavors dusted with cocoa powder and sweet spice.

Viu Manent Single Vineyard San Carlos Estate Malbec | 2007 | COLCHAGUA VALLEY

★ ★ ★ $ $ With Malbec vines that are on average 80 years old, Viu Manent is the grape's ambassador in Chile. This extraordinary wine displays equal parts fruit—crushed blackberries and raspberries—and earth flavors, culminating in a velvety finish.

south africa

Winemaking in the Cape region dates back to 1659, yet South Africa didn't become a modern winemaking power until the arrival of a fully realized democracy in the 1990s. That's when South African producers truly entered the international arena and began to reevaluate and upgrade the way they made wine. Many of the nation's vineyards are less than ten years old, a sign that South Africa is still working toward fulfilling its great potential.

Coastal Region

Atlantic Ocean

Paarl

Robertson

Cape Town
Constantia

Stellenbosch

Elgin

Walker Bay

Principal Wine Region

Indian Ocean

South Africa: An Overview

Most of the wine that South Africa exports is made in the Coastal Region and surrounding districts of the Western Cape. Northeast of Cape Town is the well-known and relatively warm region of Paarl, home to some of the country's leading producers and finest white and red wines. Cabernet Sauvignon–based Bordeaux-style blends excel in the Coastal Region's Stellenbosch district, while Sauvignon Blanc, Chardonnay and Pinot Noir do better in the region's cooler district of Constantia, as well as in Overberg, Walker Bay and Cape Agulhas to the southeast. Constantia is also the source of the nation's most famous wine, Vin de Constance, a dessert wine that garnered international acclaim in the 18th and 19th centuries. The mineral-laden, tropical-scented Chenin Blancs and fruit-forward Syrahs that are being created in the Coastal Region, however, may well be on their way to becoming South Africa's defining wines.

South African Wine Labels

The straightforward labels used by South African winemakers list the winery name, variety, region and vintage. Blends may be given proprietary names, and the varieties that went into them usually appear on the back label.

south african whites

Chenin Blanc, sometimes referred to locally as "Steen," is South Africa's most widely planted white grape. Offering more citrus and tropical flavors than traditional versions from France, South African Chenin Blancs can be excellent, yet they are not especially popular in the U.S., and are often considered old-fashioned and pedestrian in South Africa. The country's other key white grapes, Sauvignon Blanc and Chardonnay, generally yield medium-bodied wines with pronounced mineral flavors; Sauvignon Blancs sometimes display herbal and exotic fruit flavors as well.

south african white recommendations

Buitenverwachting Sauvignon Blanc | 2009 | CONSTANTIA
★★ **$** Light, refreshing and completely dry, this peachy Sauvignon Blanc is decidedly New World in style. It emphasizes bright fruit flavors with herbal nuances and has a firm mineral backbone.

DeMorgenzon Chenin Blanc | 2008 | STELLENBOSCH
★★★ **$ $** This wine possesses a delightfully complex nose of stone fruit and ginger. The palate screams apple—Granny Smith acidity coupled with Red Delicious richness—and the peach-accented finish is mouthwatering and invigorating.

DMZ Chardonnay | 2008 | WESTERN CAPE
★★ **$** Ten months aging in French oak barrels gives this Chardonnay a heady bouquet of peach, fig, roasted nuts and smoke. The round palate is equal parts juicy and flinty.

Fairview La Capra Chenin Blanc | 2009 | COASTAL REGION
★★ **$** Vibrant acidity enlivens kiwi and citrus flavors in this bright, refreshing Chenin Blanc. The zingy lime is a reminder of how pleasing Chenin Blanc can be.

Glen Carlou Chardonnay | 2008 | PAARL
★★★ **$ $** This expertly balanced Chardonnay is a stunning value, boasting an intoxicating nose of toasted oak and bright fruit and succulent, creamy flavors of caramel and apple.

Goats do Roam White | 2009 | WESTERN CAPE
★★ **$** A Rhône-style blend of Viognier, Grenache Blanc and Roussanne, this charms with aromas of melon, anise and honeysuckle. Tangy herbal notes infuse peach flavors on the soft, round palate.

Indaba Chenin Blanc | 2009 | WESTERN CAPE
★★ **$** Consultant-winemaker Bruwer Raats (see his own label's Chenin, next page) helps craft Indaba, which shows an alluring mix of fresh peach, star fruit and mineral flavors and a clean finish.

Mulderbosch Sauvignon Blanc | 2009 | WESTERN CAPE
★★★ **$ $** Mulderbosch Vineyards produces what is arguably South Africa's most celebrated Sauvignon Blanc. It's clean and crisp, with a long finish marked by grass and minerals.

Neil Ellis Chardonnay | 2009 | STELLENBOSCH
★★★ **$ $** Offering a bouquet of star fruit, subtle oak and flowers, this Burgundy-style Chardonnay is tantalizingly complex. Flavors of citrus zest, pear and peach are well balanced and delicious.

Raats Chenin Blanc | 2008 | STELLENBOSCH

★ ★ ★ $ $ Raats makes both oaked and unoaked versions of Chenin Blanc. This dry, mineral-driven version shows what the judicious use of French barrels can do for the grape. Zesty acidity enlivens flavors of apple, wet stone and juicy pear.

Thelema Sauvignon Blanc | 2009 | STELLENBOSCH

★ ★ ★ $ $ Thelema's winemaker, Rudi Schultz, is among the most respected young winemakers in South Africa. His clean, racy Sauvignon Blanc is characterized by an electric acidity rounded out by bright citrus, briny mineral and lime zest flavors.

Warwick Professor Black Sauvignon Blanc | 2009 | STELLENBOSCH

★ ★ $ $ Warwick Estate released its first vintage in 1984, and the Stellenbosch producer's wines seem to get better every year. This lovely Sauvignon Blanc displays grapefruit and lemon zest qualities uplifted by zippy acidity.

south african reds

For better or worse, South Africa's preeminent grape is Pinotage, a local crossing of the native French grapes Cinsault and Pinot Noir. With its bold, pungent aromas and decidedly eccentric, earthy taste profile, Pinotage is far from a crowd-pleaser, though carefully made, full-bodied, smooth versions have their admirers. Many winemakers attempt to balance and subdue the grape's personality by mixing it with other reds in a "Cape blend." Some producers bottle Cabernet Sauvignon alone or blend it with Merlot or Cabernet Franc to produce complex, enjoyable red wines. However, the country's most exciting red is probably Syrah (Shiraz), which can display assertive, concentrated jammy fruit flavors similar to the Australian style or earthy, smoky, meaty qualities that more closely resemble the Rhône style. Syrah is also sometimes combined with Bordeaux varieties or other Rhône varieties such as Grenache. Pinot Noir is grown in small amounts with modest success in South Africa's cooler regions, although a large portion of the yield is dedicated to the country's burgeoning production of sparkling wine.

south african red recommendations

Engelbrecht Els Vineyards Proprietor's Blend | 2007 | **STELLENBOSCH**

★ ★ ★ ★ $ $ $ There is roughly 25 percent Shiraz in this Bordeaux-fashioned blend, which imparts ripe blackberry and raspberry notes to complementary flavors of earth and red fruit, while luscious tannins round out the finish.

Fairview Pinotage | 2008 | **COASTAL REGION**

★ ★ $ $ Fairview owner Charles Back is also the man behind Goats do Roam and Spice Route. This well-crafted Pinotage is light-bodied and cherry-scented, with vanilla notes and a cascade of ripe tannins.

Glen Carlou Grand Classique | 2006 | **PAARL**

★ ★ ★ $ $ A nose of dark fruit—cassis, fig and berries—introduces this blend of Cabernet Sauvignon, Merlot, Petit Verdot, Malbec and Cabernet Franc. Chewy tannins add texture to earthy espresso notes on the fleshy palate.

Kanonkop Paul Sauer | 2004 | **SIMONSBERG-STELLENBOSCH**

★ ★ ★ ★ $ $ $ This Cabernet-dominated blend is aged for 24 months in new French oak. It's complex and generous, offering a range of red and black currant, coffee and roasted vanilla flavors that will benefit from additional cellaring.

Man Vintners Pinotage | 2008 | **COASTAL REGION**

★ ★ $ Perfect for everyday, easy drinking, this Pinotage displays fig, currant and plum flavors layered with hints of mocha. Tangy acidity and smooth tannins mark the finish.

Mulderbosch Faithful Hound | 2006 | **STELLENBOSCH**

★ ★ ★ $ $ This smoky Bordeaux blend yields aromas of spice, red currant and plum. On the palate, hints of cocoa, herb and mineral nicely highlight supple fruit flavors.

Rudi Schultz Syrah | 2007 | **STELLENBOSCH**

★ ★ ★ ★ $ $ $ Winemaker Rudi Schultz has crafted a truly extraordinary wine here. Fresh raspberry and strawberry flavors follow aromas of fig jam and mocha in this well-balanced, spicy Syrah.

Rustenberg John X. Merriman | 2007 | **STELLENBOSCH**

★ ★ ★ $ $ Named in honor of the man who helped restore Rustenberg's historic estate in the 19th century, this Bordeaux blend is layered and rich. Black cherry, earth and tobacco leap from the glass and follow through on the long, firm finish.

Rust en Vrede Estate | 2006 | STELLENBOSCH

★★★ $ $ This big but nicely balanced wine is a blend of mostly Cabernet Sauvignon, filled out with Shiraz and a bit of Merlot. Twenty-three months of oak aging adds notes of coffee and cocoa that complement its blackberry juiciness.

Simonsig Redhill Pinotage | 2007 | STELLENBOSCH

★★★ $ $ $ Those who dismiss Pinotage will change their minds after tasting this exceptional version. Ripe and ready to drink, it shows a dark plum, currant and mocha bouquet followed by intense blackberry and earth flavors that are framed by refined tannins.

Thelema Cabernet Sauvignon | 2007 | STELLENBOSCH

★★★★ $ $ $ This serious wine is approachable yet firm, introduced by mint, cocoa and black currant aromas. Soft, integrated tannins provide a nice frame for ultrarich dark plum, fig and coffee flavors through the focused, lingering finish.

Vilafonté Series M | 2004 | PAARL

★★★★ $ $ $ A very successful joint venture between American and South African winemakers has resulted in this full-bodied, Bordeaux-style beauty. Fruity but immensely elegant, it brims with layers of spice, fig and berry flavors.

Warwick Old Bush Vines Pinotage | 2007 | STELLENBOSCH

★★ $ $ This plush wine tantalizes with a mélange of sweet currant, spice and earth flavors underlined by notes of minerals that add a lovely complexity.

The Wolftrap | 2008 | WESTERN CAPE

★★ $ Always a crowd-pleaser, Wolftrap's value-priced Syrah-Mourvèdre-Viognier blend offers candied aromas of raspberry tart and violets. Lush dark fruit comes together with chalky minerality for a sweet, soft finish.

champagne & other sparkling wines

Thanks to the enthusiasm of sommeliers and winemakers, more people are realizing that sparkling wines pair incredibly well with food. Increasingly popular non-Champagne sparklers, such as refreshing Prosecco and Cava, have helped make these festive wines affordable enough for everyday drinking.

Sparkling Wine: An Overview

There are several ways to make sparkling wine, but the finest is the traditional method—*méthode traditionnelle*—in which vintners create and trap carbon dioxide bubbles in a still wine by activating a second fermentation in sealed bottles. Sparkling wines vary in the intensity of their effervescence and range in style from completely dry to very sweet. The pinnacle of all sparkling wine regions is Champagne in northern France, but France's Loire Valley, northern Italy, northern Spain and northern California's Anderson Valley and Carneros regions all make exceptional sparklers, as do many other places throughout the world with cool climates and mineral-rich soils.

champagne

Champagne is undeniably the greatest of the world's sparkling wines. Only wines made in the Champagne region of northern France (see map, p. 22) are entitled to be called "Champagne," yet despite efforts to protect the name, it is often incorrectly used to refer to any wine with bubbles, regardless of origin.

Champagne Grapes & Styles

Champagne vintners blend grapes from various vintages and villages using only three permitted varieties: Chardonnay, Pinot Noir and Pinot Meunier. *Blanc de Blancs* are made from 100 percent Chardonnay; *Blanc de Noirs* are sparkling whites produced with red grapes Pinot Noir and/or Pinot Meunier. Rosés are created by blending some red wine into white sparkling wine or by soaking pigment-rich red grape skins in pressed juice to "bleed" in some color.

Champagne Labels

Look for the word *Champagne* on the label to make sure it is the real thing. Most Champagnes are non-vintage, which means their labels don't list a year; they are blends of wines made in different vintages, a practice designed to maintain a distinctive and consistent taste from year to year. Producers make vintage Champagnes only in exceptional years; they typically age them longer before release and price them much higher than their non-vintage counterparts. Most large Champagne houses create a top-tier bottling called a *Tête de Cuvée,* usually under a proprietary name such as Moët's Dom Pérignon or Louis Roederer's Cristal. Sweetness levels in Champagne are categorized as follows, from driest to sweetest: *Brut Nature* (also known as *Brut Zéro, Pas Dosé* or *Sans-Dosage*), *Extra Brut, Brut, Extra Dry* (or *Extra Sec*), *Sec* (or *Dry*), *Demi-Sec* and *Doux*. Brut is the most widely produced and popular style.

champagne recommendations

WHITES

Alfred Gratien Blanc de Blancs Brut | NV |

★★★★ $ $ $ $ Nicolas Jaeger carries the torch as the fourth-generation cellar master at Alfred Gratien. This toast- and brioche-wafting wine boasts classic Chardonnay characteristics of quince and apple notes that develop generously in the mouth with judicious oak nuances; crisp minerals and acidity round out the delicious finish.

Bollinger Special Cuvée | NV |

★★★ $ $ $ $ This family-owned house is known for the rich style of its Champagnes. This stellar, full-bodied example is marked by brioche, buttery toast and apple aromas, bold flavors of hazelnut, honey and citrus and fine bubbles that carry through on the chalky finish.

star producers
champagne

Champagne Bollinger
Madame Lily Bollinger once said of her house's Champagne: "I never touch it—unless I'm thirsty." As ever, Bollinger's stellar wines are hard to resist.

Champagne Vilmart & Cie
Small-production Vilmart sources grapes from the Montagne de Reims region and has a cult following for its refined, elegant Champagnes.

Dom Pérignon
Named for the monk credited with perfecting the art of Champagne production in the 1600s, Moët & Chandon's *Tête du Cuvée,* or "top of the house," never fails to impress.

Jacques Selosse
Vigneron Anselme Selosse ignores many conventional Champagne practices, doing things his own way to craft wines that are distinctive, assertive and terroir-driven.

Krug
In the 19th century, many Germans went to Champagne to make wine, but none inspired as devoted a following as Johann-Joseph Krug.

Pierre Gimonnet & Fils
Pierre Gimonnet's creamy Blanc de Blancs have a distinct advantage: Most of the grapes that go into them are harvested from very old vines.

Delamotte Brut | NV |

★★ $ $ $ Sourced exclusively from Grand Cru vineyards, this is lovely Champagne with delicate candied orange peel, honey and ginger flavors. The palate has an earthy quality that is filled out with sweet citrus and bread notes.

Deutz Brut Classic | NV |

★★★ $ $ $ Using roughly equal parts Chardonnay, Pinot Noir and Pinot Meunier, Deutz always crafts a standout Brut. This is lively and fresh, with flavors of berries, lemon and apple pie highlighted with caramel, malt and buttery toast.

Gosset Excellence Brut | NV |

★★★ $ $ $ Rich, honeyed aromas lead to a palate of ripe stone fruit and juicy citrus in Gosset's exceptional Brut. There are lovely notes of lemon and grapefruit zest and a firming core of minerals on the finish.

Jacques Lassaigne Les Vignes de Montgueux Blanc de Blancs Brut | NV |

★★ $ $ $ This billows with chalky aromas, followed by star fruit, green and golden apple and pretty mandarin orange flavors that linger nicely on the yeasty finish.

eat here now

LE JARDIN The five-star hotel Château Les Crayères in the town of Reims is home to this great brasserie, which is a more affordable counterpart to the hotel's famous Le Parc restaurant. Both places are overseen by Philippe Mille (fresh from Paris's three-Michelin-starred Le Meurice). *Reims, Champagne; lescrayeres.com*

Krug Grande Cuvée Brut | NV |

★★★★ $ $ $ $ Krug crafts this terrific Champagne from up to 50 wines made over the course of six to ten years. The result is a non-vintage wine that is elegant and distinctive, with complex layers of toast, minerals, fresh and dried fruit and a yeasty, creamy texture that goes on and on.

Lamiable Grand Cru Brut | NV |

★★★ $ $ $ This Pinot Noir–dominated wine smells like a bakery: Bread dough, yeast and hints of coconut abound on the nose. Light-bodied and brisk, it delivers tart cherry and apple flavors that are well structured and spicy.

Louis Roederer Brut Premier | NV |

★★ $ $ $ Nuts and toast compete with lemon and apple on the nose of this fresh Brut. It has a chalky texture, notes of graphite and vanilla and a lingering brioche quality.

Perrier-Jouët Grand Brut | NV |

★★ $ $ $ This is lean and dry, showing tart citrus and grapefruit flavors layered with honeysuckle and minerals. The lacy texture and very fine *mousse* (effervescence) make it rather delicate on the palate, yet the flavors are quite robust.

Pol Roger Extra Cuvée de Réserve Brut | 2000 |

★★★ $ $ $ $ Pol Roger maintains cellars that are cooler than most, which contributes to this Champagne's fine mousse. The delicious 2000 vintage is golden and refined, oozing with honey, stone fruit and spice that meet a beam of vibrant acidity.

Ruinart Blanc de Blancs Brut | NV |

★★★ $ $ $ $ Ruinart holds the distinction of being the oldest existing Champagne house, founded in 1729. Made from 100 percent Chardonnay, this extraordinary Blanc de Blancs displays nice bread and yeast aromas; zippy citrus and floral notes are supple on the sweet-tart, well-knit palate.

ROSÉS

Beaumont des Crayères Grand Rosé Brut | NV |

★★★ $ $ $ Opening with an expressive array of red berry flavors, this wine is bold and round on the palate, as dried cherry and strawberry notes are joined by hints of spice, toast and pencil shavings. There's a touch of tannin on the dry, mineral-laden finish.

Henriot Rosé Brut | NV |

★★★ $ $ $ $ Hailing from a centuries-old family-owned Champagne house, this refreshing salmon-colored wine has earth and exotic spice aromas and a rich palate showing lots of raspberry, citrus and caramel notes.

Nicolas Feuillatte Rosé Brut | NV |

★★ $ $ $ A blend of 60 percent Pinot Noir, 30 percent Pinot Meunier and 10 percent Chardonnay, this red grape–dominated Champagne offers a mix of blackberry and watermelon aromas up-front. The fruit-driven palate, with wild strawberries joined by honey flavors, finishes with hints of butter and gingery spice.

Veuve Clicquot Rosé Brut | 2002 |

★★★ $ $ $ $ Clicquot has been making rosé since the 19th century, before many other houses, and its expertise shows in this beautifully crafted wine. Flower petal, strawberry and cherry aromas rise from this copper-colored rosé, and the palate reveals earth and caramel flavors alongside fresh berries.

champagne glossary

blanc de blancs White Champagne made with 100 percent Chardonnay grapes.

blanc de noirs White Champagne made exclusively with red grapes—Pinot Noir and/or Pinot Meunier—whose color-imparting skins are quickly removed after pressing.

brut Dry; the most popular style of Champagne around the world. See also *Sweetness*.

champagne Wine made by the *méthode traditionnelle* in France's Champagne region. Only these wines can list Champagne on their labels.

chardonnay One of the three grapes officially permitted to make Champagne; the only white grape among them.

méthode traditionnelle The production method that must be used to make all Champagnes, whereby the second fermentation (which creates the bubbles) takes place in the bottle.

non-vintage Champagne without a vintage year on the label; typically a blend of wines from several vintages.

pinot noir & pinot meunier The two red grape varieties winemakers are officially permitted to use in the production of Champagne.

rosé Wine with a pink hue created either by blending a small amount of red wine into the white base wine or by soaking pigment-rich red grape skins in pressed juice before fermentation to add color and flavor.

sweetness Champagne is classified by sweetness level from driest to sweetest: *Brut Nature* (also known as *Brut Zéro, Pas Dosé* or *Sans-Dosage*), *Extra Brut, Brut, Extra Dry* (or *Extra Sec*), *Sec* (or *Dry*), *Demi-Sec, Doux.*

vintage Champagne made only in exceptional years bearing a vintage year on the label. Typically, vintage Champagne is much more expensive and complex than its non-vintage counterparts.

tête de cuvée A Champagne house's top bottling, usually sold under a proprietary name such as Moët's Dom Pérignon or Louis Roederer's Cristal.

other sparkling wines

Champagne will always be the benchmark by which all sparkling wines are measured, but vintners around the world make a wide range of quality sparklers. The best tend to use the Champagne region's *méthode traditionnelle,* but more affordable versions employ different methods.

france

Beyond Champagne, France abounds with sparkling wines, most of which are made with grapes typical to each region. Seven of the country's sparkling wine appellations—the largest is the Loire—are able to use the term *Crémant* to indicate they are quality wines produced by the *méthode traditionnelle*. Other wines labeled *Brut* or *Mousseux* may or may not have been made using the Champagne method.

other french sparkling wine recommendations

WHITES

Louis Bouillot Perle d'Ivoire Blanc de Blancs Brut | NV | CRÉMANT DE BOURGOGNE

★★ $ $ Burgundy can be a good place to turn for quality sparklers at gentler prices. This Chardonnay-dominated wine has a wonderful beam of acidity, a creamy mouthfeel and flavors of red apples.

Lucien Albrecht Blanc de Blancs Brut | NV | CRÉMANT D'ALSACE

★★★★ $ $ This Alsace sparkler closely resembles Champagne, with its full body and gorgeous flavors of pear, quince and apple highlighted by brioche; the mousse is creamy and luxurious.

ROSÉ

Baumard Rosé Brut Extra | NV | CRÉMANT DE LOIRE

★★ $ $ Cabernet Franc shows a vivacious side in this rich, smooth sparkler packed with red fruit flavors that meet vibrant acidity and a hint of apricot on the finish.

italy

Italy's northern regions are the primary source of the country's *spumante* (sparkling) wines. One of the best Italian sparklers comes from Lombardy's Franciacorta zone, with its mineral-rich soil and cool nights. Made by the *méthode traditionnelle* (or *metodo classico,* as it is known locally), the sparkling wines of Franciacorta often taste similar to Champagne. Also noteworthy are Piedmont's flowery and fresh Moscato d'Asti and light red, berry-scented Brachetto d'Acqui. Affordable and tasty, the popular Proseccos of the Veneto region are produced in tanks, in a process known as the Charmat method.

italian sparkling wine recommendations

Adriano Adami Bosco di Gica Brut | NV | PROSECCO
★★ $ $ Adami grows its Prosecco vines in a south-facing vineyard with limestone-rich soils, like the terroir of Champagne. A touch of Chardonnay in the blend imparts rich, creamy notes to the Prosecco grape's pear, peach and mineral flavors.

Bortolomiol Prior Brut | NV | PROSECCO DI VALDOBBIADENE
★★ $ $ The four Bortolomiol sisters and their mother produce this zippy sparkler marked by pear and melon flavors that turn creamy toward the end and are upheld by a taut structure.

Col Vetoraz Brut | NV | PROSECCO DI VALDOBBIADENE
★★ $ $ This Prosecco is both plush and super-crisp, weaving together lush flavors of soft apple with zesty citrus.

Ferrari Brut | NV | TRENTO
★★ $ $ After studying in France, Giulio Ferrari made the unorthodox decision to plant Chardonnay in the Trentino region of Italy. More than 100 years later, this traditional-method sparkler remains 100 percent Chardonnay, showing notes of fresh-baked bread, lemon and spicy pear, tight acidity and a creamy mousse.

Massimiliano Vivalda Nettare | NV | MOSCATO D'ASTI
★★ $ $ Instead of the usual floral aromas, this sweet Moscato shows off autumnal notes—apple pie and spices—along with a full-bodied palate and great acidity.

Montenisa Brut | NV | **FRANCIACORTA**

★★★ $ $ $ Strict standards in Franciacorta—Italy's only appellation dedicated to *méthode champenoise*—make for sparkling wine of incredibly high quality. This stunning example is brimming with yeast, sweet apple and white peach aromas that evolve into nutty toast and rich fruit flavors on the palate.

Nino Franco Rustico | NV | **PROSECCO DI VALDOBBIADENE**

★★ $ $ This lively Prosecco abounds with Granny Smith apple flavors underscored by minerals; it's a refreshing, ideal summer sipper.

spain

Long marketed as less costly substitutes for Champagne, Spanish Cavas by law must be made using the traditional method. Most come from the Catalonia region near Barcelona and are made mostly from Macabeo, northern Spain's most planted white grape. In general, the best Cavas come from larger firms that control their own vinification, though some small vintners are producing high-quality examples.

spanish sparkling wine recommendations

WHITES

Agustí Torelló Mata Reserva Brut | 2006 | **CAVA**

★★ $ $ From Penedès, the heart of Spain's Cava production, Agustí Torelló Mata crafts a Cava equally generous in its fruit and spice, with a rich, long-lasting finish.

Cristalino Brut | NV | **CAVA**

★ $ Toast, vanilla and apple flavors supported by a firm backbone of acidity make this low-priced Cava a food-friendly party pour.

Elyssia Gran Cuvée Brut | NV | **CAVA**

★★ $ $ Two of Cava's classic varieties—Macabeo and Parellada—team up with Chardonnay and Pinot Noir in this wine, resulting in a sparkler with honey and almond flavors and a fine, silky mousse.

Juvé y Camps Reserva de la Familia Gran Reserva Brut Nature | 2005 | **CAVA**

★★ $ Brut Nature is the driest style of sparkling wine, yet this Cava reveals orange and vanilla aromas, a creamy mouthfeel, loads of acidity and expressive flavors that carry through the long finish.

Montsarra Brut | NV | CAVA
★★ $ $ Demonstrating the complexity that Spanish sparkling wine can achieve, this pleasing Brut is stony and minerally, with waves of lemon curd, apple and tart lime flavors.

Segura Viudas Heredad Reserva Brut | NV | CAVA
★★★ $ $ After four years of secondary fermentation, this limited-release wine develops toasted brioche qualities that marry well with the apple and quince notes through the smooth, spicy finish.

ROSÉS

Mas de Monistrol MPX Rosé Brut | NV | CAVA
★★ $ There's nothing shy about this Catalan sparkler. Consisting of 70 percent Monastrell and 30 percent Pinot Noir, it delivers bold blackberry and cherry flavors on a well-structured palate.

Mont Marçal Rosado Brut | 2007 | CAVA
★★ $ $ Mont Marçal produces this light, bright Cava from the little-known Trepat grape, which yields cherry and apple flavors, a delicate mousse and a crisp finish.

united states

The quality of American sparkling wines has been steadily improving. While the best of them still come from the cooler regions of northern California—such as Carneros and the Anderson and Green valleys—Washington State, Oregon, New York and New Mexico are making a growing number of complex, vibrant sparklers.

u.s. sparkling wine recommendations

WHITES

Argyle Brut | 2006 | WILLAMETTE VALLEY, OREGON
★★ $ $ The Willamette Valley has the ideal cool conditions for making great sparkling wines. This is a well-crafted example packed with crisp and spicy pear, clove and quince notes.

Chateau Frank Brut | 2004 | FINGER LAKES, NEW YORK
★★ $ $ Dr. Konstantin Frank helped the Finger Lakes wine region earn distinction for its Rieslings, and his son, Willy Frank, did the same for sparkling wines. This vintage continues the tradition, with a nose of flinty minerals, apple and pear flavors and a refined mousse.

Domaine Carneros by Taittinger Brut | 2006 |
CARNEROS, CALIFORNIA

★★★★ **$ $** Like its Champagnes, Taittinger's California sparklers are standouts. This vintage is simply extraordinary, with complex layers of lemon zest, red cherry, yeasty apple and chalky minerality supported by tingly acidity—all for a great price.

Domaine Ste. Michelle Blanc de Blancs | NV |
COLUMBIA VALLEY, WASHINGTON

★★ **$** Washington's famous sparkling wine producer is a reliable source for beautifully made wines. This well-priced Blanc de Blancs makes a great everyday wine for its lovely pear, apple and spice flavors enlivened by zippy mousse and a touch of quince paste.

Gloria Ferrer Blanc de Noirs | NV | CARNEROS, CALIFORNIA
★★ **$ $** Cava giant Freixenet's Ferrer family is behind this respected California label. This Pinot Noir–based sparkler shows a lovely nose of raspberries and cherries, stone fruit on the palate and a lively mousse.

Schramsberg Blanc de Blancs Brut | 2006 |
NORTH COAST, CALIFORNIA

★★★★ **$ $ $** One of the few American-owned wineries dedicated to sparkling wine, Schramsberg is a regular on White House menus. This stellar vintage is marked by biscuit and lemon curd aromas, citrus and quince flavors and a distinct minerality all the way through.

ROSÉ

Gruet Rosé Brut | NV | NEW MEXICO
★★★ **$** Frenchman Gilbert Gruet's dream of creating his own sparkling wine house was realized in the unlikely location of New Mexico. At 4,300 feet elevation, he found the perfect place for making lovely wines like this yeasty, berry-flavored, affordable rosé.

other countries

Vintners in many parts of the world make sparkling wines, ranging from countless average examples to a few great ones. In many cases Champagne producers have a direct hand in these operations. German and Austrian winemakers use Riesling and Pinot Blanc to make some fine (and a lot of mediocre) sparkling wine called *Sekt.* South Africa uses the traditional method for Cap Classique. Australia makes some delicious traditional sparklers on the cool island of Tasmania, as well as inky-purple sparkling Shiraz.

other countries sparkling wine recommendations

WHITES

Greg Norman Sparkling Pinot Noir/Chardonnay/ Pinot Meunier | NV | **SOUTH EASTERN AUSTRALIA**
★ ★ ★ **$ $** This inexpensive Australian sparkler could easily pass for Champagne with its complex apricot, toast and vanilla flavors, opulent texture and fine mousse. It's a steal for the price.

Punkt Genau Brut | NV | **WEINVIERTEL, AUSTRIA**
★ ★ **$ $** Grüner Veltliner's inherent minerality works well in a sparkling wine. This nicely crafted example shows off a racy effervescence and delicious apple flavors.

Reginato CJR Blanc de Blancs | 2008 | **MENDOZA, ARGENTINA**
★ **$** Vibrant and food-friendly, with chalky minerals, bright pear flavors and invigorating acidity, Reginato's Blanc de Blancs makes a terrific party wine.

ROSÉS

Graham Beck Rosé Brut | 2007 |
WESTERN CAPE, SOUTH AFRICA
★ ★ **$ $** This Brut rosé—made with a second fermentation in the bottle—shows broad flavors of raspberry, yeast and cream and finishes with a delightfully spicy kick.

Taltarni Taché Brut | NV | **AUSTRALIA**
★ ★ **$ $** Taltarni includes red wine in this blend, which gives it a pretty salmon color (*taché* is French for "stained"). With aromas of biscuits and apples, mild acidity and a pleasant, fluffy mousse, it's a fun, enjoyable wine.

RED

The Chook Sparkling Shiraz | NV | **SOUTH EASTERN AUSTRALIA**
★ ★ **$ $** In this exuberant dark purple Shiraz, currants and prunes on the nose carry through on the distinctive palate, where they are balanced by a zesty acidity.

fortified & dessert wines

Fortified and sweet wines typically serve as the bookends of a meal, enjoyed as an aperitif or as a delectable finale. Despite the immense versatility of these wines, with styles ranging from dry, palate-stimulating Sherries to very sweet red and white dessert wines, they remain unknown to many wine lovers. Luckily, this means it's possible to find true bargains on high-quality versions from regions around the world.

fortified wines

The practice of fortifying wines—by adding a neutral spirit, such as clear grape brandy, before bottling—began as a way to ensure the wines' stability over long ocean voyages. Traditional fortified wines include Sherry, Port, Madeira and Marsala, although variations abound. The alcohol content of these wines is higher than that of most unfortified wines, usually between 16 and 20 percent. A fortified wine's style depends largely on when the spirit is added during its production. Adding it during fermentation, as in most Port and Madeira, halts the process, and the resulting wines retain a good deal of natural grape sugar. When brandy is added after fermentation to fully fermented dry wine, the result is much drier, a good example being Fino Sherry.

FORTIFIED WINES

sherry

Sherry, perhaps the most misunderstood fortified wine, is usually associated with sweet Cream Sherry and American jug imposters. In truth, it is a distinctive, sophisticated wine with a rich heritage. Made in southern Spain's Jerez region, Sherry gains complex flavors from the area's chalky soils and a peculiar yeast that appears on the wine's surface. Sherry styles range from utterly dry to incredibly sweet.

Sherry Grapes & Styles

Most Sherries are blends of wines from different years. The dominant grape is Palomino, though sweeter styles often contain Pedro Ximénez or Moscatel. Winemakers employ a fractional blending system called *solera,* which combines barrel-aged liquids from different vintages in such a way that all Sherries bottled contain a portion of the oldest wine in that specific solera. Sherry comes in two basic varieties, *Fino* and *Oloroso,* both of which have subcategories.

- **FINO** A yeast called *flor* that grows on the wine's surface and protects it from oxygen gives Fino Sherry its unusual flavors. Two other dry sherries in the Fino category are: **Manzanilla Sherry,** which displays notes of chamomile (*manzanilla* in Spanish) and a salty tang, and **Amontillado Sherry,** a Fino that loses its flor while aging and has nutty, mineral qualities. **Pale Cream Sherry** is a Fino sweetened by adding Pedro Ximénez wine or grape juice concentrate.
- **OLOROSO** This sherry does not develop flor, and the presence of oxygen during aging creates a nutty, smoky, earthy flavor and a darker hue. Most Olorosos are sweet; some are sweetened further by adding Pedro Ximénez, which creates **Cream Sherry. Palo Cortado** is a chestnut-colored Sherry that starts to develop flor but then backtracks, ending up somewhere between Oloroso and Amontillado in style.

• **PEDRO XIMÉNEZ** Often called PX for short, this wine is produced in many Sherry houses, even though technically it is not considered to be a true Sherry. Made from grapes of the same name grown primarily in the vineyards of the Montilla-Moriles region located just outside of Jerez, Pedro Ximénez wines tend to be rich and sweet, with a viscous texture and pronounced flavors of dried fruit, such as figs, raisins and dates.

sherry recommendations

Bodegas Dios Baco Oloroso
★ $ $ Though this winery's history dates back to 1765, it has existed as Bodegas Dios Baco only since the year 1992. The Oloroso offers a delightful nose of hazelnut, spice and leather, and a concentrated palate that's subtly sweet.

Bodegas Hidalgo La Gitana Manzanilla
★★★ $ (500 ml) This is the archetype of classic Manzanilla—pale, bone-dry and briny. The nutty nose and delicate palate make it a perfect partner for green olives and Marcona almonds.

Bodegas Toro Albalá Don PX | 2007 | **Montilla-Moriles**
★★★ $ $ (375 ml) Located outside of the "Sherry triangle," Toro Albalá specializes in Pedro Ximénez–based wines. This hedonistic vintage is sweet and palate-coating, with flavors of golden raisins and sweet toffee.

Bodegas Valdivia Sacromonte Oloroso Seco 15 Years
★★★ $ $ (500 ml) Valdivia blends together wines with an average age of 15 years to make this wonderful Oloroso. It's marked by toasted hazelnut and dried citrus peel aromas, a dry, full-bodied palate and a remarkably long finish.

Lustau Los Arcos Dry Amontillado
★★★ $ $ Proof that great Sherry can be eminently affordable, this complex and irresistible wine sells for well under $20 a bottle. Dry, with flavors of caramel, nuts and burnt citrus peel, it is rich and concentrated, and its finish goes on and on.

Morenita Cream | NV |
★★ $ Hidalgo's concentrated, rich and nutty blend of Oloroso Sherry and Pedro Ximénez wine is amber-colored and off-dry, with an inviting nose of burnt caramel.

FORTIFIED WINES

port

Portugal's second-largest city, Oporto, gave its name to the country's emblematic wine. Made in the Douro Valley and fortified with brandy to arrest fermentation, Port is typically a dark, sweet wine with a high alcohol content.

Port Grapes & Styles

The grapes most often used in Port production are Touriga Nacional, Touriga Franca and Tinta Roriz (Tempranillo). Categorized by style, Port comes in two popular types, Ruby and Tawny, as well as the occasional white version.

• **RUBY** The most common style of Port, Ruby is blended from a variety of young wines. **Ruby Reserve Ports** (formerly known as Vintage Character Ports) are more complex, often bearing proprietary names like Graham's Six Grapes. **Late Bottled Vintage (LBV) Ports** are single-vintage Rubies that have been aged four to six years in barrel and are drinkable upon release, unlike most Vintage Ports. Made from the best grapes in the finest years and aged in oak for two to three years, **Vintage Ports** require decades of bottle aging to reach their maximum potential. **Single Quinta Vintage Ports** are produced with grapes from a single vineyard, usually in nondeclared vintages.

• **TAWNY** This Port, in theory, has been aged in wood longer than a Ruby and thus taken on a tawny hue. In reality, most inexpensive Tawny Ports are the same age as most Rubies; they are just made with lighter wines. **Aged Tawny Port** is authentic, however, made from blends of the highest-quality Ports that might otherwise have been bottled as Vintage Port. Tawny Port labels indicate the average age of the blend's components (10, 20 or 30 years old, for example). Tawnies are ready to drink upon release and usually exhibit delicate nutty aromas and dried fruit flavors.

• **WHITE** The best Port for summer drinking, served over a glass of ice, White Port has bright, citrusy flavors. Croft recently introduced a new style of rosé—or pink—Port.

port recommendations

Broadbent Vintage | 2007 |

★★★★ $ $ $ Bartholomew Broadbent's Port is made by Dirk van der Niepoort, one of the Douro's best winemakers. Showing perfect balance between velvety tannins and subtle sweetness, this inky wine oozes delicious ripe raspberry flavors and will age well for at least another 30 years.

Churchill's Late Bottled Vintage | 2002 |

★★ $ $ This traditional-style LBV spent four years in barrel before it was bottled unfiltered. Plum, spice and black fruit aromas abound, while chewy tannins give the wine a pleasing grip and structure.

Delaforce His Eminence's Choice 10 Year Tawny

★★ $ $ Delaforce first produced this benchmark Tawny in the 1930s. Caramel, dried apricot and sultana characterize the nose, while the palate is soft, rich and sweet.

Dow's Trademark Finest Reserve

★★ $ $ This is a great entry-level Port. With slightly sweet dark cherry, spice and plum flavors bolstered by smooth tannins, it offers great substance and elegance for the price.

Ferreira White

★ $ $ White Port is somewhat rare in the U.S., but it's very popular at home, where the Portuguese serve it as a chilled aperitif, often over ice. This off-dry version is full of baked peach and mango flavors that have a nutty finish.

Ramos Pinto Quinta de Ervamoira 10 Year Tawny

★★ $ $ $ Ramos Pinto sources all the fruit for this Tawny from a single vineyard in the Douro Superior region. Aromas of butterscotch and dried fig are echoed on the palate, where they are complemented by a nutty quality.

Warre's Vintage | 2007 |

★★★★ $ $ $ (375 ml) A stunning wine from an outstanding vintage, this is rich, full and opulent. Prune, spice, chocolate and blackberry jam compete on the nose, while firm tannins provide structure to the fleshy texture. The never-ending finish is extraordinary.

W. & J. Graham's 20 Year Tawny

★★★ $ $ $ This complex Tawny bursts with aromas and flavors of fig, nut, orange marmalade and vanilla. Smooth and polished, it is nicely framed by fine-grained tannins.

FORTIFIED WINES

madeira

An iconic drink in 19th-century America, Madeira, like other fortified wines, has fallen out of fashion. Named for the Portuguese island off the coast of Morocco where it's produced, Madeira comes in a variety of styles suitable for drinking before, during and after meals.

Madeira Grapes & Styles

Most Madeiras contain a blend of grapes, but the best carry the name of one of four: Sercial, Verdelho, Bual or Malmsey (Malvasia). Sercial is the driest; Verdelho, Bual and Malmsey are progressively sweeter. Most age designations indicate the youngest wine in the blend.

madeira recommendations

Blandy's 5 Year Alvada
★★★ $ $ (500 ml) This blend of Bual and Malmsey boasts a rich palate and a soft, satinlike texture. Though it may not have the complexity of vintage Madeira, it's got youthful charm to spare.

Broadbent 10 Year Malmsey
★★★ $ $ $ Wine importer Bartholomew Broadbent sources his Madeira from one of the finest producers. This combines strikingly concentrated aromas and flavors of caramelized fig, vanilla and walnut with a lively, fresh acidity.

D'Oliveira Malvasia | 1989 |
★★★★ $ $ $ $ Established in 1820, D'Oliveira is one of the few Madeira shippers to survive the phylloxera scourge. This off-dry beauty is hauntingly complex, with layer after layer of toasted nuts and caramel and a long, tangy finish.

H.M. Borges Sweet
★ $ $ After three years' maturation, this simple yet pleasant Tinta Negra Mole–based wine, with a medium body and moderate length, offers up flavors of rum cake and molasses.

The Rare Wine Co. Historic Series Savannah Verdelho
★★★ $ $ $ New to the Historic Series lineup, this wine is a delicious addition. Ever-so-slightly off-dry and satisfyingly full-bodied, it rewards with nuanced caramel-coated toasted nuts on the palate.

dessert wines

As the name implies, dessert wines are typically enjoyed with or in place of dessert. Sauternes from France's Bordeaux region has long held court as perhaps the most prestigious of all sweet wines and continues to command high prices. Producers in Australia make high-quality dessert wines (locally referred to as "stickies"), as do winemakers in California and Canada. Ample sweet fruit and zippy acidity characterize the best of these wines.

white dessert wines

The finest white dessert wines are intense nectars bursting with powerful flavors of flowers, spice, honey and smoke. All well-made examples possess high levels of acidity, which provides important balance and keeps them refreshing in spite of their high sugar content. In order to create dessert wines, winemakers must concentrate the sugars and flavors of the grapes, a process that can be achieved through a variety of methods.

White Dessert Wines Grapes & Styles

• **LATE HARVEST** This dessert wine is made from grapes left on the vine late into the season, when they develop especially high sugar levels. Any grape can be used to make late-harvest wines. The most famous examples come from Germany (marked *Spätlese,* which means "late," or *Auslese,* which is later and sweeter) and Alsace (where they're called *Vendanges Tardives*). California, Australia, South Africa, Chile and the Greek isle of Samos also make good versions.

• **PASSITO** An Italian specialty, passito wines are made from grapes that have been dried before pressing. Tuscan vintners use Trebbiano to make the local version, Vin Santo, while Sicilian vintners use the Zibibbo grape for their delicious passito wines.

• **BOTRYTIS** Botrytized wines owe their unique and highly praised flavors to *Botrytis cinerea,* a mold referred to as "noble rot," which concentrates the wine's fruit notes while adding intriguing hints of smoke and truffle. Some of the finest are made in the Sauternes region of Bordeaux, where Sémillon, Sauvignon Blanc and Muscadelle are blended to craft wines of exceptional flavor and longevity. Bordeaux's Barsac subregion makes many outstanding examples, while the neighboring subregions of Loupiac and Cadillac yield similar, though less costly, versions. The Loire Valley subregions of Quarts de Chaume, Vouvray, Coteaux du Layon, Montlouis and Bonnezeaux use the Chenin Blanc grape to produce their generally outstanding sweet wines. Winemakers in Alsace utilize the region's finest grapes for their *Sélection de Grains Nobles* wines, while German and Austrian vintners use Riesling and other grape varieties to craft sublime botrytized wines, which they designate *Beerenauslese* (BA) or *Trockenbeerenauslese* (TBA), according to the sugar levels of the wines (see p. 126). Winemakers in California, Australia and South Africa also make dessert wines from botrytis-affected grapes.

• **ICE WINE/EISWEIN** As its name suggests, this dessert wine is made from grapes that have been allowed to freeze while still on the vines and then are pressed while frozen, yielding very small amounts of sweet, concentrated juice. Though the finest ice wines are made in Germany and Austria with the Riesling grape, some good examples also come from Canada. Both good and poor imitations are made elsewhere using artificially frozen grapes.

• **VIN DOUX NATUREL** Fortified with brandy during fermentation, which retains the grape's sugars, these wines are made mainly in southern France. The two most noteworthy examples are Muscat de Beaumes-de-Venise from the Rhône and Muscat de Rivesaltes from Roussillon.

• **TOKAJI** This highly distinctive wine is infused with a mash of botrytis-affected grapes (*aszú*). Produced primarily in Hungary, Tokaji is graded by the amount of crushed grapes added to the base, on a scale measured by *puttonyos*—the more *puttonyos,* the more intense the wine. All Tokaji tend to exhibit delicious ripe apricot, orange and almond flavors and high acidity.

white dessert wine recommendations

Casa Larga Fiori Vidal Ice Wine | 2006 |
FINGER LAKES, NEW YORK

★★ **$ $ $** (375 ml) The Colaruotolo family in upstate New York crafts this Sauternes-like wine, which offers abundant notes of apricots and honey and a charming Old World character.

Chambers Rosewood Vineyards Muscat | NV |
RUTHERGLEN, AUSTRALIA

★★★ **$ $** (375 ml) A simply gorgeous dessert wine, this blends notes of rich, roasted nuts with toffee and coffee. Sweet dulce de leche flavors build throughout, ending in a long, caramel-laden finish.

Château de Jau | 2008 | MUSCAT DE RIVESALTES, FRANCE

★★★ **$ $** (500 ml) This concentrated wine is dripping with juicy peaches and pears that linger impressively on the ultralong finish.

Coutet Premier Cru | 2007 | SAUTERNES, FRANCE

★★★★ **$ $ $** Candied citrus aromas introduce this full-bodied sweet white, which is surprisingly refreshing, thanks to the lively acidity that offsets rich notes of thick honey and toasted almonds.

Donnafugata Ben Ryé | 2007 | PASSITO DI PANTELLERIA, ITALY

★★★ **$ $ $** Zibibbo grapes (the Sicilian name for Moscato) from the island of Pantelleria off Sicily's western coast create a wine with real personality. Classic Mediterranean notes of dried apricot and figs are layered on the sweet, full-bodied palate.

Inniskillin Vidal Icewine | 2007 | NIAGARA PENINSULA, CANADA

★★★★ **$ $ $ $** (375 ml) Inniskillin rarely disappoints, and this vintage is no exception. Luxurious and expertly balanced, thanks to a lightning bolt of acidity, it is characterized by dried apricots and candied citrus, a kick of ginger and spice and ample, luscious sweetness.

Klein Constantia Vin de Constance | 2004 |
CONSTANTIA, SOUTH AFRICA

★★★★ **$ $ $** (500 ml) This iconic estate in the Constantia region was founded in 1685. Made with Muscat Blanc à Petits Grains, this wine provides waves of beautiful fig, date and preserved peach flavors that end in a balanced, rather dry finish.

Kourtaki Muscat | NV | SAMOS, GREECE

★★★ **$** Made with grapes from the island of Samos in the northern Aegean, this Greek wine has concentrated flavors of dulce de leche, apricot and fig. Its complexity and long finish belie its low price.

Pellegrino | 2008 | **PASSITO DI PANTELLERIA, ITALY**
★★ $ $ Pellegrino's vineyards on Pantelleria endure punishing heat and fierce Mediterranean winds, yet manage to yield this luscious Moscato passito with its lovely dried nectarine, apricot and crème brûlée flavors and powerful, white pepper–accented finish.

Sheldrake Point Riesling Ice Wine | 2008 |
FINGER LAKES, NEW YORK
★★★★ $ $ $ (375 ml) Sheldrake's sustainably farmed vineyards are situated on a slope between two gorges that feed into Cayuga Lake. This Riesling is absolutely stunning, full of dried pineapple, mango, preserved peach, citrus zest and a jolt of ginger. Creamy in the mouth, it glides toward a silky, polished finish.

Weingut Blees Ferber Piesporter Gärtchen Riesling Auslese | 2008 | **MOSEL, GERMANY**
★★★ $ $ $ (500 ml) Tight and compact on first impression, this Auslese unleashes aromas of sweet pear and quince and heaps of orange, peach and apricot on the refreshingly acidic palate.

Weinlaubenhof Kracher Cuvée Beerenauslese | 2007 |
BURGENLAND, AUSTRIA
★★★ $ $ (375 ml) Chardonnay and Welschsriesling make up this blend, yielding a perfect harmony of apple, pear and apricot flavors that are creamy, spicy and tantalizingly sweet.

red dessert wines

The fame of Port and Madeira (see pp. 261 and 263) should not overshadow the red dessert wine contributions of Italy, France, California and Australia, all of which make intriguing versions ranging in style from light, bubbly and refreshing to dark and intensely rich.

Red Dessert Wines Grapes & Styles

Red dessert wines vary greatly from region to region. From northern Italy comes Recioto della Valpolicella, the sweet sibling of bittersweet Amarone (see p. 79), as well as pink Muscat (Moscato Rosa) and the lightly sparkling Brachetto d'Acqui. France's Roussillon region offers the fortified wines of Banyuls and Maury, both made with Grenache. California and Australia produce sweet late-harvest and Port-style wines from many different grape varieties.

red dessert wine recommendations

Banfi Rosa Regale | 2009 | **BRACHETTO D'ACQUI, ITALY**

★★ $ $ This Piedmont sparkling red is sweet yet ultra-refreshing, thanks to bright acidity and invigorating bubbles. It features the Brachetto grape's classic aromas of rose petals and raspberries and a charming, light body.

Bodegas Gutiérrez de la Vega Casta Diva Recóndita Armonía Monastrell | 2007 | **ALICANTE, SPAIN**

★★★ $ $ $ (500 ml) This blend of Monastrell, Syrah and Cabernet Sauvignon is made in the mountain town of Parcent. Its deceptively light, floral nose explodes into candied violet flavors that are sweet but not cloying.

Dashe Late Harvest Zinfandel | 2008 |
DRY CREEK VALLEY, CALIFORNIA

★★ $ $ (375 ml) To produce this wine, Dashe allows its Sonoma Zinfandel grapes to mature on the vine for an additional month. The result is a wine with impressive balance between black plum and chocolate-covered raisin flavors.

Familia Zuccardi Malamado Malbec | 2005 |
MENDOZA, ARGENTINA

★★ $ $ There aren't many dessert wines made from Malbec. One of Argentina's largest family-owned wineries produces this pleasurable example, which displays the aromas and flavors of coffee, caramel and toast.

Giovanni Allegrini | 2006 |
RECIOTO DELLA VALPOLICELLA CLASSICO, ITALY

★★★ $ $ $ $ (500 ml) The practice of sun-drying wine grapes in Italy's hilly Valpolicella region dates back to pre-Roman times. This modern-day version is simply irresistible, with flavors of prune jam, sweet berries and spicy sarsaparilla.

Les Clos de Paulilles Rimage | 2007 | **BANYULS, FRANCE**

★★ $ $ (500 ml) Made from Grenache, this is a light-bodied French answer to fine Port. Not-too-sweet flavors of red fruit with accents of chalk and lavender lead to a somewhat dry finish.

Seppeltsfield Cellar Nº 7 Tawny | NV | **SOUTH AUSTRALIA**

★★ $ $ This South Australian red dessert wine is the perfect sipper for a summer evening on a front porch swing. With enjoyable flavors of sweet cola, spice and root beer, it has refreshing tannins reminiscent of iced tea.

how to pair wine & food

The old adage "White wine with fish and red with meat" has been replaced with "Drink whatever you like with whatever you want." Both approaches have advantages, but you're bound to encounter pitfalls by adhering too closely to either. The trick is to pair food and wine so that neither distorts or overwhelms the other. Ideally, you want to bring together dishes and wines that highlight each other's best qualities. In the following sections, you'll find general matching rules, ideas for pairing by grape variety, 15 pairing principles with recipes to match and a pairing "cheat sheet."

general rules for matching

be body-conscious Delicately flavored food goes best with a light and delicate wine; heavy, full-flavored dishes call for heftier wines. The subtle flavors of sole meunière are going to get lost if paired with a big, oaky Chardonnay, and a light Beaujolais will seem like water if served with braised short ribs.

balance extremes If a dish is rich and creamy, you need a tart, high-acid wine to cut through the fat and to cleanse your palate. A bit of sweetness in wine balances salty or spicy foods. If you can't wait to drink those young and astringent Bordeaux, Barolos or California Cabernet Sauvignons, the protein and fat of a rich cut of meat will help moderate their tannins.

pair likes Peppery meat dishes work well with spicy red wines like those from the Rhône Valley. Play fruit sauces off rich and fruity wines. Grassy, herbal whites tend to go beautifully with green vegetables.

look to the locals Wines from a particular region often match well with foods from the same place.

mix & match The "red with meat, white with fish" rule is a good fallback when you're unsure what to pair with a dish, but it's a rule made to be broken. Try a light, acidic red such as a Burgundy with a rich fish like salmon; or pair a rich Chardonnay with grilled chicken.

bridge the gap If your table has ordered steak, salmon and sea scallops, and you have to pick the wine, choose one that offers a bit of something for each dish. Full-bodied rosés such as those from Bandol or Tavel or lighter-bodied reds like non-Riserva Chianti Classico or a light-style Oregon Pinot Noir have the subtlety not to overwhelm delicate dishes and the substance to stand up to a hearty steak.

pairing by grape

Of the thousands of different grape varieties in the world, only about 20 are regularly represented on American wine shelves. Each variety has its own particular characteristics that yield different styles of wine and result in a greater affinity with certain foods than others. Here is a guide to the most common varieties, with suggestions for dishes that pair especially well with each and a selection of wines that express each grape's typical qualities.

cabernet franc

Cabernet Franc adds spicy pepper and bright red cherry flavors to Bordeaux red wines, but it stars in France's Loire Valley, where it makes light, spicy reds. California and Long Island also make some good examples.

BEST PAIRINGS Cabernet Franc tends to be somewhat lighter and more herbal than Cabernet Sauvignon, so pair it with dishes like herb-rubbed roast chicken (or any light meat dishes involving a lot of herbs), roast pork loin or veal chops. Earthier, more structured Old World versions of Cabernet Franc—for instance, those hailing from the Chinon region of the Loire Valley—are an ideal match for roast duck or other game birds.

Clos Cristal Hospices de Saumur | 2008 | ★★ $ $ | P. 50
Domaine du Mortier Graviers | 2008 | ★★★ $ $ | P. 50
Shinn Estate Vineyards | 2007 | ★★★ $ $ $ | P. 201

cabernet sauvignon

Cabernet Sauvignon is revered worldwide for its cedary black currant and blackberry flavors bolstered by tannins, which endow it with great aging potential. The best expressions come from Bordeaux, where Cabernet Sauvignon is blended with Merlot, Cabernet Franc and Petit Verdot, as well as from California's Napa Valley, Chile's Upper Maipo Valley and Tuscany, where the grape appears on its own in some Super-Tuscans.

BEST PAIRINGS Cabernets from California, Australia and South America, with their rich fruit and substantial tannins, pair best with meat—well-marbled steaks, braised short ribs, hearty roasts. European Cabernets and Bordeaux blends tend to have higher acidity and less overtly ripe flavors; lamb is a great match for them, or game of any kind.

Angove Family Winemakers Vineyard Select | 2007 | ★★★ $ $ | P. 208

Ghost Pines | 2007 | ★★★ $ $ | P. 161

Miguel Torres Manso de Velasco Old Vines | 2006 | ★★★★ $ $ $ | P. 239

Siesta en el Tahuantinsuyu | 2003 | ★★ $ $ | P. 233

Thelema | 2007 | ★★★★ $ $ $ | P. 245

chardonnay

The Chardonnay grape grows almost everywhere, but it reaches its apex in France's Burgundy, where it produces elegant, mineral-laden whites. Elsewhere Chardonnay is responsible for full-bodied, fruit-driven wines, toasty Champagnes and dessert wines.

BEST PAIRINGS Lighter, unoaked Chardonnay and Chablis pair well with most fish, shellfish and salads. Oakier versions (most California Chardonnays, for instance) are better with more substantial dishes like roast chicken with herbs, pork tenderloin or richer fish dishes or shellfish such as salmon or lobster.

Christian Moreau Père & Fils | 2008 | ★★★ $ $ | P. 41

DMZ | 2008 | ★★ $ | P. 242

Landmark Overlook | 2008 | ★★★ $ $ | P. 151

Nicolas Maillet | 2007 | ★★★ $ $ | P. 40

Santa Ema Selected Terroir | 2009 | ★★★ $ | P. 236

chenin blanc

Full of fruit and high acidity, Chenin Blanc produces some of France's best wines, such as the Loire Valley's full-bodied, long-aging, dry whites, dessert elixirs and sparkling wines. Enjoyable examples of Chenin Blanc are also made in South Africa and California.

BEST PAIRINGS Dry Chenin Blanc is a good partner for white-fleshed fish, chicken or even light veal or pork dishes. Off-dry (lightly sweet) versions pair better with spicy foods such as Indian or other Asian dishes.

Baumard | 2006 | ★★ $ $ | P. 48
Fairview La Capra | 2009 | ★★ $ | P. 242
François Pinon Sec | 2004 | ★★★ $ $ | P. 48
Raats | 2008 | ★★★ $ $ | P. 243

gewürztraminer

The pink-skinned Gewürztraminer grape offers exuberant aromas and flamboyant flavors ranging from honeysuckle to lychee, candied apricot, mineral and Asian spice. It is an especially important grape in the white wines of Alsace and Germany.New York and California are also home to some excellent Gewürztraminer-based wines.

BEST PAIRINGS Gewürztraminer almost always pairs well with Asian and Indian food—for spicier dishes, choose an off-dry (lightly sweet) example; for less spicy dishes, dry Gewürztraminer is the better match. Gewürztraminer is also a good accompaniment for stronger cheeses such as Époisses or Muenster.

Helfrich | 2008 | ★★ $ | P. 28
Hermann J. Wiemer Dry | 2008 | ★★ $ $ | P. 200
Lucien Albrecht Cuvée Marie | 2007 | ★★★★ $ $ $ | P. 28
St. Michael-Eppan | 2009 | ★★ $ $ | P. 79

grenache/garnacha

The fresh, spicy cherry flavors of the Grenache grape are essential to many of the red wines of southern France, such as Châteauneuf-du-Pape and Côtes-du-Rhône. Spain's wine-makers rely heavily on Grenache (Garnacha in Spanish), particularly in Priorat. The variety is also important in Sardinia (where it is known as Cannonau) and shows up in wines from California and Australia.

BEST PAIRINGS Grenache, with its warm, quintessentially Mediterranean flavors, pairs well with hearty dishes like grilled sausages, lamb chops and rustic stews.

Alto Moncayo Veraton | 2007 | ★ ★ ★ $ $ | P. 105
Epicurean Bistro | 2007 | ★ ★ $ | P. 214
Monte Oton | 2008 | ★ $ | P. 106
Two Hands Yesterday's Hero | 2008 | ★ ★ ★ $ $ $ | P. 217

malbec

Malbec is the signature red grape of Argentina, where it yields wines that are bursting with lush, dark berry and rich chocolate flavors. It is no longer important in Bordeaux, its place of origin, but dominates red wine production in the French region of Cahors, where it is called Auxerrois, and shows up in the Loire Valley, California, Australia and Chile.

BEST PAIRINGS Malbec's full-bodied dark fruit flavors and light, peppery spiciness make it a natural partner for beef, lamb, venison and other substantial meats.

Bianchi Particular | 2007 | ★ ★ ★ $ $ | P. 230
Château Lagrézette Cru d'Exception | 2005 |
★ ★ ★ $ $ | P. 67
Kaiken | 2008 | ★ ★ $ | P. 232
Viu Manent Single Vineyard San Carlos Estate | 2007 |
★ ★ ★ $ $ | P. 239

marsanne/roussanne

White grapes Marsanne and Roussanne are most at home in France's northern Rhône Valley, where they are often combined to create the great wines of Crozes-Hermitage, Hermitage and St-Joseph. Many winemakers blend them with Viognier. Good versions also come from California.

BEST PAIRINGS Full-bodied, with stone-fruit and honey flavors and moderate acidity, Marsanne-Roussanne blends pair well with lighter meats in herb-based sauces and richer fish. They are also good with roast chicken and with vegetables like parsnips, fennel and celery root.

Le Plan Vermeersch Classic | 2008 | ★ ★ $ $ | P. 56
Nicolas Jaboulet Perrin Frères | 2008 |
★ ★ ★ $ $ $ $ | P. 53
Qupé Bien Nacido Hillside Estate Roussanne | 2007 |
★ ★ ★ ★ $ $ $ | P. 157

merlot

With its plum and chocolate flavors, Merlot is one of the most popular grapes in the world and is responsible for some of the greatest red wines, such as those from Bordeaux's Pomerol and Washington State. Terrific examples are also produced in California and northeastern Italy.

BEST PAIRINGS Merlot's spicy plum flavors and full body make it a good match for everything from pork chops and roasts to pasta in meat sauce and sausages off the grill.

Lonko Single Vineyard | 2005 | ★ ★ $ $ | P. 233
Michel Lynch | 2008 | ★ $ | P. 35
Pellegrini Vineyards | 2005 | ★ ★ $ $ | P. 201
Silverado Vineyards | 2006 | ★ ★ ★ $ $ $ | P. 168
Trefethen Family Vineyards | 2006 | ★ ★ ★ $ $ $ | P. 168

muscat

All Muscat, both red and white, bursts with fragrant flavors such as honeysuckle, orange blossom and musk. It's grown throughout the world, most famously in Italy as Moscato and in Spain as Moscatel, as well as in Alsace, southern France, Greece, California and Australia.

BEST PAIRINGS Most Muscat bottlings are lightly sweet; that, together with the grape's tangerine-scented fruitiness, makes it a natural partner for fresh fruit desserts.

Chambers Rosewood Vineyards | NV |
★ ★ ★ $ $ (375 ml) | P. 266
Château de Jau | 2008 | ★ ★ ★ $ $ (500 ml) | P. 266
Domaine Weinbach Clos des Capucins Réserve | 2008 |
★ ★ ★ $ $ $ | P. 28
Kourtaki | NV | ★ ★ ★ $ | P. 266

nebbiolo

Nebbiolo achieves its greatest glory in Italy's Piedmont region, where the variety's cherry, tar and tobacco flavors define the elegant, long-lived reds of Barolo and Barbaresco. A small number of vintners outside of Italy work with Nebbiolo, too, especially in California and Australia, but in these places the grape tends to express different characteristics.

BEST PAIRINGS This structured, aromatic red grape pairs particularly well with any dish involving mushrooms, but it is also good with lamb, venison and beef (beef braised in Barolo is a classic Piedmontese dish). Older vintages go perfectly with truffles.

Clendenen Family Vineyards | 2003 | ★ ★ ★ $ $ $ | P. 182
Ceretto Asij Barbaresco | 2006 | ★ ★ ★ $ $ $ | P. 72
Gaja Dagromis Barolo | 2004 | ★ ★ ★ ★ $ $ $ $ | P. 73
Piazzo Barbaresco | 2006 | ★ ★ ★ $ $ $ | P. 73
Renato Ratti Ochetti | 2008 | ★ ★ ★ $ $ | P. 75

petite sirah

Not to be confused with the Syrah grape (known as Shiraz in Australia), Petite Sirah yields wines that are lusty and dark and full of chewy tannins. A French native, hailing originally from the Rhône Valley, the grape is believed to be a cross between the Peloursin variety and Syrah, and grows well in California, Mexico, South America, Australia and parts of the Middle East.

BEST PAIRINGS Almost invariably full-bodied and bursting with blackberry and spice flavors, Petite Sirah is ideal with saucy barbecued meats or rich braised short ribs prepared with an array of sweet or savory spices.

Earthquake | 2007 | ★ ★ ★ $ $ | P. 182
Greg Norman | 2007 | ★ ★ $ | P. 182
LangeTwins Petite Sirah/Petit Verdot | 2008 | ★ ★ $ $ | P. 183

pinot blanc

Winemakers in Alsace, California and Italy craft wines from Pinot Blanc (also called Pinot Bianco) that tend to be medium-bodied with mild fruit flavors. Sometimes referred to as "the poor man's Chardonnay," Pinot Blanc goes by the name Weissburgunder ("white Burgundy") in Austria, where the variety expresses richer, more concentrated flavors and greater overall character than in the Pinot Blanc styles found elsewhere. In Alsace, Pinot Blanc is typically blended with the Auxerrois grape.

BEST PAIRINGS Pair Pinot Blanc with delicate freshwater fish such as trout or perch, or light meat dishes involving chicken breasts or veal scallops. Italian Pinot Biancos tend to be leaner and are best with raw shellfish or fresh green salads lightly dressed.

Domaines Schlumberger Les Princes Abbés | 2007 | ★ ★ $ | P. 27

Niedermayr | 2008 | ★ ★ $ $ | P. 78

St. Magdalena Dellago Weissburgunder | 2009 | ★ ★ $ $ | P. 79

Wine by Joe | 2009 | ★ ★ $ | P. 187

pinot gris/pinot grigio

In Alsace and Oregon, the Pinot Gris grape produces full-bodied, nutty white wines. In Italy, where it is called Pinot Grigio, the variety makes light, brisk whites. It also has success in California's cooler regions.

BEST PAIRINGS Light and simple Pinot Grigios make a good match for equally light fish dishes and green salads. Alsace-style Pinot Gris tends to be richer and goes better with flavorful pasta dishes or chicken in cream-based sauces; it also pairs well with modestly spiced Asian and Indian dishes.

Domaine Ostertag Fronholz | 2007 | ★ ★ ★ $ $ $ | P. 27

The Eyrie Vineyards | 2008 | ★ ★ ★ $ $ | P. 187

Kris | 2008 | ★ ★ $ | P. 78

Livon Braide Grande | 2008 | ★ ★ $ $ | P. 78

WillaKenzie Estate | 2008 | ★ ★ ★ $ $ | P. 187

pinot noir

Known as the "heartbreak grape," Pinot Noir is difficult to grow and vinify everywhere it is cultivated. At its best, the variety yields wines that are incredibly seductive, with aromas of roses, smoke, red fruits and earth. The red wines of Burgundy are regarded as the ultimate expression of the Pinot Noir grape, but excellent examples are also produced in the Loire Valley, California, New York, Oregon, Australia and New Zealand.

BEST PAIRINGS Old World Pinot Noir (Burgundy, for example) goes best with simple, flavorful dishes such as steaks, lamb chops or wild game birds. The New World's fruitier, more straightforward versions make good matches for duck, richer fish, especially salmon, and dishes involving mushrooms and truffles.

Au Bon Climat La Bauge Au-dessus | 2007 |
★ ★ ★ **$ $** | P. 169

Domaine Patrick Miolane | 2005 | ★ ★ ★ ★ **$ $** | P. 43

J. Hofstätter Meczan | 2008 | ★ ★ ★ **$ $** | P. 80

Jules Taylor Wines | 2008 | ★ ★ ★ **$ $** | P. 224

Santa Carolina Reserva | 2008 | ★ ★ **$** | P. 239

riesling

Riesling can make white wines of extraordinary complexity, with high acidity and plenty of mineral flavors, in styles that range from bone-dry to sumptuously sweet. Rieslings are made all around the world, but the best versions come from Alsace, Germany, Austria, Australia and New York. Many can age for decades.

BEST PAIRINGS Off-dry (lightly sweet) Rieslings pair very well with Asian cuisines, especially Thai and Vietnamese. Dry Riesling is a good accompaniment to freshwater fish such as trout, as well as dishes with citrus flavors.

A to Z | 2007 | ★ ★ ★ **$** | P. 187

Dr. Loosen Blue Slate Kabinett | 2008 | ★ ★ ★ **$ $** | P. 128

Penfolds Thomas Hyland | 2008 | ★ ★ ★ **$** | P. 207

Sheldrake Point Ice Wine | 2008 |
★ ★ ★ ★ **$ $ $** (375 ml) | P. 267

Theo Minges Burrweiler Schlossgarten Spätlese | 2007 |
★ ★ ★ **$ $** | P. 131

sangiovese

Sangiovese is an important grape in Italy, where it is prized for its red cherry and leather flavors and high acidity. It is most common in Tuscany, where it makes most of the red wines of Chianti and many of the exalted Super-Tuscans. The grape is also grown in California.

BEST PAIRINGS Sangiovese's bright cherry-berry flavors, firm acidity and moderate tannins are all characteristics that make it ideal for pastas with tomato-based sauces as well as pizza. Rich, starchy dishes such as risotto and full-flavored, dry-cured sausages are other good partners.

Agricola Querciabella Querciabella | 2007 | ★★★ **$ $** | P. 84
Melini Borghi d'Elsa | 2008 | ★★ **$** | P. 85
Principe Corsini Don Tommaso | 2006 | ★★★ **$ $ $** | P. 86
Seghesio Family Vineyards | 2007 | ★★★ **$ $** | P. 184

sauvignon blanc

Sauvignon Blanc's finest expressions are the lemony, herbaceous white wines of the Sancerre and Pouilly-Fumé regions of France's Loire Valley, but many New Zealand examples, with flavors of zingy grapefruit and fresh-cut grass, are also outstanding. Winemakers in parts of California, Austria and South Africa produce excellent Sauvignon Blancs as well.

BEST PAIRINGS With its bright acidity, mixed citrus (most commonly grapefruit) flavors and herbal notes, Sauvignon Blanc makes an ideal partner for raw shellfish, light fish dishes, salads and fresh vegetable dishes; it's also a classic partner for anything involving goat cheese.

Domaine Alexandre Bain Mademoiselle M Pouilly-Fumé | 2008 | ★★★ **$ $** | P. 48
Ferrari-Carano Fumé Blanc | 2009 | ★★ **$** | P. 154
Hanna | 2009 | ★★★ **$ $** | P. 154
Nobilo Icon | 2009 | ★★★ **$ $** | P. 221
Pascal Jolivet Sancerre | 2009 | ★★★ **$ $** | P. 49

sémillon

The second of Bordeaux's great white wine grapes after Sauvignon Blanc, Sémillon is the primary component of the region's luxurious, sweet Sauternes wines. The variety also appears on its own or blended with Sauvignon Blanc to make some delicious, full-bodied dry wines throughout Bordeaux and Australia.

BEST PAIRINGS Sémillon's lemon and honey flavors are ideal with light fish in butter-based sauces, as well as baked or roast fish; it's also good with light chicken dishes.

Brokenwood | 2008 | ★★ **$$** | P. 206
Château Graville-Lacoste | 2008 | ★★★★ **$$** | P. 31
Château Rahoul | 2007 | ★★ **$$** | P. 31
Coutet Premier Cru | 2007 | ★★★★ **$$$** | P. 266

syrah/shiraz

Typically rich, round, full-bodied and tannic, with berry, pepper and smoke aromas and flavors, wines made from the Syrah grape (called Shiraz in Australia) often show both power and finesse and can age for decades. Syrah's most renowned domains are the Hermitage and Côte Rôtie appellations in France's Rhône Valley, but California's Central Coast, Washington State and Australia also produce impressive versions.

BEST PAIRINGS Pair spicy, structured Old World Syrahs with steaks or game such as venison and lamb. Fruitier New World bottlings, like most from Australia, also work well with lamb and can go with rich, cheesy dishes like eggplant Parmesan or hamburgers topped with blue cheese.

Beckmen Vineyards Estate | 2008 | ★★★ **$$** | P. 174
Block 50 | 2007 | ★ **$** | P. 210
Domaine Courbis | 2007 | ★★★ **$$** | P. 54
Expatriate | 2007 | ★★★★ **$$$** | P. 210
Puydeval "Chevalier" | 2008 | ★★ **$** | P. 64

tempranillo

Grown throughout Spain, Tempranillo is best known as the variety responsible for the red wines of Rioja. Tempranillo-based wines tend to give spicy aromas, red fruit flavors and medium body.

BEST PAIRINGS Lamb in almost any form is a classic pairing for Tempranillo. Other good partners include hard sheep cheeses like Manchego and lighter roast meats like pork or veal. Tempranillo's typically cherrylike fruit also makes it nice with duck.

Bokisch Vineyards Liberty Oaks Vineyard | 2007 | ★★ $ $ | P. 181
Faustino VII | 2007 | ★★ $ | P. 106
Finca Allende | 2005 | ★★★ $ $ | P. 106
Pinord Clos de Torribas Crianza | 2005 | ★★ $ | P. 114

viognier

The basis of many of the famed white wines of France's northern Rhône Valley, Viognier has become a favorite in California for its lush peach, citrus and floral flavors.

BEST PAIRINGS Pair low-acid, lush Viognier with fruits such as apples, pears and peaches, richer shellfish such as scallops or lobster and white-fleshed fish with butter or cream sauces. France's Viogniers, which tend to be leaner and spicier, also make good partners for quail, rabbit, guinea hen or sweetbreads.

Barboursville Vineyards Reserve | 2008 | ★★ $ $ | P. 200
Christine Andrew | 2007 | ★★ $ | P. 156
Christophe Pichon | 2007 | ★★★ $ $ $ | P. 53
Cinder | 2009 | ★★ $ $ | P. 200

zinfandel

California's own red grape (by way of Croatia), Zinfandel assumes many forms, from off-dry pale rosés and simple reds to full-bodied, tannic wines with blackberry and spice flavors. Zinfandel also makes thick Port-style dessert wines.

BEST PAIRINGS Zinfandel's robust, dark berry flavors, spice notes and moderate tannins make it an ideal partner for simple, hearty meat dishes like hamburgers, sausages or lamb chops. It's also a great match for barbecue, as the wine's sweet, spicy flavors complement the sweet, spicy sauce, and for Mexican food.

Candor Lot 2 | NV | ★★ $ $ | P. 178
Claudia Springs John Ricetti Vineyard | 2007 | ★★★ $ $ | P. 178
Limerick Lane Collins Vineyard | 2007 | ★★★★ $ $ | P. 179
Porter-Bass | 2005 | ★★★ $ $ | P. 179

15 rules & recipes for perfect pairings

Listed below are pairing principles for 15 of the world's most important wines. On the following pages are 15 stellar recipes to match, developed by F&W's Test Kitchen.

1. champagne *plus* anything salty

2. sauvignon blanc *plus* tart dressings

3. grüner veltliner *plus* fresh herbs

4. pinot grigio *plus* light fish dishes

5. chardonnay *plus* rich seafood

6. off-dry riesling *plus* spicy dishes

7. moscato d'asti *plus* fruit desserts

8. sparkling rosé *plus* hearty recipes

9. dry rosé *plus* cheesy dishes

10. pinot noir *plus* earthy flavors

11. old world wines *plus* old world food

12. malbec *plus* sweet-spicy bbq

13. zinfandel *plus* pâtés & mousses

14. cabernet *plus* juicy red meat

15. syrah *plus* spiced dishes

1. champagne *plus* anything salty

Most dry sparkling wines, such as Brut Champagne and Cava, have a faint sweetness that makes them extra-refreshing with salty foods.

Crispy Udon Noodles with Nori Salt

8 SERVINGS

    4   ounces dried udon noodles
Vegetable oil, for tossing and frying
    1   sheet nori
    1   tablespoon kosher salt

1. In a medium saucepan of boiling water, cook the udon noodles until they are almost al dente, about 4 minutes. Drain thoroughly and transfer the udon noodles to a medium bowl. Gently toss the noodles with vegetable oil to keep them from sticking together.

2. Using a pair of sturdy metal tongs, hold the nori over an open flame and toast about 4 inches from the heat until the nori is darkened and crisp, about 5 seconds per side. Let cool, then crumble and transfer to a spice grinder. Add the salt and grind to a powder.

3. Take 4 udon strands and tie them in a loose knot near the end. Repeat with the remaining udon. In a large skillet, heat $1/4$ inch of vegetable oil until shimmering. Fry 4 of the bundles at a time over moderately high heat, spreading the udon out in a fan, until golden and crisp, about 1 minute per side. Transfer the bundles to paper towels to drain, then dust with the nori salt and serve.

MAKE AHEAD The fried udon bundles can be stored in an airtight container for 3 hours. The nori salt can be stored in an airtight container for 2 weeks.

WINE Brisk and refreshing sparkling wine.

2. sauvignon blanc *plus* tart dressings

Tangy dressings and sauces won't overwhelm zippy white wines like Sauvignon Blanc, Vinho Verde from Portugal and Verdejo from Spain.

Scallops with Grapefruit-Onion Salad

8 FIRST-COURSE SERVINGS

- 4 small ruby red grapefruits (about 2 pounds total)
- 3 tablespoons pickled cocktail onions
- 2 tablespoons packed flat-leaf parsley leaves

Freshly ground pepper

- 24 sea scallops (about 2 pounds)

Kosher salt

- 1 tablespoon extra-virgin olive oil, plus more for drizzling

1. Using a very sharp paring knife, peel the grapefruits, carefully removing all of the bitter white pith. Carefully cut in between the membranes to release the grapefruit sections into a bowl. Discard all but 1 tablespoon of grapefruit juice from the bowl. Stir in the pickled cocktail onions and parsley leaves and season with pepper.

2. Pat the sea scallops dry and season them all over with salt. In a large nonstick skillet, heat the 1 tablespoon of olive oil until it is shimmering. Cook the scallops over moderately high heat, turning once, until they are browned and just cooked through, about 4 minutes total. Spoon the pickled-onion-and-grapefruit salad onto small plates and arrange the scallops around the salad. Drizzle with olive oil and serve.

WINE Zingy Verdejo from central Spain.

3. grüner veltliner *plus* fresh herbs

Austria's Grüner Veltliner has a citrus-and-clover scent that's lovely with herb-rich dishes. Spain's Albariño and Italy's Vermentino are great, too.

Zucchini Linguine with Herbs

8 SERVINGS

- **4 pounds small zucchini**
- **6 tablespoons unsalted butter**
- **4 scallions, thinly sliced lengthwise**
- **Salt and freshly ground pepper**
- **1 ¹/₂ pounds fresh linguine or spaghetti**
- **2 tablespoons chopped tarragon or chervil, plus more for garnish**
- **1 tablespoon chopped lemon thyme**
- **1 teaspoon grated lemon zest**
- **8 ounces young pecorino cheese, freshly grated (2 cups), plus more for garnish**

1. Using a mandoline, julienne the zucchini lengthwise, stopping when you reach the seedy centers. You should have 12 packed cups of zucchini strands.

2. In a very large, deep skillet, melt the butter. Add the zucchini and scallions, season with salt and pepper and cook over moderately high heat, stirring occasionally, until the zucchini is just softened, about 8 minutes.

3. Meanwhile, in a large pot of boiling salted water, cook the pasta until al dente. Drain; reserve 1 cup of the water.

4. Add the pasta, chopped tarragon, thyme, lemon zest and cheese to the skillet and toss well. Add the pasta water and cook over moderately high heat, stirring, until the sauce is slightly thickened, 3 minutes. Transfer to plates, garnish with tarragon and grated cheese and serve.

WINE Aromatic, dry Grüner Veltliner from Austria.

4. pinot grigio *plus* light fish dishes

Light seafood dishes take on more flavor when they are matched with equally delicate whites, like Pinot Grigio from Italy or Chablis from France.

Seafood Tostada Bites

MAKES 24 HORS D'OEUVRES

Two 8-inch flour tortillas

- 1 cup vegetable oil
- 4 tablespoons unsalted butter
- 1 leek, white and pale green parts, halved lengthwise and thinly sliced crosswise
- 24 shelled and deveined small shrimp (about $1/2$ pound)
- $1/2$ pound sea scallops, cut into $1/2$-inch pieces
- $1/2$ pound lump crabmeat

Salt and freshly ground pepper

- $3/4$ cup dry white wine
- 2 tablespoons minced parsley

1. On a cutting board, cut the tortillas into 24 triangles, about $3/4$ inch. In a medium skillet, heat the oil over moderately high heat. Add the tortilla triangles and fry until golden, 1 minute. Using a slotted spoon, transfer the tortillas to a paper towel–lined plate.

2. In a large, deep skillet, melt 1 tablespoon of the butter. Add the leek and cook over moderate heat, stirring occasionally, until softened, about 4 minutes. Stir in the shrimp, scallops and crab and season with salt and pepper. Add the wine and simmer just until the shrimp are pink, 2 minutes. Using a slotted spoon, transfer the seafood to a bowl. Add the parsley and the remaining 3 tablespoons of butter to the skillet and simmer until the liquid is reduced to a few tablespoons, about 3 minutes. Return the seafood to the pan and toss to coat.

3. Spoon the seafood into Chinese soup spoons or shot glasses, garnish with the tortillas and serve at once.

WINE Light, nectarine-inflected Italian Pinot Grigio.

5. chardonnay *plus* rich seafood

Silky whites, such as Chardonnays from California, Chile or Australia, are delicious with rich fish like salmon or any kind of seafood in a lush sauce.

Sizzling Shrimp Scampi

8 SERVINGS

2	sticks unsalted butter, softened
3	large garlic cloves, minced
1	tablespoon plus 2 teaspoons chopped flat-leaf parsley
1 1/2	teaspoons finely grated lemon zest
1	teaspoon fresh lemon juice
1/2	teaspoon chopped thyme

Kosher salt and freshly ground black pepper

3	pounds large shrimp—shelled and deveined, tails left on
1	tablespoon thinly sliced basil leaves

Crusty bread, for serving

1. Preheat the oven to 450°. In a medium bowl, mix the butter with the garlic, 2 teaspoons of the parsley, the lemon zest, lemon juice and thyme and season with salt and black pepper to taste.

2. In a large gratin dish, arrange the shrimp, tails up, in a circular pattern. Dot the shrimp with the flavored butter and roast for about 10 minutes, until the shrimp are pink and the butter is bubbling. Sprinkle the shrimp with the remaining 1 tablespoon of chopped parsley and the thinly sliced basil leaves. Serve hot, with bread.

MAKE AHEAD The flavored butter can be refrigerated for up to 1 week or frozen for up to 1 month.

WINE Full-bodied Australian Chardonnay.

6. off-dry riesling *plus* spicy dishes

The slight sweetness of many Rieslings, Gewürztraminers and Vouvrays helps tame the heat of spicy Asian dishes.

Thai Green Salad with Duck Cracklings

8 SERVINGS

8	duck confit legs—skin cut into fine strips, meat shredded (see Note)
1	tablespoon finely chopped fresh ginger
1	large garlic clove, minced
1	serrano chile, seeded and minced
2	tablespoons light brown sugar
3	tablespoons Asian fish sauce
2	tablespoons fresh lime juice
2	tablespoons water
1 1/4	pounds baby Bibb lettuce, leaves separated
1/2	cup mint leaves
1/2	cup cilantro leaves

1. In a large nonstick skillet, cook the duck skin over moderate heat until crisp, about 8 minutes. Using a slotted spoon, transfer the cracklings to a plate. Pour off all but 2 tablespoons of the fat in the skillet and add the meat. Cook over moderate heat until tender and crispy in spots, about 7 minutes. Let cool slightly.

2. Meanwhile, in a mortar (or using a mini food processor), pound the ginger with the garlic, chile and brown sugar to a coarse paste. Stir in the fish sauce, lime juice and water.

3. In a bowl, toss the lettuce with the mint, cilantro, duck, cracklings and dressing. Transfer to plates and serve.

NOTE Duck confit is available at specialty markets and at dartagnan.com.

WINE Lightly sweet Riesling from Germany.

7. moscato d'asti *plus* fruit desserts

Slightly sweet sparkling wines such as Moscato d'Asti emphasize the fruit in the dessert, not the sugar.

Honeyed Fig Crostatas

8 SERVINGS

2 ½   cups all-purpose flour

 ¼   cup plus 1 tablespoon sugar

Kosher salt

1 ½   sticks cold unsalted butter, cut into ½-inch pieces

 ¼   cup plus 3 tablespoons ice water

1 ½   pounds fresh green and purple figs,
       each cut into 6 wedges

  5   teaspoons honey

  1   teaspoon fresh lemon juice

 ¼   teaspoon thyme leaves,
       plus small sprigs for garnish

  1   egg beaten with 1 tablespoon of water

1. In a food processor, pulse the flour, sugar and ½ teaspoon of salt. Add the butter and pulse until the mixture is the size of peas. Add the ice water; pulse until the dough comes together. Pat the dough into a disk, wrap in plastic and chill for 30 minutes.

2. On a lightly floured surface, roll out the dough ⅛ inch thick. Cut out eight 5-inch rounds; reroll the scraps if needed. Transfer to a parchment-lined baking sheet and refrigerate for 30 minutes.

3. Preheat the oven to 375°. In a bowl, toss two-thirds of the figs with 3 teaspoons of the honey, the lemon juice, thyme leaves and a pinch of salt. Arrange the figs on the rounds, leaving a ½-inch border all around. Fold the edges over the figs; brush the dough with the egg wash. Chill for 30 minutes.

4. Bake for 35 minutes, until the crusts are golden. Let stand for 10 minutes.

5. Toss the remaining figs with the remaining 2 teaspoons of honey. Transfer the crostatas to plates, top with the figs and thyme sprigs and serve.

WINE Subtly sweet sparkling wine.

8. sparkling rosé *plus* hearty recipes

Although most people drink sparkling rosé with hors d'oeuvres, these wines have the depth of flavor to go with a wide range of main courses.

Beet Risotto

8 SERVINGS

- **7** cups chicken stock or 3 1/2 cups low-sodium broth mixed with 3 1/2 cups of water
- **4** tablespoons unsalted butter
- **1/4** cup extra-virgin olive oil
- **1** large sweet onion, finely chopped
- **2** large beets (12 ounces each), peeled and coarsely shredded, plus thinly sliced beets for garnish
- **3** cups arborio rice (1 1/4 pounds)
- **6** ounces young pecorino cheese, freshly grated (1 1/2 cups)
- **2** teaspoons poppy seeds, plus more for garnish

1. In a saucepan, bring the stock to a simmer; cover and keep warm. In a medium enameled cast-iron casserole, melt the butter in the oil. Add the onion and cook over moderately high heat, stirring, until softened, 5 minutes. Add the shredded beets and cook, stirring, until the pan is dry, 12 minutes. Spoon half of the beets into a small bowl.

2. Add the rice to the casserole and cook, stirring, for 2 minutes. Add 1 cup of the warm stock to the rice and cook over moderate heat, stirring, until the stock is nearly absorbed. Continue adding the stock 1 cup at a time, stirring constantly, until the rice is al dente and a thick sauce forms, 22 minutes. Stir in the reserved cooked beets, the cheese and the 2 teaspoons of poppy seeds. Cook, stirring, until heated through; add a few tablespoons of water if the risotto is too thick. Spoon the risotto into bowls, garnish with the sliced beets and poppy seeds and serve.

WINE Sparkling rosé from California.

9. dry rosé *plus* cheesy dishes

Some cheeses go better with white wine, some with red; yet almost all pair well with dry rosé, with its balance of acidity and fruit.

Triple-Decker Baked Italian Cheese Sandwiches

8 SERVINGS

- 8 plum tomatoes, halved
- 1/4 cup extra-virgin olive oil

Kosher salt and freshly ground pepper

- 1 teaspoon thyme leaves
- 2 white Pullman loaves—ends discarded, each loaf cut into twelve 1/2-inch-thick slices
- 1 pound sliced provolone cheese
- 1 pound Fontina cheese, coarsely shredded (about 5 1/2 cups)
- 1/2 cup freshly grated Parmigiano-Reggiano cheese

1. Preheat the oven to 325°. On a large rimmed baking sheet, toss the tomatoes with 2 tablespoons of the oil and season with salt and pepper. Bake the tomatoes cut side up for 1 1/2 hours, until soft and starting to brown. Sprinkle with the thyme and bake for 30 minutes longer, until the tomatoes are very tender and slightly shriveled but still juicy. Let cool.

2. Increase the oven temperature to 375°. Brush 16 bread slices with the remaining 2 tablespoons of olive oil; arrange 8 of the slices oiled side down on a large rimmed baking sheet. Top with the provolone and the unbrushed bread slices. Cover with the tomatoes, 4 cups of the Fontina and the remaining 8 bread slices, oiled side up. Press gently on the sandwiches and bake for about 15 minutes, until the bread is toasted and the cheese is melted.

3. Preheat the broiler. Toss the remaining Fontina with the Parmigiano-Reggiano and sprinkle on the sandwiches. Broil 3 inches from the heat for about 1 minute, until the cheese is melted. Transfer to plates and serve.

WINE Dry, fragrant rosé from Provence.

10. pinot noir *plus* earthy flavors

Ingredients such as mushrooms and truffles taste great with Pinot Noir and Dolcetto, which are light-bodied but full of savory depth.

Leek-and-Pecorino Pizzas

8 SERVINGS

All-purpose flour, for dusting

$1 \frac{1}{2}$ **pounds pizza dough, cut into 8 pieces**

$\frac{1}{4}$ **cup plus 2 tablespoons extra-virgin olive oil, plus more for brushing**

2 **large leeks, sliced $\frac{1}{4}$ inch thick**

Salt and freshly ground pepper

$\frac{3}{4}$ **pound ground lamb**

32 **cherry tomatoes, halved**

$\frac{1}{4}$ **pound truffled pecorino cheese, thinly sliced**

1. Preheat the oven to 500°. Heat a pizza stone on the bottom of the oven for 45 minutes. (Or heat a large inverted baking sheet on the bottom rack of the oven for 5 minutes.)

2. On a lightly floured work surface, roll out each piece of dough to a 7-inch round. Oil 3 large baking sheets and place the rounds on the sheets. Cover with plastic wrap and let rest for 15 minutes.

3. Meanwhile, in a large skillet, heat $\frac{1}{4}$ cup of the olive oil. Add the leeks, season with salt and pepper and cook over moderate heat until softened, about 8 minutes; transfer to a plate. Add the 2 tablespoons of olive oil to the skillet. Add the lamb, season with salt and pepper and cook until no pink remains, 5 minutes.

4. Generously flour a pizza peel. Place a dough round on the peel and brush with olive oil. Top with some of the leeks, lamb, tomatoes and pecorino cheese. Slide the dough round onto the hot stone or baking sheet and bake for about 4 minutes, until bubbling and crisp. Repeat with the remaining ingredients and serve.

WINE Light-bodied, spicy Pinot Noir from Oregon.

11. old world wines *plus* old world food

Foods and wines that have grown up together over the centuries are almost always a good fit.

Pappardelle with Veal Ragù

8 SERVINGS

3 ½ to 4 pounds boneless veal shoulder,
    cut into 3-inch chunks

Salt and freshly ground pepper

All-purpose flour, for dusting

- ½   cup extra-virgin olive oil
- 1   large sweet onion, chopped
- 4   garlic cloves, minced
- 1 ½   teaspoons ground coriander
- 1 ½   teaspoons ground fennel
- 1 ½   cups dry red wine

Two 28-ounce cans Italian whole tomatoes,
    drained and chopped

- 4   cups chicken or veal stock
- 1 ½   tablespoons minced rosemary
- 2   pounds fresh pappardelle

Freshly grated Parmigiano-Reggiano

1. Season the veal with salt and pepper and dust with flour. In a large enameled cast-iron casserole, heat ¼ cup of the oil. Add the veal and cook over moderately high heat until browned all over, about 12 minutes; transfer to a plate.

2. Add the remaining ¼ cup of oil to the casserole. Stir in the onion, garlic, coriander and fennel; cook over low heat for 5 minutes. Add the wine and boil until reduced to ⅓ cup, 5 minutes. Add the tomatoes and cook over moderately high heat for 5 minutes. Add the stock and rosemary and bring to a boil. Add the veal, cover partially and cook over low heat until very tender, 2 hours. Remove the meat and shred it. Boil the sauce until slightly reduced, 10 minutes. Stir in the meat.

3. In a large pot of boiling salted water, cook the pasta until al dente. Drain and return to the pot. Add the ragù; toss over low heat until coated. Serve, passing the cheese at the table.

WINE Cherry-rich Chianti Classico.

12. malbec *plus* sweet-spicy bbq

Malbec, Shiraz and Côtes du Rhône are big and bold enough to drink with foods that are brushed with heavily spiced barbecue sauces.

Chicken Drumsticks with Asian Barbecue Sauce

8 SERVINGS

- 2 **tablespoons vegetable oil**
- 1 **teaspoon Chinese five-spice powder**
- 16 **chicken drumsticks (3 pounds)**

Salt and freshly ground pepper

- ³/₄ **cup hoisin sauce**
- ¹/₄ **cup sweet Asian chile sauce or hot pepper jelly**
- ¹/₄ **cup unseasoned rice vinegar**
- ¹/₄ **cup chicken stock or broth**
- 2 **tablespoons minced fresh ginger**
- 2 **large garlic cloves**
- 1 **teaspoon toasted sesame oil**
- 1 **cup toasted sesame seeds**

1. Preheat the oven to 425°. In a bowl, mix the vegetable oil and five-spice powder. Add the chicken drumsticks, season with salt and pepper and toss. Arrange the chicken on a foil-lined baking sheet. Roast for about 35 minutes, turning twice, until cooked.

2. Meanwhile, in a blender, puree the hoisin sauce, chile sauce, rice vinegar, stock, ginger, garlic and sesame oil until smooth. Transfer to a saucepan and simmer until slightly thickened, 5 minutes.

3. Transfer the chicken drumsticks to a bowl and toss with the sauce to coat.

4. Preheat the broiler and position a rack 8 inches from the heat. Return the chicken to the baking sheet and broil for about 10 minutes, brushing with the sauce and turning occasionally, until glazed and sticky.

5. Add the sesame seeds to a bowl. Dip the chicken in the seeds to coat; serve.

WINE Ripe, spicy Argentine Malbec.

13. zinfandel *plus* pâtés & mousses

The words *rustic* and *rich* describe chicken-liver mousse as much as they do wines like Zinfandel, Italy's Nero d'Avola and Spain's Monastrell.

Creamy Chicken-Liver Mousse

8 TO 10 SERVINGS

4	teaspoons yellow mustard seeds
2 1/2	sticks unsalted butter, softened
3	large shallots, thinly sliced
2	pounds chicken livers, halved

Kosher salt and freshly ground black pepper

1/4	cup Cognac
1/4	cup chopped flat-leaf parsley
10	caperberries, thinly sliced

1. In a large skillet, cook the mustard seeds over moderately high heat until toasted, about 1 minute. Transfer to a plate. Heat 4 tablespoons of the butter in the skillet. Add the shallots and cook over moderate heat until softened. Add the livers, season with salt and pepper and cook until barely pink inside, 8 minutes. Add the Cognac and simmer for 1 minute. Scrape into a food processor; let cool.

2. Add 1 1/2 sticks of the butter to the livers and puree until smooth. Transfer to a bowl. Fold in 3 teaspoons of the mustard seeds, 3 tablespoons of the parsley and 8 of the sliced caperberries and season with 1/2 teaspoon each of salt and pepper. Spread the mousse in a 6-cup soufflé dish and top with the remaining parsley, mustard seeds and caperberries.

3. In a small bowl, melt the remaining 4 tablespoons of butter in the microwave. Skim the foam from the surface. Spoon the clear butter evenly over the mousse, leaving behind the milk solids; tilt to distribute the butter. Cover and refrigerate overnight.

SERVE WITH Baguette toasts.

WINE Robust, dark-fruited Zinfandel from Sonoma County.

14. cabernet *plus* juicy red meat

California Cabernet, Bordeaux and Bordeaux-style blends go terrifically well with steaks or chops: Their tannins refresh the palate after each bite.

Korean Sizzling Beef

8 SERVINGS

- 1/4 **cup soy sauce**
- 2 **tablespoons sugar**
- 2 **tablespoons dry white wine**
- 2 **large garlic cloves, very finely chopped**
- 1 **tablespoon toasted sesame oil**
- 2 **teaspoons crushed red pepper**

One 2 1/2-pound beef flank steak, cut across the grain into twenty 1/4-inch-thick slices

- 16 **scallions**

Vegetable oil, for rubbing

Salt

Steamed rice, for serving

1. In a large, shallow dish, combine the soy sauce with the sugar, white wine, chopped garlic, toasted sesame oil and crushed red pepper, stirring to dissolve the sugar. Add the steak slices and coat thoroughly in the marinade. Cover and refrigerate the steak for at least 4 hours or overnight.

2. Light a grill or heat a griddle. Rub the scallions with vegetable oil and grill them over high heat, turning once, until just softened, about 2 minutes. Season with salt.

3. Working in batches, grill the steak over high heat until richly browned and medium-rare, about 30 seconds per side. Transfer the steak to a platter and serve with the grilled scallions and steamed rice.

WINE Structured, cassis-rich and tannic Bordeaux.

15. syrah *plus* spiced dishes

For heavily seasoned meat, look for a red with spicy notes, like Syrah from Washington State, Cabernet Franc from France and Xynomavro from Greece.

Cumin-Spiced Burgers with Harissa Mayo

8 SERVINGS

- 3 pounds ground chuck

Kosher salt and freshly ground black pepper

- 1/4 cup plus 2 teaspoons harissa
- 2 1/2 teaspoons ground cumin
- 2 teaspoons garlic powder
- 1 teaspoon dried thyme
- 1 large red onion, sliced 1/4 inch thick
- 1 tablespoon extra-virgin olive oil

Eight 6-inch oval rolls, split

- 1 cup mayonnaise
- 1 teaspoon caraway seeds

Tomato and cucumber slices

1. In a large bowl, mix the chuck with 1 tablespoon of kosher salt, 1 teaspoon of black pepper, 2 tablespoons plus 2 teaspoons of the harissa, the cumin, garlic powder and thyme. Form the meat into eight 3/4-inch-thick oval patties. In a medium bowl, toss the onion slices with the oil and season with salt and pepper.

2. Heat a grill pan. Cook the onions over moderate heat, turning once, until tender, about 10 minutes. Transfer to a plate and keep warm. Grill the burgers over moderately high heat, turning once, until medium, about 8 minutes. Grill the rolls until lightly toasted, about 2 minutes.

3. Meanwhile, mix the mayonnaise, caraway and the remaining 2 tablespoons of harissa; season with salt and pepper.

4. Spread the mayo on the rolls. Top with the burger patties, grilled onions, tomato and cucumber; close the sandwiches and serve.

WINE Spicy Washington Syrah.

wine & food pairing cheat sheet

CLASSIC DISHES	THE WINES
RAW OYSTERS	Muscadet
TUNA STEAK	Rosé
GRILLED SALMON	Pinot Gris
SALAD WITH VINAIGRETTE	Sauvignon Blanc
LOBSTER	Chardonnay
CRAB CAKES	Pinot Grigio
ROAST CHICKEN	Pinot Noir
PORK TENDERLOIN	Merlot
HAMBURGERS/SAUSAGES	Zinfandel
SPAGHETTI WITH RED SAUCE	Sangiovese
STEAK	Cabernet Sauvignon
PIZZA	Barbera
INDIAN CURRIES	Gewürztraminer
SPICY ASIAN FOOD	Off-dry Riesling

WHY THE MATCH WORKS	BOTTLE TO TRY
This white has an almost briny note that's great with raw shellfish.	**Clos des Briords Cuvée Vieilles Vignes Sur Lie** | **2008** | ★★★ **$ $** | P. 48
Rosés have the fruit to stand up to meaty fish, but lack tannins that can make fish taste metallic.	**Quivira Vineyards and Winery Grenache Rosé** | **2009** | ★★★ **$** | P. 158
Salmon and other rich fish can pair with either full-bodied whites or lighter reds.	**The Eyrie Vineyards** | **2008** | ★★★ **$ $** | P. 187
A salad with a tangy dressing will overwhelm low-acid whites but not tart whites.	**Nobilo Icon** | **2009** | ★★★ **$ $** | P. 221
The sweet and luscious flavor of lobster calls for a substantial white.	**Thorn-Clarke Terra Barossa** | **2008** | ★★★ **$** | P. 205
Tangy, high-acid whites cut through the fat of pan-fried or deep-fried seafood.	**Livon Braide Grande** | **2008** | ★★ **$ $** | P. 78
Pinot Noir is light enough for white meat, yet flavorful enough for dark.	**Jules Taylor Wines** | **2008** | ★★★ **$ $** | P. 224
Medium-bodied Merlot is a good red wine for lighter meats like pork or veal.	**Twenty Rows** | **2008** | ★★★ **$ $** | P. 168
Big, juicy reds have the substance to match robust meats.	**Sobon Estate Rocky Top** | **2007** | ★★★★ **$ $** | P. 180
Red wines with bright acidity complement tomato-based pasta sauces.	**Querceto Riserva** | **2005** | ★★★ **$ $** | P. 86
The tannins in Cabernets balance the richness of well-marbled beef.	**Irony** | **2007** | ★★★ **$** | P. 163
This Italian red has enough acidity to cut through cheesy pizza slices.	**Marziano Abbona Rinaldi** | **2007** | ★★★ **$ $** | P. 75
Gewürztraminer's exotic aromas complement Indian spices like cumin and coriander.	**Lazy Creek Vineyards** | **2007** | ★★★★ **$ $** | P. 157
The light sweetness of an off-dry Riesling can help cool the heat of spicy foods.	**Covey Run** | **2008** | ★★ **$** | P. 193

bargain wine finder

Great wine does not have to be expensive. Good value for money was an important consideration in the process of selecting the wines recommended in this guide. Following is an index of many different wines whose quality (★) to price ($) ratio makes them exceptional values and well worth stocking up on.

Whites
★★★★ $ $

Château Graville-Lacoste, Graves, France, p. 31

Honig Sauvignon Blanc, Napa Valley, California, p. 154

Lazy Creek Vineyards Gewürztraminer, Anderson Valley, California, p. 157

Reichsgraf von Kesselstatt Josephshöfer Riesling Kabinett, Mosel, Germany, p. 131

R. López de Heredia Viña Tondonia Viña Gravonia Crianza, Rioja, Spain, p. 105

Saint Clair Family Estate Pioneer Block 1 Foundation Sauvignon Blanc, Marlborough, New Zealand, p. 222

Salentein Reserve Chardonnay, Uco Valley, Argentina, p. 229

★★★ $

A to Z Riesling, Oregon, p. 187

Big Woop! White Wine, South Eastern Australia, p. 206

Crios de Susana Balbo Torrontés, Salta, Argentina, p. 228

Ironstone Obsession Symphony, California, p. 157

Markham Vineyards Sauvignon Blanc, Napa Valley, California, p. 155

Mercouri Estate Folói, Pisatis, Greece, p. 143

Muga, Rioja, Spain, p. 105

Penfolds Thomas Hyland Riesling, Adelaide, Australia, p. 207

Santa Ema Selected Terroir Chardonnay, Casablanca Valley, Chile, p. 236

S.A. Prüm Essence Riesling, Mosel, Germany, p. 131

Shaya Old Vines Verdejo, Rueda, Spain, p. 116

Thorn-Clarke Terra Barossa Chardonnay, Eden Valley, Australia, p. 205

Torres Viña Esmeralda Moscato/ Gewürztraminer, Catalonia, Spain, p. 113

Rosés
★★★ $

Bieler Père et Fils Sabine, Coteaux d'Aix-en-Provence, France, p. 65

Quivira Vineyards and Winery Grenache Rosé, Dry Creek Valley, California, p. 158

Reds
★ ★ ★ ★ $ $

Blason d'Issan, Margaux, France, p. 32

Bodega Inurrieta Sur, Navarra, Spain, p. 106

Churchill's Estates, Douro, Portugal, p. 121

Domaine Patrick Miolane Pinot Noir, Bourgogne, France, p. 43

Domaine Terlato & Chapoutier Shiraz/Viognier, Victoria, Australia, p. 210

Doña Paula Estate Malbec, Mendoza, Argentina, p. 231

Juan Gil Monastrell, Jumilla, Spain, p. 111

Layer Cake Primitivo, Apulia, Italy, p. 98

Limerick Lane Collins Vineyard Zinfandel, Russian River Valley, California, p. 179

Mendel Malbec, Mendoza, Argentina, p. 233

Quinta do Vallado, Douro, Portugal, p. 123

Ruffino Modus, Tuscany, Italy, p. 92

Sobon Estate Rocky Top Zinfandel, Amador County, California, p. 180

Tir Na N'og Old Vines Grenache, McLaren Vale, Australia, p. 216

Torbreck Cuvée Juveniles, Barossa Valley, Australia, p. 216

★ ★ ★ $

Cantore di Castelforte Donna Maria Primitivo, Salento, Italy, p. 98

Cascina Bruciata Rian, Dolcetto d'Alba, Italy, p. 74

Clos Siguier, Cahors, France, p. 67

d'Arenberg The Stump Jump Grenache/Shiraz/Mourvèdre, South Australia, p. 214

Irony Cabernet Sauvignon, Napa Valley, California, p. 163

Kiona Lemberger, Red Mountain, Washington State, p. 196

Layer Cake Shiraz, South Australia, p. 211

Monte Antico Sangiovese/Merlot/ Cabernet Sauvignon, Tuscany, Italy, p. 91

MontGras Reserva Carmenère, Colchagua Valley, Chile, p. 239

Porta dos Cavaleiros, Dão, Portugal, p. 123

2 Up Shiraz, South Australia, p. 213

Sparkling Wines
★ ★ ★ ★ $ $

Domaine Carneros by Taittinger Brut, Carneros, California, p. 256

Lucien Albrecht Blanc de Blancs Brut, Crémant d'Alsace, France, p. 252

★ ★ ★ $

Gruet Rosé Brut, New Mexico, p. 256

Fortified & Dessert Wines
★ ★ ★ $

Bodegas Hidalgo La Gitana Manzanilla Sherry, Jerez, Spain, p. 260

Kourtaki Muscat, Samos, Greece, p. 266

index of wines

d

e

f

g

j

k

m

n

S

t